HARRIER

Francis K. Mason

2nd edition

NAVAL INSTITUTE PRESS

Published and distributed in the United States of America and Canada by the Naval Institute Press, Annapolis, Maryland 21402

Library of Congress Catalog Card No: 82-62644

ISBN 0-87021-829-8

Printed in Great Britain

Frontispiece *Sidewinder-equipped Sea Harrier about to land on HMS* Hermes *after patrol in the South Atlantic as a Royal Fleet Auxiliary prepares to transfer stores and equipment* (Ministry of Defence).

Front endpaper *Full-standard Harrier T Mark 4 with LRMTS/FE541 and RWR equipment, shown here at Wittering in the markings of No 233 OCU* (British Aerospace Corporation, Neg No 796073).

Rear endpaper *A pair of AV-8A Harriers of US Marine Corps VMA-231 ('Ace of Spades' Squadron),* 158385 *and* 158390 (Courtesy US Marine Corps.)

Contents

Introduction

The surprising feature of the Harrier's history is that it ever survived. On the other hand one could probably make the same observation about almost every other advanced British military aircraft project conceived during the past thirty years, and it is sadly true that of every three such projects which have reached the metal-cutting stage (having already absorbed huge sums of private and public money), only one has reached profitable service. It is an unfortunate truism that the more radical or relatively sophisticated an aircraft's concept appears to be, the more certain it is that it will attract political cynicism, if not downright opposition. The path has become littered with fallen artefacts, yet the Harrier survived against all odds to become a shining example of British genius, ingenuity and perseverance—in the face of undisguised hostility, lack of political and professional backbone and, possibly worst of all, ignorance where intelligence should abound.

Against this cynical scenario—not always reflected by politicians alone—the demand for progress in the air is constant, whether it be in aircraft performance, weapon lethality or just plain cost-effectiveness. When indigenous efforts to meet the demand fail, there is public outrage no less than when the remedy is sought abroad. And when radical means are proffered to achieve progress the opposition is more often than not voiced, not by the lay public—the ultimate beneficiaries—but by those whose profession is to encourage profitable advance: the governments and their administrative staffs.

It may be argued that the public servant is not in office to indulge in risks but to seek conventional efficiency by the established processes of administration; to do otherwise, and fail, is to endanger the system. In matters of defence, where the nation's only voice lies ultimately in the ballot box, the administration of future planning is entrusted on the one hand to professional Service officers with a lifetime of personal experience behind them and on the other to an all-powerful Treasury. The one demands, the other sanctions.

The process is not infallible for, despite the in-built committee-decision safeguard, Service Staffs are inevitably vulnerable to the effect of lobbying—whether of a deliberate or unconscious nature, for political or economic considerations. Nor is Britain alone in this manifestation of human nature.

The tasks of Britain's Air Staffs between 1930 and 1955 remained relatively straightforward. The nation's air defence responsibilities were seldom open to misinterpretation, and the rate of technological progress lay well within the bounds of Treasury sanction and political approval. The strategists and planners had pursued their customary demands from the aircraft of the future—greater speeds, weapons, engine power and so on—and Britain's air forces had sustained their defence responsibilities admirably: to a great extent the gradual post-war contraction of Britain's worldwide defence responsibilities offset the growing cost of technology. In the mid-1950s, however, a point was reached at which the pattern changed.

To keep abreast of America (as had been possible in the immediate post-war period) proved to be beyond the capacity of government research funding. No longer was the British Air Staff able to apply conventional parameters of performance improvement and timescale planning with any likelihood of automatic Treasury sanction. The machinery of operational requirement came close to breakdown and it was on this that the Government in 1957 seized to provide an excuse to change direction in British defence planning altogether. Yet who was to say at that time that the Government's vision of an all-missile air defence system was any more attainable or realistic than any other proposal? The Air Staff clung doggedly to conventional aircraft (albeit shying away from the anathematised 'manned fighter'), but the aircraft industry had other ideas. Was it any wonder that Hawker found it difficult to sell the concept of a no-runway air force?

No one today yet believes in a 'no-runway air force'. Yet the Royal Air Force, Royal Navy and United States Marine Corps have demonstrated emphatically that the V/STOL combat aeroplane is a vital weapon in the overall defence armoury—indeed, in some circumstances it may be the only surviving weapon available. It is difficult to imagine how Great Britain could have resolved the situation in the South Atlantic in 1982 without giving way to naked aggression had her air forces not been equipped with the Harrier for, as if this scenario had been specially conceived with the V/STOL combat aeroplane in mind, the British forces found themselves in a 'no-runway' environment throughout that brilliantly fought campaign.

The road from the original P 1127 of the early 1960s to the Sea Harrier and AV-8B of the 1980s has been tortuous and beset with design cul-de-sacs and misconceived diversions, and it has proved impossible to produce a straightforward narrative of events in chronological sequence. I hope therefore that I may be forgiven if—to describe such events—I have had to resort to cross-referencing both forward and backward in time and chapter.

Acknowledgements

In the course of preparing this book over the past twenty years I have been aware that many of my former colleagues at Hawker Aircraft Limited—now grandiloquently identified as British Aerospace Corporation, Aircraft Group (Kingston-Brough Division)—have unwittingly assisted me in the course of our everyday conversations. I have, however, been careful to avoid implicating them in possibly contentious opinions expressed in the book, relying instead on contemporary documentation which found its way into public consumption through legitimate channels. Such opinions, unless specifically attributed elsewhere, are mine (but not necessarily mine alone), and I take full responsibility for their expression.

On the other hand, in unravelling the often-contradictory policies being expressed twenty years ago, I have been most generously assisted by my old friends Ralph Hooper and John Fozard, both of whom have inevitably climbed the dizzy heights of their profession at Kingston. Both have made available to me countless documents without which this work could not have been produced. I am also indebted to others at Kingston and Dunsfold, among them R.H. Chaplin, John Chudleigh, John Coombs, R.G. Dare, John Gale, Eric Hayward, Tony Lewis, G.R. Lillistone, Fred Sutton and Graham Wilmer, for providing considerable documentary and illustrative material; much of this is unique and has never seen the light of day in published form. David Core generously gave much of his leisure time to the preparation of the minutiae which forms the basis of Appendix 5.

Turning elsewhere I acknowledge with gratitude the assistance lent by David Hall, Pegasus Sales Manager at the Aero Division of Rolls-Royce Ltd, Bristol, and to Bill Bedford who did so much of the early V/STOL flying at Hawker.

In the United States of America numerous people have contributed material and opinions, invaluable in arriving at what I hope is a balanced view of the complicated policies regarding V/STOL. At McDonnell Douglas, Mr Gerald J. Meyer, Corporation Director, and Mr John J. McGrath, Aircraft Company Director, have been particularly helpful and generous with their assistance, as has Doree Martin in Saint Louis and my old friend Geoffrey Norris in the company's UK Office. I have also been fortunate in collaborating with a number of officers in the US Marine Corps, in particular Lieutenant Colonel Tod A. Eikenbery, commanding Marine Attack Squadron 231 at Cherry Point, and Gabrielle M. Santelli at the Marine Corps Headquarters, Washington, DC.

Finally I must acknowledge the assistance I have derived from documents which were given into my care by the late Sir Sydney Camm—from whom 'all things Hawker' sprang for forty momentous years. These provided the inspiration: all else was contributory, but none the less gratefully received.

Chapter 1

Towards the vertical

The introductory passages of this book have sought to outline the apparently never ending trend among military aviation strategists and planners to demand and satisfy greater aircraft capacities and capabilities, a trend that has in turn warranted engines of ever-increasing power and fuel consumption if air bases and runways are to remain within the bounds of realism. For many years the vulnerability of huge runways to accommodate the modern warplane was considered of little embarrassment so long as efficient airfield defence existed, but even as long ago as the Second World War, in which swiftly moving armies demanded tactical use of combat aircraft based close to the front line, the vulnerability to air or ground attack of large fixed airfield facilities rendered such air support somewhat tenuous.

The arrival in service of tactical surface-to-surface guided- or self-navigating missiles after the Second World War gave cause for serious reflection as to alternative means of operating combat aircraft without total dependence upon geographically-fixed facilities whose exact position would always be known to an enemy, which could not be effectively concealed and—in the case of the ballistic missile—could not be adequately defended. It might be thought that the helicopter offered an immediate solution, but it should be remembered that this aircraft was still relatively young, expensive and slow for some 15 years after 1945 and that the assault gunship (the fast attack helicopter) only evolved into a realistic combat weapon at the beginning of the Vietnam conflict in the 1960s. To this day it still constitutes an exceptionally fragile weapon in the presence of ground defences.

Early studies of practical vertical launching of manned combat interceptors started in Germany during the war and included the development of the Bachem Natter, a rocket-powered manned craft which was to be launched vertically in flying attitude to intercept incoming Allied bombers. A battery of nose-mounted rocket projectiles would be discharged towards the target, after which the cockpit capsule would descend by parachute. Although several Natters were launched experimentally, none is thought to have been employed operationally.

An early German vertical take-off and landing (VTOL) aircraft project was the Focke-Achgelis Fa 269 shipborne fighter using thrust vectoring; a single BMW 801 radial engine in the fuselage drove a pair of large-diameter propellers aft of the wing, which could be rotated downwards to provide vertical thrust, and rearwards for horizontal flight. Intended to achieve a speed of 354 mph, a prototype of the Fa 269 was commenced but this and all details and drawings were destroyed in an Allied air raid in 1943, and the project was abandoned. The aircraft had been intended to operate from platforms on merchant vessels.

Undismayed by the complex problems of stability during transition from vertical to horizontal flight, the US Navy Department in 1951 issued a requirement for a VTOL

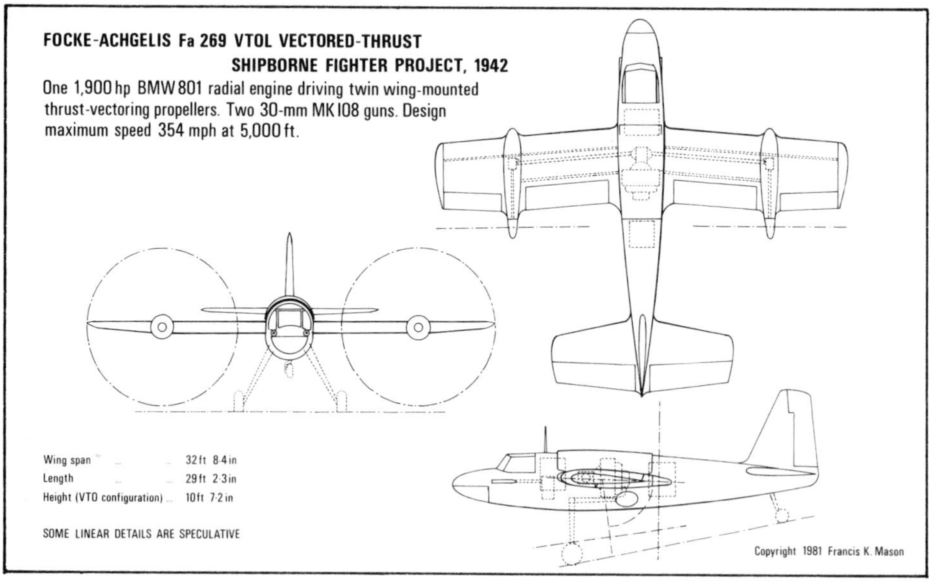
FOCKE-ACHGELIS Fa 269 VTOL VECTORED-THRUST
SHIPBORNE FIGHTER PROJECT, 1942
One 1,900 hp BMW 801 radial engine driving twin wing-mounted
thrust-vectoring propellers. Two 30-mm MK 108 guns. Design
maximum speed 354 mph at 5,000 ft.
Wing span ... ... 32 ft 8·4 in
Length ... ... 29 ft 2·3 in
Height (VTO configuration) ... 10 ft 7·2 in
SOME LINEAR DETAILS ARE SPECULATIVE
Copyright 1981 Francis K. Mason

fleet fighter. Unlike the 'flat rising' Fa 269, whose lateral and longitudinal control at zero forward speed does not appear to have been investigated successfully at the time the project was abandoned, the new American fighter project envisaged a 'tail-sitter' using a powerful turboprop with large contraprops to eliminate torque. The aircraft, using a simple two-axis autostabiliser, would simply be flown vertically off the ground and be 'pushed over' into horizontal flight; to land, the aircraft would hang vertically on its propellers and gradually sink backwards on to its tail castors.

Two contenders were accepted for development in March 1951, the Lockheed XFV-1 (of which two prototypes, *138657* and *138658,* were ordered) and the Convair XFY-1 (three ordered, *138648-138650*). Both designs employed the 5,850-hp Allison T40-A-14 driving large six-blade contraprops, and the Convair XFY-1 made its first flight in August 1954, following with a full transition to horizontal flight on November 2 that year.

Notwithstanding the apparent success of those early trials, the US Navy in 1956 abandoned its quest for vertical take-off combat aircraft. Reasons for this decision were not entirely motivated by technical or operating problems. (The stability and control response parameters during transition were difficult to define; the aircraft as a combat weapon was wholly compromised by its weird configuration; and the attenuation of hot gas blast on the deck of a ship proved apparently insoluble.) There was still a powerful, senior element within the US Navy dedicated to the proliferation of the aircraft carrier as the major fleet element. Thus, so long as funding could be provided for ever larger carriers, the pattern of naval combat aircraft would be determined accordingly, and not *vice versa.* As will be shown in due course, the natural attrition among 'capital ship strategists' has brought to senior rank men more willing to conceive of powerful fleets comprising smaller yet equally effective vessels. That is not to say that the very large aircraft carrier may not continue to exercise an important rôle in naval affairs for years to come; the vertical/short take-off combat aircraft so far developed still only represents part of an air force's essential armoury. However, more and more navies have come to appreciate the cost and vulnerability of deploying such leviathans as the fleet carrier and are beginning to accept the V/STOL combat aircraft as being the *only* suitable weapon in many circumstances.

Above *The Convair XFY-1 vertical take-off fleet escort fighter of the 1950s* (General Dynamics, Convair Aerospace Division).

Right *The Lockheed XFV-1 vertical take-off fighter designed for the US Navy; this aircraft differed from the Convair XFY-1 design principally in featuring conventional wings and a separate cruciform tail* (Lockheed Aircraft Corporation).

U.S. ARMY
24506

U.S. AIR FORCE
41620

Hitherto, apart from the Natter expendable rocket-powered interceptor, only propeller-driven aircraft have been mentioned here, and from 1955 onwards such projects multiplied, particularly in the United States of America. The aims and emphasis of these projects inevitably moved towards the evolution of VTOL transport aircraft in which high performance was not at a premium, and as such—for all their interest and ingenuity—do not lie within the scope of this book. Tilting wings and engines have all been pursued with success by a growing number of manufacturers, but the nature of the associated structures and their weight penalties have combined to move them outside the realms of combat aircraft, at least for the time being.

The first significant interest in 'pure-jet VTO' was evinced by the Ryan Aeronautical Company of San Diego, California, in 1947. To investigate methods of varying jet thrust for directional control the company suspended an Allison J33 turbojet in a horizontal test rig, following this with a vertical rig, and ultimately evolving a tethered 'bedstead' with cockpit, reaction controls and two-axis autostabiliser. Using this bedstead a set of control response parameters was obtained and some development work was carried out on reaction control design. It should be emphasised that no effort was made to vector the thrust line of the engine whose exhaust was permanently directed vertically downwards.

In 1953 Ryan received a USAF contract to build a prototype aircraft, the X-13 Vertijet. Powered by a Rolls-Royce Avon, the X-13 was a small, squat, delta-wing aircraft intended to be launched from its own self-contained servicing trailer which incorporated an hydraulically-operated inclining launch ramp. The first aircraft flew on December 10 1955 fitted with a temporary fixed tricycle undercarriage to allow normal horizontal take-off, flight and landing. Its first tail-sitting take-off was made on May 28 1956, followed by simulated hook-on 'landing' by engaging a nylon rope suspended between two vertical steel towers.

A second X-13 was produced and completed a full sequence of vertical take-off, transition to horizontal flight and reverse transition to vertical landing on April 11 1957.

As suggested by its experimental designation, the X-13 was never intended to represent the basis of an operational aircraft design, but served to demonstrate the feasibility of vertical take-off by an aircraft powered by an engine whose installed thrust exceeded its weight by a margin adequate to allow installation in a viable airframe. The 9,100-lb thrust Avon engine had been installed in an aircraft whose all-up weight was around 7,500 lb; fuel carried was sufficient for no more than about twelve minutes' running at full power.

Meanwhile, in Britain the Rolls-Royce company itself had been conducting its own experiments with vertical thrust engines, also using a bedstead rig. As early as 1953 the Rolls-Royce Thrust Measuring Rig (generally known as the TMR or 'flying bedstead') commenced jet-lift trials. In this vehicle two 5,000-lb thrust Rolls-Royce Nene turbojets were installed horizontally at opposite ends of the rig with their tailpipes directed vertically downwards near the rig's mass centre. Stability and control was provided by high pressure air tapped from the engines' compressors and directed downwards through

Top left *One of many American experimental vertical take-off essays was the flat-rising Ryan XV-5A. Employing the 'fan-in-wing' principle, the XV-5A was powered by two General Electric J85 turbojets in the fuselage driving lift fans in the wings and in the nose for vertical take-off. It first flew on May 25 1964* (US Army, via British Aerospace Corporation).

Centre left *The Ryan X-13 Vertijet performing its 'hook-on' act; the helmeted figure perched on the tower is guiding the pilot by means of visual signals. Seeing is believing!* (Rolls-Royce Ltd, Neg No E223819).

Left *The Rolls-Royce Thrust Measuring Rig (the 'Flying Bedstead')* (Rolls-Royce Ltd, Neg No E223818).

valves located on arms to provide moments equivalent to those of forces which would otherwise act on conventional flying control surfaces.

In France SNECMA embarked on a four-stage programme of tail-sitting test vehicles powered by the Atar turbojet. The first such rig, the C.400 P-1, was a remotely-controlled unmanned rig comprising a vertically-mounted Atar in a nacelle on a tubular structure incorporating a four-wheel undercarriage; a total of 205 'flights' was made, commencing on September 22 1956. The C.400 P-2 was a manned version of the P-1 featuring a pilot's ejector seat on top of the rig; tethered hovering started on April 8 1957, and the first free flight was made on May 14. The P-3 was similar to the P-2 but was designed to be mounted horizontally on a railway truck with the Atar's tailpipe directed forward; at towed speeds of up to 50 mph, tests were carried out to determine jet blast effects during a simulated rapid vertical descent.

The final stage of the SNECMA tests involved a fully-enclosed Atar 101E.V in a fuselage structure, itself surrounded by an annular wing to permit transition from tail-sitting vertical take-off to horizontal flight. The first flight of this, the SNECMA C-450 Coléoptère, was made on April 17 1959, but on July 25 that year the aircraft was destroyed in a crash; the pilot, Auguste Morel, lost control while attempting to stabilise the aircraft for a vertical descent from about 200 ft, but managed to eject safely. This effectively ended French experiments with tail-sitting VTOL aircraft.

First evidence of Russian interest in the jet-lift principle was provided at the big 'Day of the Soviet Air Fleet' display at Tushino on July 20 1958. The vehicle shown was a bedstead rig designed by A. Rapahaelyantz, featuring a single vertically-mounted turbojet (probably of about 6,500-lb thrust) with four long transverse arms carrying the reaction control pipes and valves and the four-wheel undercarriage. Two fuel tanks were located beside the engine and the pilot was accommodated in a lightweight cockpit but was not provided with an ejector seat.

★ ★ ★

Thus by 1958 four nations, the United States, Britain, France and the Soviet Union, were actively engaged in research into various aspects of vertical take-off and jet-borne flight. However, only in Britain had serious thought been given to the ultimate viability of a practical application of jet lift, a situation universally accredited to Rolls-Royce's world leadership in gas turbine technology.

The purpose of the Rolls-Royce TMR, which had appeared in 1953, had been to prove the theory of Dr A.A. Griffith, Chief Scientist at Rolls-Royce Limited, that the supersonic airliner of the future (as forecast at that time) would be of slender delta wing form, optimised for high-speed cruise, and using a large battery of fixed vertical-lift turbojets for take-off and landing. The Anglo-French Concorde supersonic airliner confirmed Dr Griffith's theories as correct only in its overall aerodynamic configuration, but the application of vertical take-off principles to mainline passenger air travel has so far proved impractical. Just as the US Navy had decided that the operating base configuration would continue to dictate the nature of the aircraft (and not *vice versa*), so the nature of commercial airport design—as expensively evolved over decades in the light of international requirements—would preclude any radical alteration in take-off and landing procedures. In short, the development of a wholly new concept in airliner design could never be supported in opposition to the massive vested interests of relatively low-cost, conventional airliners, while no worthwhile revenue would be forthcoming to underwrite the development costs. An exactly parallel example of the resistance to fundamental technological innovation in commercial aviation has, of course, been afforded by Concorde itself.

Early configuration of the Short SC1 in hover over a special operating platform (Short Bros, Neg No AC5-3723).

Nevertheless, such were the widening potentialities of vertical take-off deemed to be in the early 1950s that Dr Griffith in 1954 initiated the development of a specialist lightweight lift turbojet, the Rolls-Royce RB 108, with a thrust-weight ratio of about 8:1 (compared with, for example, the Avon's 3:1). At the same time the Ministry of Supply issued a Specification, ER 143, for a small VTO flat-rising research aircraft capable of taking off vertically under the thrust of a battery of vertically-mounted lift engines and becoming fully supported by a conventional aerofoil in forward flight made possible by an independent, rearward-directed turbojet.

Short Brothers & Harland submitted the design of a small delta aircraft incorporating four vertically-mounted Rolls-Royce RB 108s, grouped around the aeroplane's centre of gravity, and a fifth RB 108 exhausting rearwards in the tail. (Because the RB 108's lubrication system was designed for vertical installation, the rear engine had to be inclined sharply in the airframe but still provided adequate thrust for conventional forward flight.) The Short tender, designated the SC1, was accepted and two prototypes (*XG900* and *XG905*) were ordered in August 1954.

For all its small size, the SC1 was an exceedingly complex aeroplane, involving considerable development effort to perfect a three-axis autostabiliser, powered controls, integrated reaction controls and specialised fixed landing gear. An analogue computer, produced by the Precision Engineering Division, was used in the design of the hydraulic and electronic control systems which employed magnetic amplifiers in place of the customary thermionic valves.

At first sight it might be thought that the provision of four lift engines would provide a substantial safety margin in the event of a single engine failure while jet-borne, yet such a failure—apart from reducing the lift element by 25 per cent in hover—would create an instant asymmetric lift force, demanding immediate corrective action by the relevant reaction controls. The autostabiliser was designed to permit instant reversion from automatic to manual control, and its fail-safe design included three parallel-circuited channels so that a runaway by any one channel would be overpowered by the other two until the

Later configuration of the SC1 hovering at Sydenham, Belfast (Short Bros, Neg No AC5-3878-1).

pilot could assume manual control. Thus, in theory, no single fault in the control system would be catastrophic.

The fixed tricycle undercarriage, utilising long-travel oleo legs, could be raked forward to provide the aircraft with its optimum ground angle for conventional take-offs and landings or, by operation of a two-position hydraulic jack acting as a drag strut, moved to the vertical position for vertical take-offs and landings. The undercarriage was designed to withstand a vertical velocity of 18 ft/sec at normal all-up weights.

Engine running with only the rear RB 108 installed in *XG900* started on December 7 1956 at Sydenham, Belfast, and, with Tom Brooke-Smith at the controls, taxying ten days later. On April 2 1957, having been shipped to the Aircraft and Armament Experimental Establishment (A&AEE) at Boscombe Down in Wiltshire, *XG900* made its first conventional take-off and landing. The second aircraft, *XG905,* was then completed with lift engines installed and on May 23 1958 carried out its first tethered hover in a large gantry.

It had, of course, long been an established feature of the gas turbine's operating characteristics that its overall efficiency depends upon the ambient air temperature, and that in high temperatures the engine's power output is reduced. It was therefore realised in advance that hot gases being directed vertically down underneath a VTOL aeroplane would create a local area of high ambient temperatures all around the aircraft. So as to allow the lift engines to operate as efficiently as possible (there was still theoretically a lift-thrust margin of only about 600 lb over the SC1's all-up weight under ideal atmospheric conditions), the initial tethered hovering flights were made over a raised platform with open-grid decking so as to disperse the exhaust gases and avoid their re-circulation.

After five months of tethered hovering tests the gantry was discarded and *XG905* embarked on free hovering—still over the grid. In November 1958 Brooke-Smith achieved a vertical landing on unprepared ground. At the 1959 Society of British Aircraft Constructors' (SBAC) Display at Farnborough, it was intended to demonstrate vertical and horizontal flight; however, the grass on the operating area, which had been mown but

The Short SC1's voracious appetite for loose grass, as shown at Farnborough in September 1959 (Short Bros, Neg No AC8-3637).

not removed, rose in clouds around the aircraft and became clogged in the debris guards over the lift engines, giving the SC1 a distinctly 'thatched' appearance. Brooke-Smith, experiencing some loss of power, had to descend and land somewhat hurriedly. Full accelerating and decelerating transitions were eventually achieved by *XG905* on April 6 1960.

At about this time *XG900* emerged once more, now with all five RB 108s installed, improved reaction controls and automatic intake louvres over the lift engines. Together the two SC1s started a series of rolling take-off trials on unprepared surfaces; the objects of these trials were to avoid surface erosion and, by utilising some degree of wing-lift in forward motion, to take off at increased weights—the short take-off manoeuvre (STO). By now several pilots had flown the SC1 apart from Tom Brooke-Smith, who had been joined by Jock Eassie at Sydenham, and who was succeeded by Denis Taylor from the Royal Aircraft Establishment (RAE), Bedford, on the former's retirement from test flying in December 1960. Alex Roberts of Shorts had also flown the SC1 many times, as had Squadron Leader S.J. Hubbard of the RAE.

In June 1963 another RAE pilot, J.R. Green, joined Shorts to undertake development flying in *XG905,* now modified with improved all-weather autostabiliser. More than 80 flights were made at Belfast using the new equipment, but on October 2, as Green was approaching to land, a fault developed in the gyro input of the autostabiliser. The pilot immediately assumed manual control, but all three gyros failed to cage and diverged to their stops, giving a false vertical reference which caused the autostabiliser to fly the aircraft into the ground. The SC1 somersaulted on to its back, killing Green.

XG905 required extensive repairs, but it re-emerged again in 1966 equipped with a modified autostabiliser in which the gyros would always cage under all combinations of attitude and acceleration. It was also fitted with a pilot's head-up display and ground/air data link for all-weather/night trials with the Blind Landing Experimental Unit (BLEU).

* * *

The fortunes of the Short SC1 have been described at some length for a number of reasons. It was, after all, the first demonstrably reliable and realistic VTOL aeroplane to be produced anywhere in the world, despite its tragic accident in 1963. It established a pattern of research and experimental flying by which other designers and planners could forecast development requirements; a mass of parametric data was made available from which component design could progress.

However, the true value of the SC1 was misconstrued almost from the outset. Too many people both in Britain and elsewhere attempted to seek exaggerated significance in the multiple-lift turbojet thesis. As already explained, the original purpose of the Ministry of Supply's 1954 Specification was simply to exploit the theory of multiple lift-engine take-off and landing; there had been nothing implicit in the requirement to suggest that it provide the basis for military aircraft application.

Yet, although by 1957 the original Griffith multi-lift-jet hypothesis for supersonic airliners was seen to be commercially fallacious, it was entirely understandable that Rolls-Royce should employ its undoubted influence to exploit the principle in other applications, not least in combat aircraft which might incorporate multiple lift turbojets as well as powerful horizontal-thrust Rolls-Royce engines.

Fortunately—or unfortunately, depending on one's viewpoint—the very considerable and extensive lobbying of political, industrial and military interests that stemmed from Rolls-Royce's determination to perpetuate the multiple lift-jet concept occurred at a time of total disarray among those responsible for future military aviation planning.

The Suez Crisis of 1956 had demonstrated to Britain the vulnerability of her lifelines to the East and had firmly aligned certain key Middle East nations in a potentially hostile camp. It had also shown the necessity for Britain to integrate her defence interests more closely with the Western defence bloc—NATO— and in forecasting (incorrectly) almost total dependence upon an armoury of unmanned guided missiles, the 1957 Defence White Paper brought to a standstill almost all work on future conventional combat aircraft, other than the English Electric Lightning, then suggested as being the ultimate manned interceptor.

There is little doubt that the fallacies of the White Paper were first appreciated by the NATO planners whose overall defence responsibilities for Europe were quite different from those of the insular British Government. Thus while disarray existed in the military departments of Whitehall, operational requirements continued to be studied and issued by the offices of NATO, and it should be recalled that at that time Britain's aircraft industry was still by far the largest and most prosperous in Europe. Therefore any approach, with either military or commercial connotations, by Rolls-Royce in respect of NATO requirements would be bound to carry considerable weight of argument.

Thus it was in the absence of any material support for a VTOL combat aircraft evident in Britain that an approach by Rolls-Royce to the French company, Générale Aéronautique Marcel Dassault, to collaborate in a VTOL tactical combat aircraft, appeared to give rise for optimism among the multi-lift-jet protagonists.

In truth, the lack of interest by the Air Ministry in this concept had been entirely misconstrued. The Operational Requirements (OR) Branch at the Air Ministry in 1958, by now realising that a 'manned' Royal Air Force would indeed continue to flourish into the distant future, had seized upon and was totally engrossed in a major new requirement which had been originated by NATO and was now to obsess the Air Staff for the next six years. It was indeed the magnitude of the TSR-2 strike aircraft requirement, which threatened to absorb almost every penny of the Treasury's allotment for defence, that so besotted the minds at Air Ministry's OR Branch that scarcely any other projects were permitted consideration.

The multi-lift-jet principle *was* practical, yet to the purists among designers of conventional tactical aircraft in Europe and America the idea of employing engines solely for take-off and landing seemed wholly unnatural. By necessity the airframe could not possibly be optimised for the aircraft's primary combat rôle, but would involve compromise brought about by so much dead weight. The complexity inherent in the multi-engine installation and the mandatory autostabilisation was the very antithesis for tactical employment of VTO in the field where simplicity is the keyword. The carriage of heavy weapon and/or fuel loads would only be possible when performing the short rolling take-off manoeuvre, a manoeuvre demanding complex handling techniques with both lift and horizontal thrust engines, and total dependence upon the autostabiliser. Problems of ground erosion and hot gas re-circulation still defied solution.

This then was the technical, military and political environment that persisted in Britain towards the end of the 1950s. VTOL had been shown to be practical, though the means were yet controversial. If the Royal Air Force was preoccupied with negotiating a crossroads in its own affairs, America and her European partners in NATO appeared less inhibited.

Chapter 2

Flat risers with a difference

As previously explained, the British aircraft industry was thrown into some disarray as a result of the 1957 Defence White Paper, particularly in respect of its forecast demise of the manned interceptor fighter.

Hawker Aircraft Limited, the Kingston-upon-Thames company whose name had been synonymous with interceptor fighters for more than thirty years, was at the time of the White Paper's publication almost entirely committed to quantity production of the Hunter which, to the Government and public at large, was regarded as a 'fighter', pure and simple. It mattered not one jot to a Treasury intent on pruning defence expenditure with little regard to technical niceties, that the Hunter was then being developed, and indeed being introduced into service as a ground attack aircraft. Production of the aircraft was peremptorily halted for the RAF and outstanding orders cancelled—and had it not been for export orders, henceforth diligently sought by the company, Hawker Aircraft might have withered and died in 1957.*

Dependence by a company upon a single product in the aircraft industry is to invite disaster, particularly when placed at risk by the vagaries of political misology, and as a prime contractor for military aircraft to the British Government Hawker was unquestionably treading on thin ice. However as a member of the giant Hawker Siddeley Group, the company was able to retain its skilled labour force through the sub-contracting of components for other Group aircraft (tail sections for the Avro Vulcan, for example) and perseverance with another of its own projects, the P 1103/P 1121. This large aircraft had started life as an air superiority fighter in the mid-1950s as the P 1103; powered by a reheated de Havilland Gyron engine, a prototype had started manufacture at Kingston, supported by the private funds of the Hawker Siddeley Group, and to some extent by encouragement from Government and Service departments. When, however, the 1957 White Paper appeared any association with 'fighter' aircraft became an anathema in the eyes of Government, public and Group shareholders alike, while erstwhile enthusiasts in the higher ranks of the Royal Air Force became suddenly conspicuous by their absence. Not even when Hawker was able to demonstrate by use of the Rolls-Royce Conway bypass engine or Bristol Olympus that the newly-styled P 1121 would provide a potent answer to an RAF tactical strike requirement were the Government authorities any more inclined towards support for the Hawker project. Truth to tell, the Operational Requirements Branch at Air Ministry was already hard at work on the TSR 2.

This brief summary of the work being undertaken by Hawker Aircraft in 1957-58 is necessary to illustrate the means by which the company was able to survive at a time when the very nature of its own speciality—the fighter—threatened to be its downfall. The

* *See* Hawker Hunter: Biography of a thoroughbred, *also by Francis K. Mason and published by Patrick Stephens Limited.*

P 1121 died from national neglect, and with it was lost several million pounds of privately-subscribed investment. However, the P 1121 must be seen as having contributed very little in technological progress, being of fairly conventional construction, and could conceivably have *retarded* development of modern weapons systems in Britain during the 1960s by repeatedly invoking compromise; and, as is now widely said of the ill-fated TSR 2, it would certainly have overstrained the increasingly limited resources of the aircraft industry as a whole. One can be wise after the event.

Unlike Sweden, wherein wholehearted determination to defend the nation's political and military non-alignment had encouraged development of the Viggen multi-rôle fighter (the most advanced European combat aircraft for over a decade), Britain's aircraft industry was already under considerable political pressure to contract in the yet-unsubstantiated belief that thereby could costs be reduced.

In one vital respect the P 1121 contributed to Hawker's survival: it ensured the retention of its design force, the assemblage of highly experienced design specialists, the project and research engineers, aerodynamicists and metallurgists, systems managers, stressmen, weapons specialists and others. These men and women were individually at the very pinnacle of the mechanical engineering profession, and collectively represented the most valuable single asset of a great aircraft manufacturing company.

* * *

This then was the situation at Hawker Aircraft Limited when, in mid-1957, the company entered the field of vertical take-off aircraft design. Some three years earlier another member of the Hawker Siddeley Group, A.V. Roe & Co, had unsuccessfully tendered a proposal to employ the Avro 707B delta research aircraft for the Ministry of Supply's ER 143 T jet-lift Specification, and in 1955-56 Sir W.G. Armstrong Whitworth Aircraft Limited was working on its AW 956 project with ten lift engines and two Orpheus cruise

Wooden mock-up of the Hawker P 1121 supersonic air superiority strike aircraft in the Kingston experimental shops (Hawker Aircraft Ltd, Neg No EXP228/57).

engines. One is again reminded that all serious consideration of vertical take-off was being applied at this time to multiple jet-lift powerplant configuration.

However, it was at this time that a French engineer, Michel Wibault, began toying with the idea of employing the vectored-thrust principle to divert the gases from a turbojet downwards for take-off and landing, and rearwards for horizontal cruising flight. Wibault, whose company had built commercial aircraft between the World Wars, had spent the war years in America but returned to France in poor health afterwards and established an engineering consultancy. His scheme for vectored-thrust from a turbojet envisaged centrifugal blowers at right angles to the aircraft's fore-and-aft datum, driven by a gas turbine, the volute casings being rotatable so as to direct the exhaust from the turbine vertically downwards or horizontally aft. After unsuccessful attempts to interest the French and American governments in his scheme, he was advised to approach the Mutual Weapons Development Team (MWDT) in Paris, an organisation headed by Colonel (later General, retired) Bill Chapman, USAF, to examine and encourage promising European military projects which might otherwise have withered and died through lack of funds.

The MWDT was already working with Bristol Engines on development of the Orpheus turbojet for the NATO Light Strike Fighter—which eventually emerged as the Fiat G.91—and it was therefore not unnatural that Chapman should approach Dr Stanley Hooker, then Bristol's Technical Director, for his views on Wibault's proposals in 1956. The initial response was unenthusiastic owing to the relative inefficiency of the centrifugal blowers but Hooker, mindful of his company's gratitude for MWDT's support in helping to get the Orpheus off the ground, promised to undertake a constructive examination of the project. A design was initiated (as the BE 52) in which the centrifugal blowers were replaced by an axial compressor whose total flow was to be discharged through a pair of rotatable 'bent pipes'. This scheme was considered to show promise and in January 1957 a provisional patent was applied for in the joint names of Michel Wibault and Gordon Lewis (then a Bristol project engineer and later Assistant Managing Director (Bristol), Rolls-Royce (1971) Ltd). In due course Bristol adopted the Orpheus gas producer driving the first three stages of the Olympus compressor through a low pressure turbine added at the rear end of the Orpheus, this engine becoming the BE 53. A brochure outlining these proposals was passed to MWDT early in 1957.

Hawker became involved quite fortuitously when the company's Chief Designer, Sir Sydney Camm, was being conducted around the Paris Air Show in June that year. By chance his guide, 'Gerry' Morel*, was the French agent for both Hawker Aircraft and Bristol Engines, and while watching the 'flying Atar' being demonstrated he asked Camm whether he was aware of Hooker's work on the BE 53. Camm admitted that he was not, and within a day or so a copy of the engine brochure arrived on his desk at Kingston.

At first no one at Hawker took the engine proposals too seriously as it was thought that an Orpheus-based engine producing over 11,000 pounds thrust was wishful thinking. It fell, however, to Ralph Hooper, one of Camm's senior project designers, to examine the scheme and to decide what, if any, type of aircraft might conceivably be realistically designed about it. Vertical take-off was out of the question at that time as the gas producer's exhaust was not deflected downwards. However, Hooper was immediately impressed by the inherent simplicity of the proposal, and embarked on the initial scheming of a three-seat STOL battlefield liaison aircraft—believing that the limited

* *Major Gerard Morel, to whom the British aircraft industry owes a special debt of gratitude, had served with outstanding courage with the Special Operations Executive (SOE) during the war. Despite recurring ill-health he was one of the first agents to be landed in France, survived imprisonment by the Germans and Vichy authorities and twice escaped to England through Spain. Sadly, he died shortly after the events described above.*

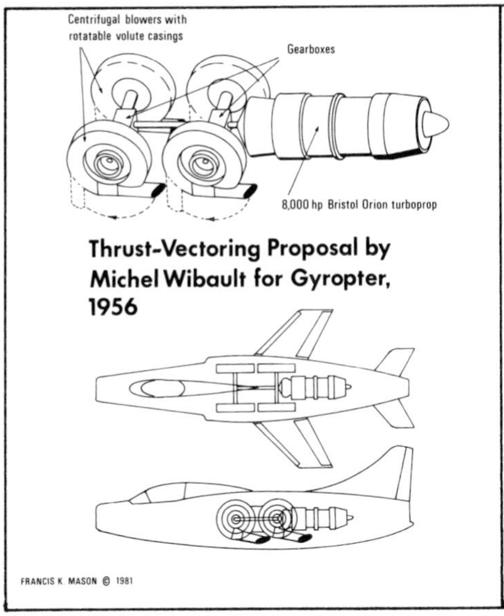

Thrust-Vectoring Proposal by Michel Wibault for Gyropter, 1956

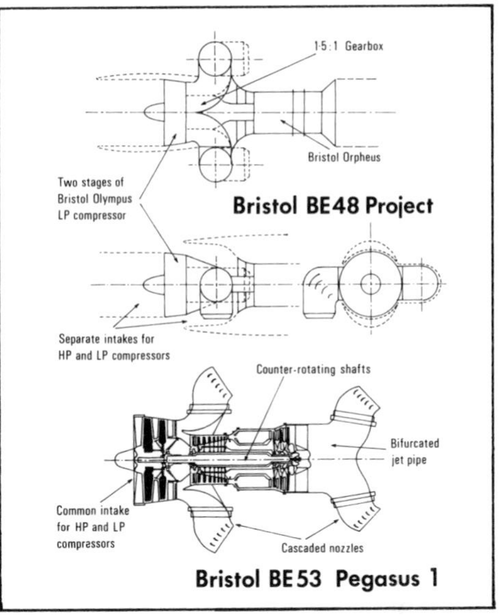

Bristol BE48 Project

Bristol BE53 Pegasus 1

thrust available would preclude carriage of a worthwhile weapon load. No doubt there were also feelings at Hawker at this time that thoughts of a 'fighter' aircraft would attract little sympathy outside the company. This scheme, dated June 28 and allotted the project number P 1127, was little more than a thumbnail sketch and incorporated nose air intake, tailwheel undercarriage and exaggerated on-ground attitude. Within a week, after further calculations had shown engine thrust to be inadequate, a further scheme was produced in which only two tandem seats were included together with lateral air intakes and nose-and-tail reaction controls. (See drawings on page 31.)

In the meantime Dr Hooker had visited Kingston to discuss the BE 53 and he suggested that, provided financial support could be found, a flight engine might be available two years hence. As work went ahead in Camm's project office it was becoming obvious that aircraft weight was likely to overtake engine performance, so much of the engine's potential vertical component of thrust being wasted in the horizontal at take-off. It 'suddenly' occurred to Hooper that to bifurcate the hot end of the Orpheus (as in the Hawker Sea Hawk's Nene engine, whose split tailpipes were covered by Hawker patents) would allow *all* the hot thrust to be vectored downwards, and at the end of August Bristol, who were preparing a final tender for MWDT, gave qualified approval for this proposal, and went so far as to suggest that Hawker should join forces in dealing with Colonel Chapman.

The first P 1127 brochure, depicting a single-seat ground attack/reconnaissance aircraft, was prepared in August and shown to Colonel Chapman during his visit to the Farnborough Display the following month. His reaction was generally favourable, but it was clear that NATO requirements would demand a doubling of the aircraft's range. To achieve the necessary 2,000-lb thrust increase from the engine to cater for the additional fuel, Hawker suggested to Bristol adopting water injection at take-off, the engine company confirming that this would achieve the target power output.

Another aspect of the engine characteristics which troubled Hawker at this time was the substantial gyroscopic effect from co-rotating Olympus fan and Orpheus gas producer. It had always been part of Hawker's 'battlefield concept' for the P 1127 that simplicity of control system was of paramount importance, it being a design aim to dispense with mandatory three-axis autostabilisation, although some degree of back-up auto-pilot was anticipated. All available information, particularly from the Short SC1 and the Rolls-Royce 'flying bedstead', suggested that such autostabilisation would be essential. Yet the view prevailed at Kingston that if the fan and gas producer of the BE 53 could be made to counter-rotate, the gyroscopic couple would be virtually eliminated. Bristol, whose engine proposals were to some extent based on the cost-saving use of the existing Olympus fan, naturally pointed to the high cost of re-blading the fan to reverse its rotation, and also suggested that doubling the spin rate of the intershaft bearings might be unacceptable.*

It was at this point (November 1957) that work on the P 1127 temporarily stopped. Instead it was decided to pool all the Kingston design resources with those of Avro to submit a tender for the Air Staff Operational Requirement (OR 339)—which later became the TSR 2. It was also in November that Sir Sydney Camm was formally informed by Controller (Air) at the Ministry of Supply that the company could not expect any support for the P 1127 from the British Government. Pre-occupation by the Ministry with the jet-lift Short SC1—which was, after all, already flying and had been developed to meet a specific requirement—effectively closed the door on Treasury funding of the BE 53 engine. Coming so close on the heels of the demise of the P 1121, not to mention the other Hawker Siddeley projects axed in 1956-57 (including the Avro 720 rocket-powered interceptor whose prototype had been 90 per cent complete), there was little private capital available for speculative support of high-cost engine development.

Notwithstanding this lack of enthusiasm by the British Government, the tide of the P 1127's fortunes changed early in 1958. A further visit to the MWDT by Camm and Hooper was paid in January during which it was learned that American funding was virtually assured for the engine development. A revised version of the aircraft, the P 1127B, was outlined in a new brochure; the new design was somewhat smaller and featured Hawker vaned nozzles in place of the 'bent pipes'. At the same time the engine had undergone considerable change with the inclusion of a new two-stage transonic fan which supercharged the high-pressure compressor thus effectively making the BE 53 a high bypass fan in which the bypass gases exhausted through the front 'cold' nozzles.

The bulk of the engine now demanded considerable further redesign of the P 1127 (the P 1127C) in which a conventional undercarriage had to be abandoned. Hooper recalls that in order to finalise the new proposals for a further visit to Colonel Chapman on March 24, he had to work throughout the preceding weekend, but the design 'became quite exciting as it was clear that things fitted together much better.'†

The engine's improved specific fuel consumption, resulting from its higher pressure ratio, permitted the fuel capacity to be reduced from 500 to 430 gallons. A zero-track tricycle undercarriage with nose and mainwheels retracting into the fuselage on the centreline demanded balancing outriggers at the wing tips; the marked wing anhedral

* *There is evidence of some disagreement between Hawker and Bristol as to who first 'thought of' bifurcating the tailpipes and including counter-rotating spools. Certainly the Bristol patent application drawings (Patent No 881662 of January 29 1957, ie, before collaboration with Hawker commenced) include both features. However, it is likely that Hawker was not shown the patent drawings but simply a rudimentary brochure; in the interests of cost-limiting neither feature was probably considered vital at this stage.*

Equally beyond dispute is the fact that the bifurcated tailpipe was the subject of a Hawker patent—vis-a-vis *the Sea Hawk 12 years earlier—and Hooper clearly advocated this, as well as spool counter-rotation, independently. The application of these features in the P 1127 was thus arrived at independently and agreed by Bristol when their ramifications had been fully studied. What is not disputed is that the concept of jet-thrust vectoring as a feature of the BE engine projects was entirely Bristol's (in the joint names of Wibault and Gordon Lewis).*

† *Cf 19th Chadwick Memorial Lecture, RAeS, 1974*

Early wooden display model of the P 1127 (Hawker Aircraft Ltd, Neg No EXP172/58).

now adopted stemmed from the need to limit the length of the outrigger legs with the wing being mounted as a continuous structure across the top of the engine.

The new design met with an enthusiastic reception by the MWDT and the following month design office effort at Kingston was considerably increased, being aimed principally at trying to find an alternative to the zero-track undercarriage (about which Camm was not particularly enthusiastic), but without success.

In May the company was informed by Dr Walter Cawood at the Ministry of Supply that although some tunnel testing facilities might in due course be made available, there was little chance of obtaining a research contract for the P 1127 as there appeared to be no civil potential, and Hawker was obliged to embark on a hand-to-mouth existence, employing locally-constructed models in the Kingston Technical College's low-speed tunnel. However, under the supervision of Hawker's Chief Systems Engineer, Ellis Gabbay, the design and manufacture of a series of ground-board models, with both cold and hot blowing (and later intake suction) for ground effects investigation, was put in hand for testing in the company's Experimental Department.

Not surprisingly the whole vexed question regarding support for the P 1127 continued to worry the group and company management. It was, of course, very encouraging that development of the Bristol engine was virtually assured, but the strictly parochial development of a potentially operational aeroplane was something as unsatisfactory from a commercial viewpoint as it was politically damaging. At the previous year's annual Anglo-American Aeronautical Conference at Folkestone Mr M.O. McKinney had presented a paper describing the work already done in America on vertical and short take-off aircraft*, from which it had emerged just how American interest in the field had grown. The 1958 Conference, held during late July in the USA, was attended by Mr E.T. Jones, Deputy Controller (Overseas Affairs) at the Ministry of Supply, and the Hawker management took pains beforehand not only to brief Mr Jones on the P 1127's potential but also to emphasise the advisability of investing some British Government share in the project in the event that the aircraft successfully achieved operational status.

* NACA Research on VTOL and STOL Aeroplanes. *M.O. McKinney, 1957*

Left *One-tenth scale low-speed tunnel model with rotatable engine nozzles; this model was also used for ground effects investigation* (Hawker Aircraft Ltd, Neg No PROJ16/61).

Right *One-tenth scale static ground effects model; the central large-diameter duct drew air through the engine intakes, and the other ducts discharged cold and hot air vertically downwards through front and rear nozzles respectively* (Hawker Aircraft Ltd, Neg No EXP121/58).

Below right *First prototype P 1127 wing during manufacture; the wing spars of the second aircraft are in the jigs in the background* (Hawker Aircraft Ltd, Neg No EXP180/59).

That these arguments were beginning to bear fruit was evidenced by growing interest in the project at the RAE where, following an instruction given by Mr Handel Davies (Director-General, Scientific Research (Air), at the Ministry of Supply) in June, tunnel facilities were now to be put at Hawker's disposal, while Lewis Nicholson, the RAE's Head of Aerodynamics, and David Williams, the RAE's Deputy Chief Scientific Officer (Structural Research), visited Hawker to discuss the P 1127's design and the nature of tunnel tests required. At the end of the month Hugh Vessey, Head of the RAE's Transonic Tunnel Department, started discussions on the high-speed test programme.

With tangible evidence of Ministry involvement in the research programme now being planned, the Hawker management in August 1958 authorised a start on the detail design of the P 1127 wing in the company's Experimental Design Office.

Probably spurred by the increasing interest being displayed by MWDT in the Hawker project—in September Major Severski, USAF, Technical Adviser to NATO, had recommended bypassing a Fiat G.91 replacement with an aircraft possibly based on the P 1127—not to mention undisguised American enthusiasm for the project, the RAF (and the Admiralty) started to display symptoms of interest in the whole subject of V/STOL aircraft in October with the preliminary drafting of Requirements for a VTOL fighter and a VTOL transport. The former, however—owing to widely differing views still held within the OR Branch—was to undergo countless fundamental alterations before it was eventually issued some two years later as the GOR 345. These constant alterations proved to span almost every imaginable facet of performance, equipment, weapons and even the ultimate combat rôle, to such an extent that it was just as well that the Requirement was not allowed to influence the P 1127's fundamental design progress, otherwise it is very doubtful whether any final design would have emerged.

It may have been the absence of Government funding for the project as a whole,

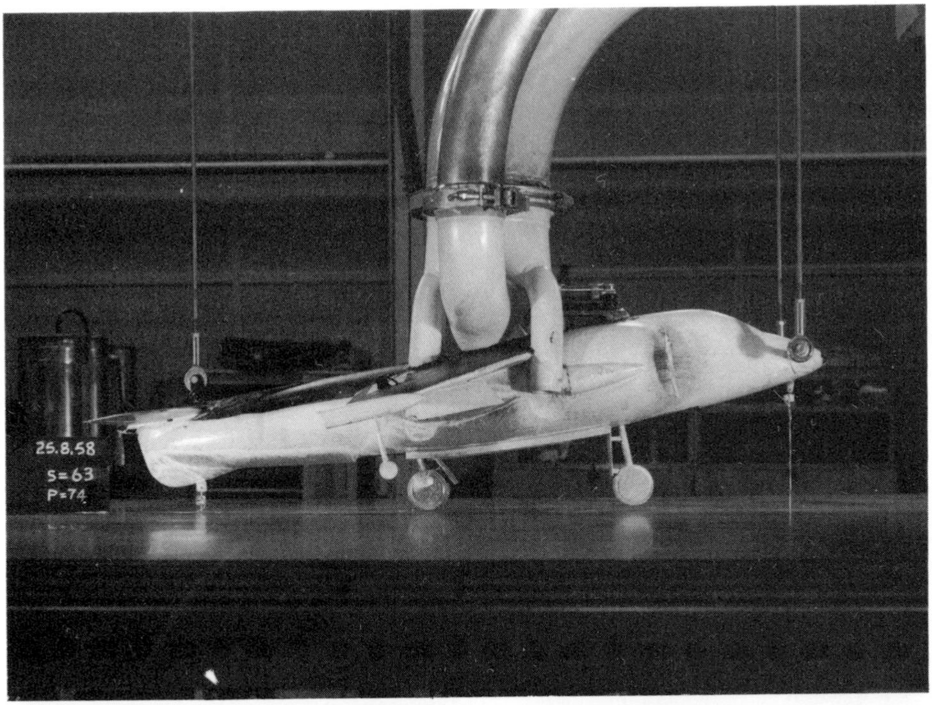
25.8.58
S=63
P=74

together with Camm's own preference for an uncomplicated operational design concept (a concept that was, incidentally, beginning to gain widespread support) that excluded sophisticated control systems in the P 1127 from the outset, so that the inclusion of a relatively simple three-axis autostabiliser was not allowed to override the ultimate objective of achieving manual control in all modes of flight. Such a policy might have seemed inconceivable to those at the RAE and the National Physics Laboratory who were already entirely sympathetic with the relatively complex control system of the Short SC1 (and those who were always prepared to produce calculations to prove that it is impossible to ride a bicycle without an autostabiliser); nevertheless, agreement was reached in October that such a manual system could, with careful development work, probably be accomplished. Accordingly, under the supervision of a Hawker project engineer, Robin Balmer, work started on development of a control response simulator—in effect an Avro-Ferranti Pegasus analog computer modified to reproduce control-load characteristics in real time according to aircraft dynamic inputs. This ingenious device represented a rudimentary flight simulator, capable of reproducing the P 1127's—or any other aircraft's—control 'feel' while the aircraft still existed only on paper.

First indications that some form of Government support for the P 1127 was being considered were unofficially disclosed to the company's management early in January 1959 with a hint that the newly-styled Ministry of Aviation had in mind the purchase of two prototypes, and later that month Mr R.A. Shaw, Assistant Director (Aircraft Research), MoA, visited the company to be briefed on the project's progress. The reason for this reversal of official policy soon became apparent during a discussion between the Deputy Chief of the Air Staff (Operational Requirements), Air Vice-Marshal W.H. (later Sir Wallace) Kyle, and Camm on January 23 1959 when it was stated that, having got its way with the TSR 2 Requirement (OR 339), the Air Staff now felt free to take an active interest in other projects, and that the RAF intended to seek an aircraft such as the P 1127 to replace the Hunter in the tactical ground support rôle. A week later Hawker was officially informed that an RAF Specification existed in draft form and was being examined by various Government departments.

An entirely new situation now arose. As British support for the P 1127 appeared to be assured (although no Contract cover had materialised), Hawker became aware that it would be very difficult to obtain tangible support from MWDT for NATO's employment of the aircraft. Owing to powerful influences existing within the SHAPE/NATO infrastructure, a policy of 'internationalisation' was being adopted whereby preference was expressed for project-sharing between two or more nations, and it was explained by SHAPE's OR department that the P 1127, with airframe and engine both being designed and developed in Britain, would meet with opposition from France, and the company was therefore encouraged to enter negotiations with a Continental manufacturer to share the development and eventual production of the P 1127.

Such a policy—subsequently pursued successfully with such aircraft as the SEPECAT Jaguar, Panavia Tornado and, in the commercial field, the BAC-Aérospatiale Concorde—might have appeared logical in that it would possibly have generated wider interest among NATO member nations in the P 1127 as well as alleviating development costs of the project. However, as matters stood in 1959, Hawker was itself anxious to secure its own survival through eventual quantity manufacture of the P 1127 and, with the engine development firmly rooted in Britain with MWDT support, saw a likelihood of losing the airframe manufacture to a Continental company if such an agreement were to be conditional for SHAPE/NATO support.

Already Rolls-Royce was involved in negotiations with Marcel Dassault to collaborate in the development of a V/STOL adaptation of the Mirage fighter (later to materialise as the Dassault Mirage 'Balzac' prototype) with jet-lift engines. There is little doubt but that it was this project-sharing between the British engine company and the French airframe manufacturer that was to muddy the waters of Hawker's erstwhile relations with MWDT. Moreover—as with the RAF's VTO fighter Requirement—the new NATO second-generation light fighter OR was still extremely nebulous, and there was still no firm indication whether the ultimate Requirement would be for a 'simple' aircraft, such as the Fiat G.91 which the aircraft would in due course be required to replace, or for a much more sophisticated aircraft including supersonic performance and perhaps multi-rôle capability.

On balance Hawker was certainly wise in its decision to continue to 'go it alone' for the time being, and pursue the research aspect of the P 1127 to demonstrate the feasibility of vectored-thrust before becoming enmeshed in meeting Operational Requirements; after all, there was still no telling whether the RAF and NATO Requirements might not emerge as diametrically conflicting in their operational demands; the P 1127 might fall between both, and satisfy neither. Subsequent events confirmed the wisdom of Hawker's decision.

In fairness to those in Paris and Whitehall, the decisions regarding operational employment of V/STOL aircraft were daunting in their implications. In its eagerness to pursue commercial interests, a section of the aircraft industry was, after all, suggesting adoption of a radically new operational concept—ingenious and attractive though it might eventually prove to be—which would ultimately demand considerable re-organisation, training and re-alignment of operational responsibilities not only among combat elements of the armed forces but throughout the support and administrative branches. Whatever the attractions of the so-called 'no runway' philosophy might be, the implications of introducing a new specialist element into an Air Force's weapon arsenal could only be countenanced with caution as each radical stage was confirmed by successful demonstration and experience.

Thus was the Hawker management left with the unenviable situation in which it was obliged to persevere with the P 1127 as a research vehicle, knowing that it represented by far the most realistic approach to the basis of an operational aircraft being considered anywhere in the world, yet without any coherent Operational Requirement in being and without any Contract cover for the necessary research. Yet faith in its decision to persevere prompted Hawker to issue manufacturing drawings to its Experimental Department in March 1959, and the first metal was cut the following month.

Meanwhile a number of decisions had been taken affecting production of the initial aircraft; these included the adoption of a simple autostabiliser and full-power controls in the prototypes, and use of some Sea Hawk undercarriage components in the first aircraft to save time and cost.

In April 1959 the company was given its first sight of the RAF's draft GOR 345, intended to outline the requirements for a Hunter replacement in the ground attack and fighter-reconnaissance rôles during 1965. Although still very much blurred by conflicting ideas held by senior RAF planners, the OR had clearly been 'written around' the P 1127, and its demands were at least realistic and not, as had been feared, beyond the capabilities of an eventual development of the aircraft.

On the 23rd the company was formally asked by the MoA to prepare costs and a manufacturing programme for two prototypes, and within a week these had been submitted through Handel Davies. At the same time a draft Research Specification, ER 204D, was prepared at the MoA, and this was first shown to the company on May 13.

This unaccustomed burst of administrative activity, disclosing the British Government's determination to become identified at long last with the P 1127, appears to have taken SHAPE by surprise and almost immediately Hawker was invited to attend a meeting in Paris with Bristol and MoA representatives to discuss possible adaptation of the aircraft to meet NATO requirements, such as they were. It was generally accepted that the P 1127 was now so far ahead of competitors in its potential operational concept that it still demanded consideration in the context of NATO's second-generation 'light fighter' requirements. However, at the meeting, held on June 16, it became abundantly clear that the emphasis had moved right away from the 'lightweight' concept and that a much more sophisticated all-weather capability was being demanded. This effectively ended any immediate likelihood of NATO interest in the P 1127.

Notwithstanding this turn of events, Colonel Chapman still maintained his enthusiasm for the project and turned his influence to foster closer collaboration between Hawker and the American aircraft industry, and it was not long before representatives of that industry were visiting Kingston to learn more of the project at first hand.

As the Hawker management now authorised overtime working in all departments with a first flight target date set for July 1960, Robert Marsh (Hawker's Head of Projects) and Ralph Hooper visited the United States on July 21 for discussions with the Bell Aircraft Corporation and NASA at Langley Field. Bell Aircraft were at the time investigating three concepts of vertical take-off aircraft, apart from their extensive involvement in helicopter work; these were the tilting-rotor convertiplane, the ducted-propeller VTOL aeroplane and the jet-deflection turbojet-powered aircraft. The latter, a small twin Viper-powered research aeroplane designated the X-14, was of extremely simple design employing thrust diverters behind the engines to deflect the jet efflux downwards to provide vertical thrust. In this respect, and in its system of reaction controls, the X-14 approximated to the P 1127 in concept—albeit handicapped by a fairly serious gyro couple—and it was obviously of mutual interest that some interchange of opinions should be initiated. The same friendly atmosphere of willingness to collaborate was found at Langley Field where Mr John Stack on his own authority initiated a programme of free-flight model testing of the P 1127. Following the Hawker project engineers' visit it was agreed with the MoA that NASA should also undertake transonic tunnel testing of the aircraft. On October 21 Hawker received a preliminary 'holding' Contract from the MoA for £75,000 to cover the cost of design work now being done on the aircraft.

By the end of 1959, against a background of overseas interest*, the first P 1127 prototype was beginning to take shape in the Experimental Department. The BS 53/2 had been ground-run successfully at Filton and the first phase of low-speed tunnel tests completed at the RAE. Design studies were in hand by outside contractors for cockpit instrument display systems, while the Sperry Gyroscope Company and Ferranti Limited were working on navigation and reconnaissance systems.

While progress continued to be made with the P 1127, events elsewhere still threatened to complicate the situation vis-a-vis the NATO VTOL requirement. As already stated this had by now been generally accepted as demanding an aircraft of considerably greater complexity and sophistication than was likely to be satisfied by the P 1127 or a relatively straightforward derivative. Indeed, such was the scale of equipment likely to be demanded (including advanced weapon delivery and navigation equipment, not to mention heavy weapon load and even supersonic interceptor capability) that Bristol had projected a 'Stage 2' version of the BS 53 with a thrust of almost 20,000 lb. Moreover, the increased aircraft size and weight implicit in the NATO aircraft now encouraged Rolls-Royce to redouble its efforts to canvas support for the multi-jet-lift principle, pursuing the theory

* *Representatives from the air forces of the USA, Canada, Australia, Switzerland, Holland and Germany had all visited Kingston, stating that V/STOL requirements were being formulated in their respective countries.*

The Bristol Siddeley Pegasus turbofan was flight-tested mounted under the bomb bay of a Valiant bomber, WP199, *during 1963-64* (Rolls-Royce Ltd, Neg No E68776).

that the lift-jets permitted greater flexibility with regard to aircraft weight and performance. And this philosophy was still attracting many advocates—not least in the RAF's OR Branch.

The upshot of this distraction was a formal request by the MoA in February 1960 that Hawker commit itself to a formal declaration as to whether or not the P 1127 could be considered seriously to meet the NATO Requirement. The company replied that there was no likelihood of the P 1127—in its initial configuration—meeting such advanced operational demands but that in due course, by using the Stage 2 BS 53 with greatly increased power output, a developed version might satisfy the NATO demands. More will be told in Chapter 5 of this Requirement.

As it was, Hawker's reluctance to become prematurely involved in what was still a wholly nebulous requirement seems to have been entirely justified, particularly as the Bristol engine had yet to fly even in its earliest form. Furthermore, it was at this very point that Bristol Siddeley informed Camm that its power outputs were already behind schedule and that it seemed unlikely that more than 10,000 lb thrust would be available from the first flight engine. This was a severe blow to the Hawker designers who were already forecasting an all-up weight for the prototype of around 10,000 lb. After some alterations to the engine, however, Dr Hooker was able to revise his estimates and told

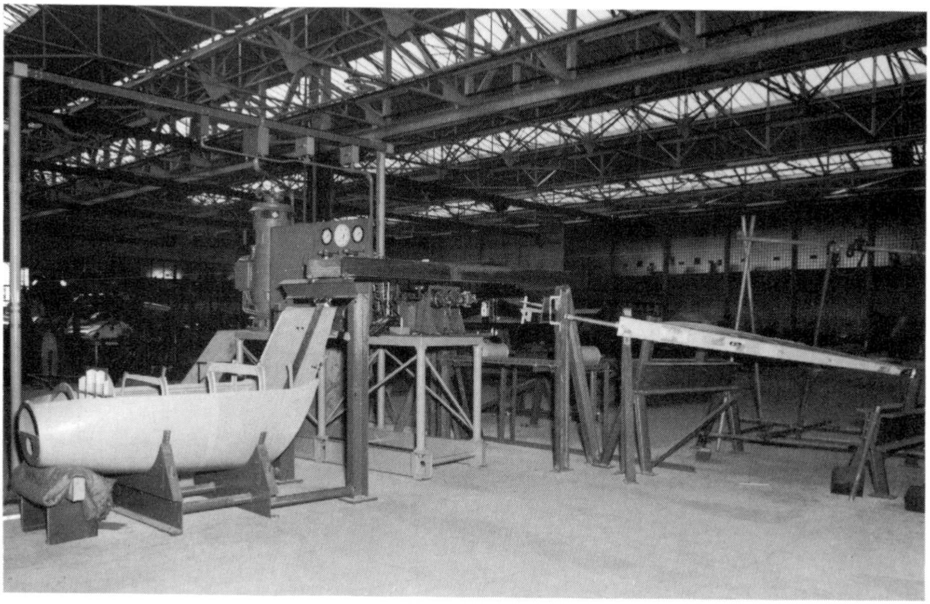

Flying control rig during manufacture at Kingston (Hawker Aircraft Ltd, Neg No EXP34/60).

Camm on March 29 that recent bench running had confirmed a thrust of 11,500 lb; this seemed to be marginally sufficient for the initial hovering trials, but *only* marginally so in view of demands made in April for increased bleed for the reaction controls.

The latter expedient was considered necessary to cope with increased roll power during hover following an accident with the Bell X-14 on April 1 involving Hugh Merewether, Hawker's Chief Experimental Test Pilot, who was in America to gain experience in the aircraft. During a vertical landing in this aeroplane the pilot 'ran out' of roll power owing to the high gyroscopic couple and damaged the undercarriage; Merewether was unhurt, and the Americans at Ames generously explained that in any case the X-14 was scheduled to be grounded to have more powerful engines fitted.

While manufacture of the first aircraft approached completion at Kingston, the Short SC1 achieved its first transitions from vertical to horizontal flight during May. At Filton the first bench-running of the Pegasus 2, with a higher mass flow compressor to permit use of high pressure air for the aircraft's reaction controls, had started in February and was now cleared for flight at an uninstalled thrust of 11,000 lb.

Model testing was also beginning to return most encouraging results, accelerating and decelerating transitions being achieved by the one-tenth scale free-flight model at Langley, Virginia (also in February), while a peroxide-powered transonic model programme was underway at NASA. In March the one-tenth scale low-speed model started its second phase of tunnel tests at the RAE, and at the end of the following month endurance tests on the reaction control ducts and valves commenced at the Gloster Aircraft Company's Brockworth facility.

Despite no Contract yet existing to cover the first two P 1127s, the Ministry of Aviation approached Hawker on April 12 with a request for tender on four further prototypes, and on May 3 the cost and timescale estimates were submitted. Three days later the first Pegasus engine (No 905) was delivered by Bristol to Kingston for installation in the first prototype.

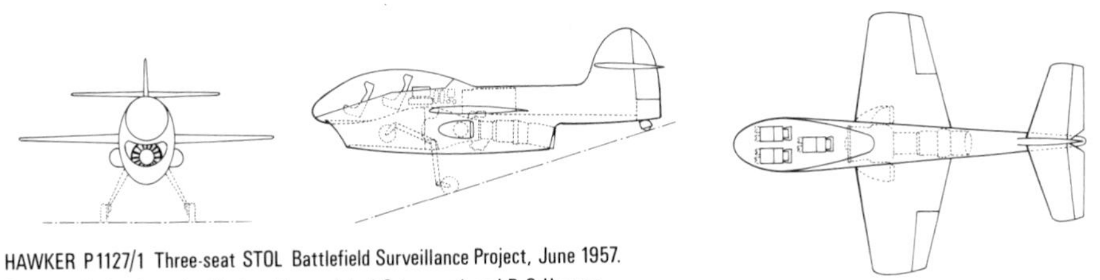

HAWKER P1127/1 Three-seat STOL Battlefield Surveillance Project, June 1957.
Semi-annular intake and mid-wing. From original Scheme, signed R.S. Hooper.

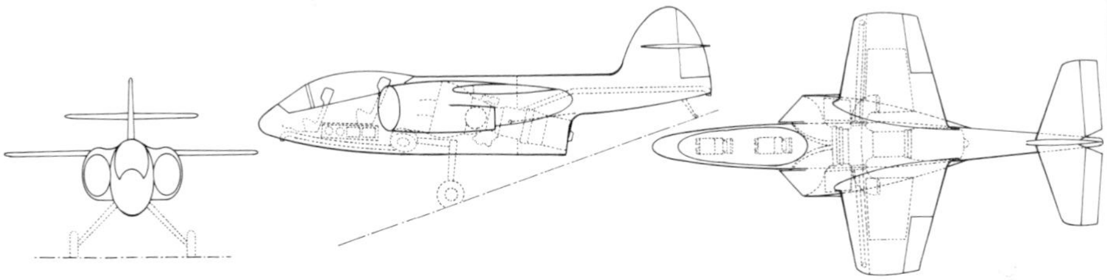

HAWKER P1127/2 Two-seat STOL Tactical Support Project, July 1957.
Lateral intakes and shoulder wing. From original Scheme, dated 5th July 1957, signed R.S. Hooper.

Summary of models employed in P 1127 development back-up

1 $\frac{1}{16}$th-scale static ground effects model; cold efflux; common supply to fore and aft nozzles; no intake flow. Used to establish flow patterns and measure ground suction loss. Led to adoption of strakes to reduce ground loss.

2 As above but with intake suction added.

3 $\frac{1}{16}$th-scale static hot model. Front and rear efflux at correct temperature and velocity; intake flow included. Temperature surveys only.

4 $\frac{1}{10}$th-scale static ground effects model. Correct intake and jet conditions. Forces and temperatures measured together. Transient conditions investigated.

5 $\frac{1}{10}$th-scale low-speed tunnel model; cold efflux; common supply to fore and aft rotatable nozzles; intake flow available but not to full RPM mass flow; model mounted on air bearings. Also used as ground effects model.

6 NASA $\frac{1}{7}$th-scale free-flight model. Manufactured and tested at Langley Field, Va, USA. Cold jets with common supply. Reaction nozzles with bang-bang control. Model hovered and carried out quasi-static transitions in tunnel. Performed STOs and scale-time transitions on rotating crane rig.

7 NASA $\frac{1}{8}$th-scale transonic tunnel model. Model with peroxide jets inducing intake flow, hence all jets at approximately the same conditions.

8 ARA $\frac{1}{10}$th-scale transonic tunnel model. Model with compressed cold air jets including intake flow. Common supply.

9 ARA $\frac{1}{4}$-scale transonic half-model. Free flow through intake and jet exits. Used for wing development and tailplane flow investigations.

Chapter 3

The idea succeeds

The arrival at flight stage by the P 1127 was extraordinary tribute to the engine and airframe design leaders to whom the aircraft was not simply a new project but a new concept. Conventional demarcation between airframe and engine development had simply not existed and this led to integrated flexibility of thought and reduced boundaries of responsibility. Unquestionably such freedom of action resulted in a unique level of collaboration between the contractors' staffs in a manner that would have been stifled under conventional Ministry-invigilated conditions.

That the P 1127/Pegasus project now moved into the formal environment of Government sponsorship, yet continued to progress in an atmosphere of confidence and inherent enthusiasm, was entirely due to the attitudes of integration and shared responsibilities that had hitherto thrived under the initial commercial management. No one was more conscious than Camm's and Hooker's staffs that the entire success or failure of the V/STOL concept was about to be decided as the first P 1127 approached completion during the late summer of 1960.

As the whole *raison d'être* of the P 1127 lay in its ability to perform vertical and short take-offs and landings, it was decided to devote all initial engine running time on the first prototype to the hovering mode so as to examine all problems associated with control at zero forward speed and 'flight' under jet-borne power. To begin with, it was accepted that not only would the early engines' lives be strictly limited, permitting very abbreviated hovering duration, but also that an extremely slender margin of installed thrust over aircraft weight would be available. As it was essential to avoid additional thrust loss due to recirculation, work started at Dunsfold beside the western extremity of the runway to provide a large gas dispersal recess covered by a steel slatted grid over which initial hovering would be carried out. Unlike the earlier Short SC1 trials, use of an overhead gantry was dispensed with.

On June 22 the Ministry of Aviation got around to signing a Contract for the first two prototypes, to be numbered *XP831* and *XP836.* The following month the Ministry established a P 1127 Management Board and Assessment Group to monitor and supervise progress.

The first prototype, *XP831,* was delivered to Dunsfold on July 15 for final assembly and systems checks, and the complete aircraft was first 'rolled out' on August 31 for initial weighing and its first engine runs with engine No 905 in a specially modified silencing pen. During the course of these a small fire occurred following an oil leak at the rear nozzle, but damage was imperceptible owing to the prompt action of an attendant fireman.

The next stage was to run the engine over the grid on September 22 when it was found that excessive airframe temperatures, suffered when using exhaust collector shrouds in the silencing pen, were no longer experienced. Engine No 905 was then returned to

Right *The Dunsfold hover-grid showing the cascade vanes and some sections of gridded platform in place* (Hawker Aircraft Ltd, Neg No PRO211/60).

Below *The Dunsfold ground-running pen during manufacture, showing the below-surface ducts for disposing of exhaust efflux* (Hawker Aircraft Ltd, Neg No PRO207/60).

Left *First roll-out picture of* XP831 *taken at Dunsfold on August 31 1960, prior to initial engine running. Note the fixed bell-mouth air intake fairings* (Hawker Aircraft Ltd, Neg No EXP253/60).

Below left XP831 *in the special ground-running pen with exhaust shrouds in place* (Hawker Aircraft Ltd, Neg No EXP250/60).

Right *Close-up of* XP831 *during the initial hovering phase, showing the temporary bell-mouth intake fairing; note absence of wheel doors and that the port outrigger, although fully extended, is clear of the ground* (Bristol Siddeley, Neg No E52495).

Filton having ended its cleared life before examination, and on October 13 the first flight engine, Pegasus 2 No 906 developing 11,300 lb thrust on the bench, was run for the first time in *XP831*.

The point had now been reached when everything seemed set to take to the air. Unfortunately Bill Bedford, Hawker's Chief Test Pilot, had just had an argument with a tree while being driven in a car in Switzerland and was hobbling about with his leg encased in a large plaster cast, and it was in this uncomfortable state that he climbed into *XP831* on October 21. The aircraft had been stripped of all unessential equipment in the interests of weight saving, including radio equipment, undercarriage doors, outrigger fairings and nose pitot boom. Only 35 gallons of fuel were provided—adequate for just two minutes' hovering at full throttle! With the engine nozzles locked in the vertical, Bedford started up and fairly briskly opened the throttle to maximum power; *XP831* rose off the grid to the full extent of its wing-tip tethers—just twelve inches. As the nominal length of the tethers was reached an increasing number of metal weights was lifted, thereby smoothly increasing the restraint. All went well and as Bedford came to the end of his fuel he closed the throttle and *XP831* settled back on the grid.

Unforeseen problems arose during the next hover when the tether length was extended to four feet: the main undercarriage leg extended more than the outriggers on lift-off and, as the aircraft rose, the horizontal lift force component moved the aircraft sideways and slewed it round in yaw. This could have been countered by increased reaction control power—but this simply didn't exist in the Pegasus 2 at the time.

During the first five weeks 21 hovers were successfully accomplished and on November 19 *XP831* rose from the grid freed of tethers. It was at once clear that some of the minor problems encountered thus far had, in fact, been *caused* by the action of the tethers.

Hovering had first been carried out with the autostabiliser switched out on the 4th, and

Above XP831 *during its second, tethered hover over the Dunsfold grid (restricted to about 4 ft). Of interest is the wool tufting on the rear fuselage, telemetry cables under the tail, radio telephone line behind the nearest wingtip tether (the radio had been omitted) and the absence of wheel doors and nose boom* (Hawker Aircraft Ltd, Neg No EXP340/60).

Left *The first prototype performing untethered hovering over the grid; the cable suspended from the starboard outrigger is the radio telephone link* (Hawker Aircraft Ltd, Neg No EXP334/60).

Below *The first P 1127 on arrival at the RAE, Bedford, complete with low-profile intake lips and all undercarriage fairings* (Dennis T. Waller, Neg No L742, dated March 14 1961).

Another view of XP831 *during its first visit to the RAE. Since the initial hovering tests all wheel doors and fairings have been fitted and the blunt intake lip fairings have been removed for the conventional flight trials; a tail parachute has also been fitted. The ram-air turbine, forward of the fin, is shown extended* (Dennis T. Waller, Neg No L741, dated March 14 1961).

on the 15th a brief tethered hover over solid ground was achieved without trouble although there was some slight overheating of the mainwheels.

Runway taxying up to 70 knots started on November 9 and, as was perhaps to be expected with such a radical undercarriage arrangement, these gave rise to some new problems, particularly with the nosewheel steering. The fully castoring outriggers tended to shimmy and were eventually locked for later trials. The aircraft also tended to bank from side to side while taxying in a side-wind; in due course the outriggers' travel was increased to ensure that both were in contact with the ground simultaneously. High-speed taxying which started on February 3 1961 resulted in serious wheel judder and cracking of the mainwheel leg. The undercarriage was removed from the second prototype—nearing completion at Kingston—for strengthening by Dowty, and on the 14th further taxying tests proved successful. *XP831* was then delivered by road to the RAE at Bedford to embark on conventional flight trials, arriving on the 27th.

In the meantime (on November 2) the Ministry of Aviation had signed a Contract for four further prototypes—*XP972, XP976, XP980* and *XP984*. It was intended that minor airframe and engine improvements would be progressively introduced in these as flight experience was accumulated.

Taxying by *XP831* up to 150 knots started at the RAE on March 1 (interrupted two days later by a small fire following an engine flameout on the runway), and on the 13th Bill Bedford made a successful first conventional flight of 22 minutes' duration. Eight further such flights were made up to 400 knots ASI, and 4 g at 30,000 ft (both Bedford and Merewether participating) before *XP831* was returned to Dunsfold by air on the 25th.

After the next two flights, which extended the clearance to Mach 0.8 and 4.7 g, the two pilots reported that lateral control was good, but longitudinally the aircraft was statically unstable and suffered pitch-up at high incidence; it was satisfactory directionally except with undercarriage down when it was slightly unstable. Use of flap and airbrake caused excessive trim change and there was a marked nose-down trim-change when in ground effect so that full stick-back was required while landing 'horizontally'. Cockpit noise and buffet were unacceptably high. The engine had functioned satisfactorily within the very stringent limitations imposed to avoid resonance of the fan blades owing to the very short air intakes. However, most of the handling and stability shortcomings had been foreseen

Left *Bill Bedford disembarks from* XP831 *during the first RAE tests* (Bristol Siddeley, Neg No E46889).

Below *High-speed taxying at Bedford; just beyond* XP831 *is the fire tender whose crew was called upon to extinguish a small fire on March 3 1961* (Bristol Siddeley, Neg No E46895).

Right *A view of* XP831 *in horizontal flight. Note the cutaway on the landing flaps (later found to be unnecessary)* (Hawker Aircraft Ltd).

Below *Conventional (ie, horizontal) runway landing by* XP831 *at Bedford, with a Hunter 7 two-seat chase-plane in attendance* (Bristol Siddeley, Neg No E46897).

The second prototype P 1127 XP836, *landing at Dunsfold* (Hawker Aircraft Ltd, Neg No 64/61).

and a series of wind tunnel tests at the Aircraft Research Authority with a half-model suggested that wing vortex generators would go a long way to improve stability.

Between May and June *XP831* returned to the hovering mode and 51 such 'flights' were made, now powered by a 12,000-lb thrust Pegasus 2. Increased control bleed was provided and this proved perfectly adequate during hovering above 50 ft, but below 20 ft—where the aircraft suffered in the ground effect—yaw control was strictly marginal. This was also affected at low forward speeds due to high intake momentum drag of the large engine airflow ahead of the aircraft's centre of gravity.

Meanwhile much attention had been given to alleviating hot gas recirculation near the ground. For the first series of hovering tests in 1960 the engine intake lips had been 'blunted' by use of fixed, bulbous fairings to reduce ingestion of hot gases by the engine; these were removed for the conventional flight trials at Bedford, but a compromise (ie, less prominent fairings) was effected for the second phase of hovering with rather more engine power available. In due course inflatable-bag lips—to provide the blunt profile for hovering and sharp profile for level flight—were adopted, as will be shown later.

On June 20 *XP836* was delivered to Dunsfold for flight preparation and on the 7th of the following month it flew the first of a series of conventional flights aimed at extending the flight envelope at both the high and low ends of the speed range. In the upper range it achieved 538 knots, Mach 1.02, 40,000 ft and 6 g, and at the lower end decelerated to a partially jet-borne minimum horizontal speed of 95 knots. As *XP831* had achieved acceleration to 95 knots from the hover, clearance for full accelerating and decelerating transitions was given. On September 12 (alas, just too late for the SBAC Air Display that year), complete transitions were carried out in each direction by both Bedford and Merewether. The 'gap' had been closed in well under one year—despite the aircraft being grounded for roughly a quarter of this period owing to the necessity for constant substitution of experimental engines with their very short maintenance limitations.

In fact, although representing a most significant landmark in the V/STOL story, the Hawker test pilots reported that the transitions had proved extraordinarily simple and straightforward. After lift-off at full throttle, the adjacent nozzle lever was pushed slowly forward until the nozzles pointed directly aft and the aircraft was fully wing-borne. If the nozzles rotated aft too quickly the aircraft lost height; if too slowly then the aircraft climbed unnecessarily high.

On September 22 vertical lift-offs from solid ground, with subsequent transitions, were successfully achieved.

The short take-off

The P 1127 now embarked on what was to become one of the most vital phases of its concept, that of rolling, or short take-off. While the vertical take-off manoeuvre would be of inestimable value for an aircraft operating from restricted sites (ie, helicopter pads and woodland clearings) in the tactical support rôle, with either reduced weapon or fuel loads, the ability to carry full load would often be required. By allowing the aircraft to roll forward under take-off power until the wings achieved some lift before the thrust was vectored downwards, the generation of this lift would make up the deficiency of engine thrust when required to fly at substantially higher all-up weight. After lift-off the pilot simply completed the latter part of an accelerating transition.

Still with an engine providing only 12,000 lb thrust, *XP831* completed its first 'short take-off' from the Dunsfold runway on October 28, proving the manoeuvre to be entirely straightforward. During the following month Squadron Leader J.M. Henderson, one of the RAE pilots engaged in flying the Short SC1, carried out a brief low-speed assessment of the P 1127, including transitions without use of the autostabiliser, contributing an extremely favourable verdict on the aircraft. Immediately afterwards *XP831* commenced operation from grass surfaces with both vertical and short take-offs. Although some scorching of the grass was evident there was no significant ground erosion and no damage to the engine from debris.*

However, conventional flight still continued to present a number of problems and the next phase of flying was devoted to their solution. It had been discovered on *XP836* that from Mach 0.90 upwards the aircraft displayed marked wing-drop but this was now cured with the addition of 13 vortex generators on the upper surface of each wing at about quarter-chord, and on December 12 this aircraft achieved supersonic speed in a shallow dive with much improved flying qualities.

Two days later, however, while Bill Bedford was making a high-speed low-level run over Wiltshire in *XP836,* the port fibreglass 'cold' nozzle failed and was blown off, prompting a quick decision to make an emergency landing at the Royal Naval Air Station at Yeovilton. Without time to carry out low-speed handling checks at a safe height, Bedford started a straight-in approach to the runway, but on selecting flap at about 300 ft the aircraft commenced an uncontrollable roll—probably due to the violently asymmetric thrust—and the pilot immediately ejected (leaving the aircraft almost horizontally to one side); mercifully Bedford escaped with no more than a severe shaking, but the aircraft struck a storage barn and was totally destroyed.

The exact cause of the failure of the fibreglass nozzle could not be fully established (the nozzle, being badly damaged, was found almost four miles to one side of the flight path), and it was immediately decided to develop steel nozzles (as of course were already employed for the rear, 'hot' exhaust).

Fortunately the loss of *XP836* did not seriously retard the flight programme, and apart from temporarily strengthening the fibreglass nozzles on the first prototype, flight trials continued almost uninterrupted on this aircraft.

On March 24 1962 the first Pegasus 3, developing a nominal 13,500 lb thrust, was run in *XP831* and on April 5 this engine-aircraft combination was first flown, and hovered in its fully-equipped condition. On the same day the third prototype, *XP972,* was also flown for the first time, with a Pegasus 2 prepared initially for conventional flight only.

* *It is worthwhile quoting here an observation by J.M. Fozard. 'Regular operation away from paved runways has not been a feature of high performance fighter deployment for at least two decades. The airmanship of operation from unprepared bases, familiar to all concerned a generation ago with aircraft of a few thousand horsepower, has in the meantime been neglected and largely forgotten . . . The 30,000 jet horsepower of the Pegasus in V/STOL has provided a great leap forward (and upward) . . .' cf Ref No 25 in the Bibliography.*

Above *Hugh Merewether's aircraft,* XP972, *after his brilliant force landing at Tangmere on October 30 1962* (Hawker Aircraft Ltd, Neg No EXP251/62).
Far left *Tell-tale shimmy marks left by a failed outrigger during high-speed taxying on the Bedford runway* (Hawker Aircraft Ltd, Neg No EXPR80/61).
Above left *Damaged outrigger showing separated tyre tread and fouled fairing* (Author's collection).
Below left *Deep rutting of the Dunsfold grass after a short take-off* (Author's collection).

XP831 was severely restricted during its hovering trials (owing to fan blade faults) but successfully completed a series of STOL trials from grass surfaces, and on June 13 two NASA pilots completed an entire V/STOL programme from paving and grass, expressing very complimentary impressions of the whole concept. The following day *XP831* was flown before the public at Upavon during the RAF's Display of historic aircraft—operating from the small grass airstrip.

On July 12 the fourth aircraft, *XP976,* which incorporated local alterations to the wingtip leading edge to improve transonic characteristics, was flown for the first time, and this aircraft was initially used to familiarise Hawker's two Production Test Pilots, Duncan Simpson and David Lockspeiser, on the P 1127. They made their first conventional flights on August 25 and 29 respectively, becoming the fifth and sixth pilots to fly the aircraft. (On Lockspeiser's first flight the undercarriage failed to lower, but a successful landing was made at Boscombe Down using the back-up lowering system.)

XP831 and *XP976* were displayed at the SBAC Display at Farnborough early in September, Bedford and Merewether performing vertical and short take-offs and landings, transitions and high-speed runs past the crowds. Shortly afterwards the first serving RAF pilots, Wing Commander Roger Topp (of 'Black Arrows' fame*) and Squadron Leader J.D. Barwell from Boscombe Down, converted on to the P 1127 in less than 15 minutes' total jet-borne flight.

Disaster befell *XP972* on October 30. Hugh Merewether was flying the aircraft on a 550-knot low-level run over Hampshire when, on entering a turn (thought to be about 5 g),

* *As a Squadron Leader, Roger Topp had commanded and led No 111 (Fighter) Squadron during the late 1950s when the squadron had performed its memorable sequences of large-formation aerobatics in Hawker Hunters.*

Hawker P.1127

XP980

Hawker
P.1127

Left *Bill Bedford hovering* XP831 *above the deck of HMS* Ark Royal *during the P 1127's first carrier trials in February 1963* (Hawker Aircraft Ltd, Neg No R13/63).

Centre left *The fifth P 1127 prototype,* XP980, *on the Dunsfold grid. Note the bag-type intake lips partially inflated, and the engine nozzles' position* (Hawker Aircraft Ltd, Neg No R80/63).

Bottom left XP980 *performing a vertical take-off from grass; the intake lip bags are fully inflated* (Hawker Aircraft Ltd, Neg No R66/64).

the engine suffered a bearing failure following surge, causing the high-pressure compressor blades to foul and catch fire. With complete loss of power, Merewether made an emergency landing at Tangmere but the undercarriage failed to lock down and the aircraft was badly damaged by a titanium fire in the engine bay.* This brought flying on the Pegasus 3-powered aircraft to a temporary standstill while assurance could be gained that surge limits on this engine were adequate in the hover.

The next landmark was reached on February 8 1963 when *XP831* successfully performed the first V/STOL operations from an aircraft carrier at sea. For some months the Admiralty had been expressing increasing interest in obtaining an advanced V/STOL carrier-borne interceptor with which to replace its de Havilland Sea Vixens and had already drafted such a Requirement (see Chapter 5). To demonstrate the practicability of such operations, Bedford and Merewether performed vertical and short take-offs and vertical landings on HMS *Ark Royal* at sea in the English Channel off Portland. These trials lasted five days and gave rise to the pilots' opinion that carrier operation was, if anything, simpler than on land owing to the carrier's bridge superstructure providing an excellent height reference. Among the vital tactical benefits to emerge from these pioneer trials was the ability of the carrier to recover the aircraft without having to alter course into wind. Perhaps the most remarkable aspect of the trials was that neither pilot possessed any previous experience of deck flying whatsoever. And at no time was more than one-third of the deck space used by the P 1127. Although the Royal Navy's interest in V/STOL operation was rendered premature by economic pressures, these early trials represented the first rung on a ladder that was to reach extensive worldwide maritime V/STOL operations over the next 20 years.

The fifth P 1127, *XP980,* made its first flight on February 24, joining *XP831* and *XP976* in the continuing flight programme. *XP980* differed from the previous aircraft in featuring hydro-mechanical nosewheel steering and, like *XP976,* was powered by a 13,500-lb Pegasus 3.

As will be shown in later chapters, 1963 represented a vital watershed in the entire V/STOL concept. At Kingston the P 1150/P 1154 supersonic V/STOL project was underway, having been declared the design winner of the important NBMR-3 international design contest (see Chapter 5) and the first metal was about to be cut for the first P 1154 prototype. As it transpired, with the eventual cancellation of the P 1154, a more modest V/STOL design approach was adopted by the RAF, and as an initial step the decision had already been taken to introduce a less radical adaptation of the P 1127—the Kestrel—into service with a three-nation evaluation squadron (as told in the following chapter).

Thus it may be seen that Hawker had everything to gain by demonstrating to the world the extraordinary operating flexibility of V/STOL operations, and hardly a day passed without demonstrations and 'presentations' being given before foreign visitors at

* *The damaged carcase of* XP972 *was returned to Kingston for examination, but it was decided not to undertake repairs. For some time negotiations with German aircraft manufacturers were pursued in case the airframe might provide the basis of a new design incorporating lift-jets—bearing in mind that the centre fuselage would have to be re-built in any case. These were abandoned in due course.*

Above *Interesting in-flight view of* XP831, XP976 *and* XP980. *All three aircraft feature the inflatable-bag intake lips, but* XP831 *has the original 'pen nib' rear nozzle heat shields, anhedral tailplane, semi-delta wing without vortex generators, but with underfuselage strakes;* XP976, *leading the formation, features the modified 'spade' type heat shields, straight tailplane, delta wing without vortex generators but no fuselage strakes; while* XP980 *has the anhedral tailplane, streamwise wingtips, vortex generators and fuselage strakes. The pilots on this occasion were Bill Bedford, Hugh Merewether and Duncan Simpson* (Hawker Siddeley, Neg No 115/63).

Below XP980 *hovering at about 50 ft* (Hawker Aircraft Ltd, Neg No R67/64).

A fine study of XP831 *in snowy surroundings early in 1963; later that year this historic aircraft suffered an accident at the Paris Air Show* (Hawker Siddeley Aviation, Neg No R56/63).

Kingston and Dunsfold. France, in particular, was considered to be a fertile area in which to demonstrate the efficacy of the vectored-thrust principle following that nation's stated decision to persist with the lift-jet alternative—NBMR-3 notwithstanding.

It therefore came as a bitter blow to Hawker's pride when, on Sunday June 16, while performing immediately in front of the Paris Air Show crowds, *XP831* crashed. The irony of the event was further heightened by the fact that the accident's cause was of such insignificant nature—a small foreign object entering the nozzle actuation motor caused the nozzles to rotate slightly aft during hover, resulting in loss of lift thrust. Bedford, who was performing a perfectly straightforward low hover, simply had no alternative but to set the aircraft down on its belly in a fairly heavy landing, striking a concrete obstacle. *XP831* was fairly badly damaged and this historic aircraft did not recommence flying for more than a year.

Despite the extrinsic setback at the Paris Air Show, work continued at full pace to prepare for the future evaluation of the P 1127, and on September 1 Bristol delivered the first Pegasus 5 engine (No 922) for installation in the last of the six P 1127s, *XP984,* this aircraft having been selected to represent the aerodynamic prototype of the evaluation version. As such it featured a new swept wing with modified streamwise wingtips to alleviate transonic wing drop. The new Pegasus 5—with ultimate thrust development to 18,000 lb—was rated at 15,000 lb in *XP984* and included a number of fundamental changes from the Mark 3 version. The low pressure compressor now featured three stages (in place of two) and the previous inlet guide vanes were dispensed with; variable inlet guide vanes were introduced to the high pressure compressor, and cooling was now provided for the first stage of the turbine; and an annular combustion chamber replaced the original cans. At its 15,500-lb thrust-rating the Pegasus 5—although a much heavier engine—still returned the same thrust/weight ratio (at 4.58 lb/lb) as the original Pegasus 2.

Also included in *XP984* were toe-operated wheelbrakes, two pylon attachments for underwing drop tanks, and a 5-ft diameter tail parachute for stalling and spinning trials. The complete aircraft was delivered to Dunsfold on October 7, but engine running was halted on the 19th when loose objects in the airframe damaged the fan, and the engine was returned to Bristol for repair. However, before it could be re-installed in *XP984,* it failed during bench-running following fouling of a bearing seal, and it was not until December 24 that a new Pegasus 5, No 924, was delivered to Hawker, and on February 13 1964 *XP984* was first flown without incident.

By now, however, the first evaluation aircraft were approaching completion, and within a month the Kestrel had flown. It is therefore convenient now to describe the course of events which had been followed in preparation of this operational version of the P 1127.

Chapter 4

Three-nation evaluation

Having regard for the lugubrious attitudes struck by the British Air Staff towards Hawker's radical proposals for V/STOL as early as 1958, a cynic might be forgiven for marvelling at Britain's eventual ability to evolve a realistic operational end product. The same observer might be tempted to suggest that the narrow-minded pursuit of a single, highly sophisticated expedient—with all the obvious economic, technical and political risks attending such a military project as TSR 2—brought the Air Staff no more than its just deserts as events unfolded.

As already suggested, it was only after the future of TSR 2 had apparently been assured late in 1958 that the Air Ministry evinced real interest in the P 1127 as the possible basis of a combat aeroplane. Indeed, it was these first signs of Service interest that prompted the Ministry of Aviation to make its first serious enquiries in January 1959 about purchasing two P 1127 prototypes. By the end of that month the first draft of GOR 345 for a tactical ground support aircraft to replace the Hunter in service was being examined by Government Ministries, the Air Ministry department responsible for this Requirement being OR 10, headed by Wing Commander G.H. Nelson-Edwards, DFC.*

In February the first of many high-level visits was paid to Kingston by senior Government and Service officials to discuss the likely development of an 'RAF P 1127' when Sir Frederick Brundrett† and Air Marshal Sir Geoffrey Tuttle‡ visited the Hawker management. It was at once clear that Sir Frederick Brundrett had grasped the full portent of the V/STOL philosophy, and in the short time remaining before his retirement later that year he unquestionably imposed his influence of unqualified support upon the Ministry of Defence.

At all events it was obvious that GOR 345 had been drafted with the P 1127 foremost in mind and that realistic performance demands were being made. Although countless changes came to be made during the course of the next two years, it is not intended to dwell on these as, in the main, they reflected no more than partisan ideas and in due course the Requirement stabilised in much the same form as it first appeared. Red herrings proliferated, not least in the Air Ministry where potentially hostile propaganda abounded, and such incorrect beliefs as a lack of altitude performance had constantly to be painstakingly corrected.

Following NATO's focusing upon its supersonic requirement, the RAF in 1960 was able to crystallise more modest demands for a 'first generation' aircraft, especially when

* *Wing Commander Nelson-Edwards, a Battle of Britain veteran, retired from the Service in January 1960, his place at OR 10 being taken by Wing Commander J.I. Parker.*

† *Scientific Adviser to the Minister of Defence and Chairman of the Defence Research Policy Committee.*

‡ *Air Marshal Sir Geoffrey Tuttle, KBE, CB, DFC, was Deputy Chief of the Air Staff until his retirement in December 1959 when he was appointed a director and general manager of Vickers-Armstrong (Aircraft) Ltd, prime contractor for the TSR 2.*

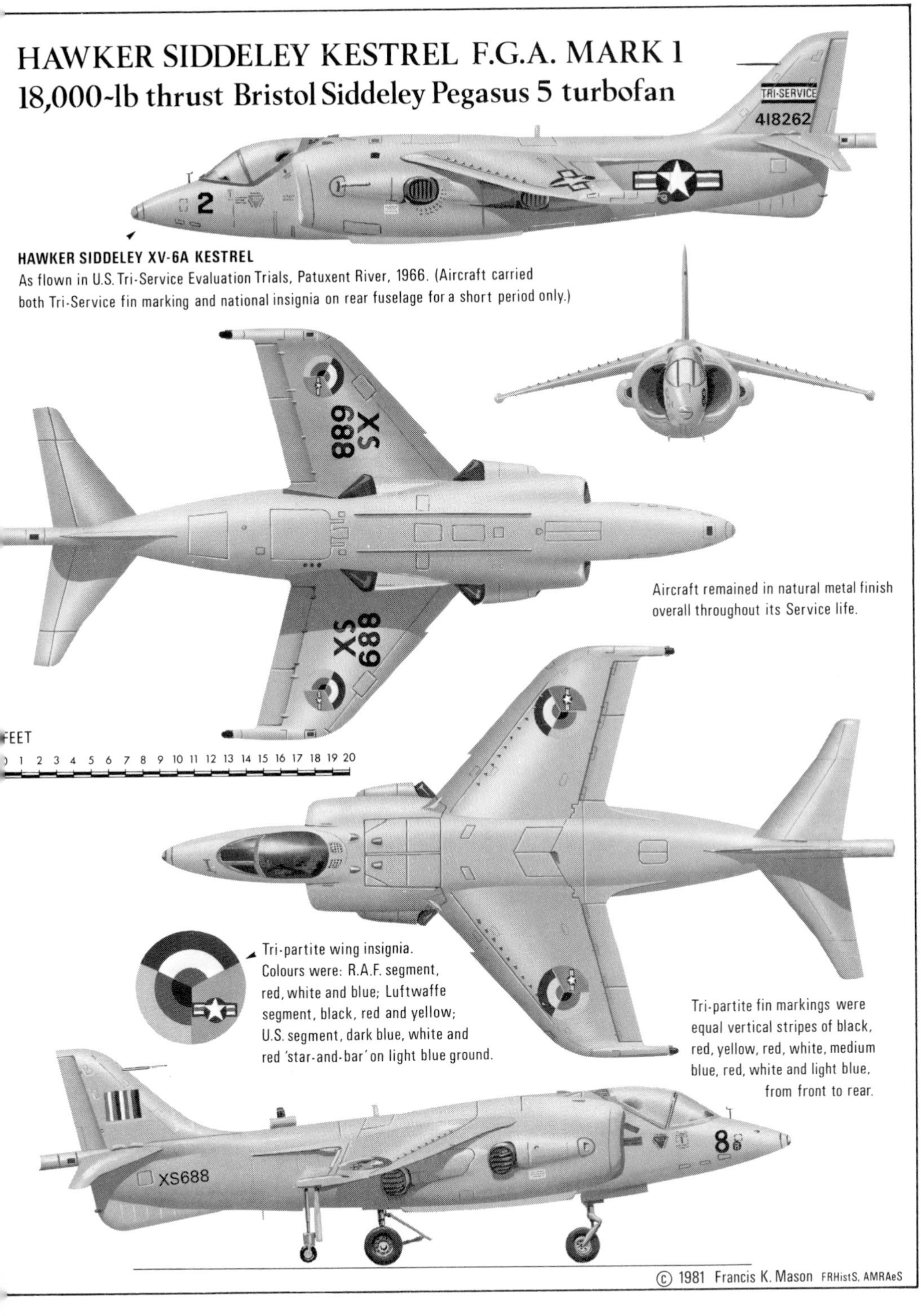
HAWKER SIDDELEY KESTREL F.G.A. MARK 1
18,000-lb thrust Bristol Siddeley Pegasus 5 turbofan
TRI-SERVICE
418262
2
HAWKER SIDDELEY XV-6A KESTREL
As flown in U.S. Tri-Service Evaluation Trials, Patuxent River, 1966. (Aircraft carried both Tri-Service fin marking and national insignia on rear fuselage for a short period only.)
XS 688
XS 688
Aircraft remained in natural metal finish overall throughout its Service life.
FEET
1 2 3 4 5 6 7 8 9 10 11 12 13 14 15 16 17 18 19 20
Tri-partite wing insignia.
Colours were: R.A.F. segment, red, white and blue; Luftwaffe segment, black, red and yellow; U.S. segment, dark blue, white and red 'star-and-bar' on light blue ground.
Tri-partite fin markings were equal vertical stripes of black, red, yellow, red, white, medium blue, red, white and light blue, from front to rear.
XS688
8
© 1981 Francis K. Mason FRHistS, AMRAeS

the idea of a Service evaluation version was first mooted. In January that year the RAF's Central Fighter Establishment was instructed to carry out an immediate study of the operational aspects of a V/STOL combat aircraft. On March 25 Hawker was informed by OR 10 that recommendations had been made to establish a special evaluation squadron within the RAF, and the following month members of the Kingston Project Office visited the CFE at West Raynham, Norfolk, to discuss the P 1127. On June 20 GOR 345 was officially issued (although many changes still remained to be made).

Despite attempts made by Duncan Sandys, the British Minister of Aviation, to negotiate a joint development agreement with France and Germany earlier in 1960, it soon became apparent that the French Government was determined to pursue an independent line (almost certainly centred upon the Dassault/Rolls-Royce mixed powerplant concept). However, with several German manufacturers maintaining an unbiased approach in their initial design studies, it soon became evident that future multinational collaboration with Britain would centre on Germany and the United States—the latter now contributing as much as 75 per cent of the engine development costs. And when Herr Strauss, the German Minister of Defence, during a visit to Dunsfold on September 8 gave his opinion that the P 1127 represented the best single solution to NATO's tactical combat needs, it was abundantly clear where Hawker's best support in Europe lay.

It was now that events took a most unfavourable turn. During the past 18 months, while GOR 345 had been undergoing gestation, the customary demands for additional equipment had run their course, and from the original, relatively simple concept had grown a fairly advanced weapon system which was fast overhauling the capabilities of even the most optimistic engine performance prophets. In terms of conventional aircraft this natural weight growth can be accommodated with some sacrifice of take-off performance; it does not appear to have been fully appreciated by the Service authorities that there must come a point in weight growth of the VTOL aeroplane where take-off simply would not be possible!

When *XP831* made its first hovering flight—only achieved after stripping of all extraneous equipment—the Service and Ministry of Aviation expressed astonishment at the narrow power limitations, and all manner of doubts as to the aircraft's ultimate operational value were expressed. When the company quoted a cost of £56m (or £76m, depending on the extent of engine development) for 100 aircraft—including all equipment and development costs—the Air Staff expressed horror, bearing in mind the 'small performance advance' offered. When one reflects that refurbished Hunters—amortised over 2,000 production examples—were costing around £300,000 each, the objection to a unit price for a radically new weapon with greatly increased operational flexibility of £560,000 is difficult to understand.*

It was not until March 29 1961, during a visit to Kingston by the Chief of the Air Staff, Air Chief Marshal Sir Thomas Pike, that Camm was informed that realisation was dawning in the Air Ministry that any Service version of the P 1127 must be kept relatively simple to remain within the limited parameters of initial engine development. He asked Camm to prepare cost estimates for delivery of 30 simplified aircraft capable of performing support/reconnaissance duties. Discussions along these lines continued for

* *In particular, Air Marshal Sir Ronald Lees, KCB, CBE, DFC (another Battle of Britain pilot), newly-appointed Deputy Chief of the Air Staff, expressed his opposition to the project, and joined with other Air Staff members in suggesting that 'if Hawker had kept the P 1127 simple, the company would already have received an order for 25 aircraft'. Camm reminded them that it had been the OR Branch demands for increased equipment that was responsible for ill-controlled weight growth, and hence increased engine power demands and development cost escalation.*

about three months during which a figure of about £10m for the 30 aircraft and £18m for engine development (including the American funding) emerged. However, despite this shift in the Air Staff's approach, it was evident that it now compromised the Air Ministry OR Branch demands now being inserted in GOR 345—amounting to a strike capability against both hard and soft targets. In any case these costs were still regarded as being too high!

The whole unhappy situation was further exacerbated with the issue in mid-1961 of NATO's NBMR-3 (see the following chapter) calling for a highly sophisticated V/STOL aircraft. Not surprisingly, this encouraged the various parties to nail their colours to the mast; what was perhaps extraordinary was that so many senior RAF officers should do so when the outcome of the NATO Requirement seemed likely to favour Hawker's design concepts.

The OR Branch once more executed an about-turn late in September, and Group Captain D.T. Witt, DSO, DFC, DFM, paid a visit to Camm and stated that his Branch was beginning to have doubts about both NBMR-3 *and* GOR 345! By the end of 1961, faced by total disarray, the Air Staff ordered GOR 345 to be withdrawn, and henceforth efforts were made to evolve an RAF Requirement more in line with the provisions of NBMR-3.

* * *

It is necessary here to return briefly to 1960. The key factor in GOR 345's performance demand had been the sortie radius of action, a demand which Hawker had been at pains to explain was unattainable on account of the fuel required—and hence the engine power available, then anticipated at 15,000-lb thrust. The breakthrough occurred when Dr Hooker informed Camm that by introducing an extra stage to the low-pressure fan, and other improvements, the Pegasus could be expected to produce about 18,000 lb within about 30 months. This would enable the P 1127 to carry sufficient fuel to meet GOR 345's critical sortie demands.*

During the long period of uncertainty which followed, Hawker could do little more than keep abreast of development of this new engine (eventually to materialise as the Pegasus 5); in the event it came to be scheduled for installation in the final P 1127, *XP984*, as related in the previous chapter.

Meanwhile plans had gone ahead to establish an evaluation squadron in the RAF. When GOR 345 was finally pronounced dead the British Government returned to its efforts to secure a collaborative agreement with the United States and Germany to participate in the financing of a small production batch of evaluation P 1127s, and on May 22 1962 Hawker received an Instruction to Proceed with nine such aircraft. By mid-September the Specification had been received at Kingston and at this point it was decided to employ the projected Pegasus 5 engine.

On January 16 1963 the Tripartite Agreement—between Britain, the United States of America and the Federal German Republic—was signed in Paris on the basis of the cost of three aircraft and one-third of the development costs being borne by each nation.†

* *GOR 345/1 Amendment 1 required a radius of action of 150 nautical miles, with 2,000-lb weapon load, and a take-off distance to 50 ft of 1,000 ft in 'hot-high' conditions. The P 1127 with 18,000-lb thrust Pegasus 5 was expected to have an all-up weight of 16,966 lb. In 'hot-high' conditions the Pegasus 5 was expected to produce an installed thrust of 17,250 lb.*

† *When first proposals were made for the Tripartite P 1127s, 18 aircraft had been suggested as being necessary. The figure was reduced to nine but the German authorities continued for some months to question whether this number would be adequate.*

Hawker Siddeley P1127

XS688
Hawker Siddeley P1127

XS689

Left *An early in-flight view of the first Kestrel,* XS688, *when still fitted with the short tailplane and without the wing vortex generators; note the inflatable intake bags, still fitted, and the incorrect port wing Tripartite marking* (Hawker Siddeley Aviation, Neg No 1127-114/64).

Centre left *The first Kestrel,* XS688, *taxying with drop tanks at Dunsfold; note the bag-type intake lips still fitted* (Hawker Siddeley Aviation, Neg No R265/64).

Bottom left XS688 *performing a short take-off* (Hawker Siddeley Aviation, Neg No R264/64).

Owing to the need to incorporate the latest design experience with the P 1127 prototypes, manufacture of the Tripartite P 1127s was delayed until the last possible moment, and did not get underway until mid-1963. In the meantime it was agreed with the Ministry of Aviation that all pre-Service trials by the A&AEE, normally carried out at Boscombe Down, would be performed at Dunsfold, and the first A&AEE pilots underwent conversion on the P 1127 under Hawker's guidance. Such was the ease with which pilots were converting to the new aircraft that it was decided to omit the autostabiliser/autopilot from the Tripartite aircraft altogether.

In January 1964 the names of the ten pilots who would constitute the Tripartite Evaluation Squadron were announced. They were: Wing Commander D. McL. Scrimgeour, RAF, Commanding Officer; Oberst Gerhard Barkhorn, *Luftwaffe,** Deputy Commanding Officer; Commander J.J. Tyson, Jr, US Navy, Deputy Commanding Officer; Squadron Leader F.A. Trowern, RAF; Major J.K. Campbell, USAF; Major Paul R. Curry, US Army; Major John A. Johnston, US Army; Flight Lieutenant R.J.A. Munro, AFC, RAF; Flight Lieutenant D.J.McL. Edmonston, RAF; Leutnant V. Suhr, *Luftwaffe.*

Of these, the Americans were test pilots while those from the RAF and *Luftwaffe* were line squadron pilots for, whereas the United States regarded the evaluation programme as a semi-technical development exercise, Britain and Germany saw it as an operational trial. In view of later events it is perhaps surprising that not one pilot from the US Marine Corps was involved in the evaluation, while the inclusion of two US Army pilots was of illusory significance as will be explained later.

The first Tripartite aircraft *(XS688)* commenced taxying tests on March 5, and made its first flight two days later; at the same time the first American evaluation pilot (Major Campbell) started his conversion on *XP980.*

The new aircraft differed from the prototypes in featuring a fuselage lengthened by 9 in to match the aerodynamic centre with the Pegasus 5's thrust centre, and operational equipment was confined to a nose camera, although space was provided for a Doppler navigator. The same wing (with swept leading and trailing edges), as had been flown on the last prototype, was retained on the evaluation aircraft and provision was made to carry a pair of underwing drop tanks.

There followed a short flight programme to seek improvement of the aircraft's longitudinal stability, commencing with a slightly increased-span tailplane on *XP984* on May 1; when this gave no improvement the tailplane was extended to 14-ft span, and a Dowty q-feel 2-lb/g bob-weight was included in the longitudinal control circuit. After flight on June 29 the aircraft was declared acceptable; the big tailplane was henceforth adopted on all evaluation aircraft and *XS688* was modified accordingly.

The next problem arose with failure of the inflatable bag-type intake lips, these being fitted on the surviving P 1127 prototypes and on the evaluation aircraft either flying or nearing completion. *XS688*'s bags failed at Mach 0.85 on July 28, followed by those on

* *Among these pilots Gerhard Barkhorn possessed an outstanding operational record, having attained the second-highest victory score of all time as a wartime* Luftwaffe *fighter pilot. His tally of 301 enemy aircraft destroyed was achieved entirely on the Eastern Front, and he was a holder of the Knight's Cross with Swords and Oakleaves.*

Above *Dramatic flashlight photo of the sixth Kestrel during Bill Bedford's first night demonstration of V/STOL on February 1 1965* (Hawker Siddeley Aviation, Neg No R54/65).

Below XS688 *in high hover. Although the aircraft is clear of ground effects, light ground debris is still much in evidence* (Hawker Siddeley Aviation, Neg No R207/64).

One of the first Kestrels about to take off from the grass at Dunsfold; note the intake lips have inflated and the engine nozzles are in the aft position (Hawker Siddeley Aviation, Neg No R206/64).

XS690 at 300 knots on August 5. In due course it was decided to dispense with these bags altogether and a fixed, raised-profile fairing was adopted for the evaluation aircraft.

On August 26 Wing Commander Scrimgeour and Commander Tyson started their conversion on to the P 1127, by which time three evaluation aircraft had flown.

On September 30 the evaluation P 1127 was officially named the Kestrel FGA Mark 1, and on October 13 *XP831* rejoined the flight programme after repair following its accident at the previous year's Paris Air Show. By the end of the year six Kestrels had flown and the majority of the handling, performance and store clearance trials had been completed under all manner of operating conditions, and by mid-January 1965 five of the Service evaluation pilots had completed their conversion on to the Kestrel.

Another flight landmark was reached on February 1 with the first night flying by a V/STOL aircraft, Bill Bedford performing conventional take-off, overshoot and landing, three vertical take-offs and vertical landings, a transition and two 180-degree turns at the hover.

The West Raynham trials

On February 26 the remaining Evaluation Squadron pilots completed their conversion to the Kestrel, and on March 5 the last of the production aircraft, *XS696,* was flown for the first time at Dunsfold. By the end of the month aircraft were being delivered to the Central Fighter Establishment at West Raynham.

Apart from the obvious relevance of the CFE to the Service evaluation of a new RAF aircraft, West Raynham itself was fortuitously located in an area conveniently endowed with numerous disused airfields nearby, as well as an extensive army battle exercise area, apart from being relatively sparsely populated.

The first stage of the evaluation comprised straightforward assessment of the Kestrel as a close support aircraft, operating from the parent airfield at West Raynham*, together with limited operational training. Thereafter the squadron moved 'into the country',

* *On April 1* XS696, *being flown by one of the American pilots, ground-looped during a short take-off and veered sideways off the runway at about 60 knots. The engine could not be throttled down and at some personal risk Wing Commander Scrimgeour, Wing Commander H. Bennett and Flight Lieutenant F. Coulton managed to extricate the pilot from the cockpit, for which they were awarded the Queen's Commendation for Valuable Services in the Air. The aircraft was extensively damaged.*

5
4
9

XS694
4
2
5
0
9

5

Left *Fine formation flying by pilots of the Tripartite Squadron* (Hawker Siddeley Aviation, Neg No 687-261).

Centre left *Line-up at West Raynham of six Kestrels of the Evaluation Squadron. The absence of* XS696 *suggests that the photo was taken in mid-1965* (Hawker Siddeley Aviation, Neg No 113/65).

Bottom left *Sylvan setting for a Kestrel.* XS695 *dispersed in a Norfolk wood* (Hawker Siddeley Aviation, Neg No 687-161).

operating from a number of semi-prepared sites, including the disused airfield at Bircham Newton whose old runways allowed only restricted areas for take-off and landing. A prototype portable operating pad, comprising interlocking aluminium planks and measuring 70 ft square, was evaluated with a Kestrel performing low hovers and vertical take-offs from it. Portable steel planking was laid in confined areas at Buckenham Tofts to allow dispersal of the Kestrels in remote areas and a number of realistic exercises were carried out without significant problems arising. In some instances the P 1127 prototypes were flown to Norfolk by the Hawker pilots to demonstrate advanced operating techniques, after which the Service pilots applied them to their everyday tasks.

The West Raynham trials continued throughout the summer of 1965 and were adjudged an unqualified success, particularly by the RAF. An average of seven aircraft was deployed during the six months of the trials and a total of about 600 hours' flying was completed, based on 24 flights per aircraft per month, the programme being divided into a number of tasks including flight operating procedures and techniques, comparison of various modes of take-off and landing capabilities, instrument flying and night operations. Take-off and landing trials were conducted at seven different sites on a variety of surfaces including the aluminium pad, glass-fibre mats, aluminium tracks, light PVC/Terylene and Neoprene/Nylon membranes, as well as grass and other semi-prepared surfaces. 340 take-offs were made from grass and 930 sorties, simulating strike and reconnaissance missions, were completed—constant use being made of the Kestrel's nose camera.

It was shown that in conventional flight the Kestrel possessed similar weather limits to any other operational aircraft, but also had the additional potential of operating in lower weather minima due to its unique ability to decelerate rapidly when breaking from cloud.

When the squadron was disbanded in November 1965, six of the Kestrels were delivered to the United States where they underwent Tri-Service trials and research programmes at NASA, Langley Field and at Edwards Air Force Base. The other two surviving Kestrels were retained in Britain where they joined the P 1127s* in development work for the forthcoming P 1127 (RAF) production version, later to be named the Harrier (see Chapter 6).

* *On March 19 1965* XP984 *was fairly badly damaged in an accident at Thorney Island. Following repair of a persistent fuel leak the aircraft was being flown by Hugh Merewether on an engine handling sortie; during a dive at Mach 1.15 from 30,000 ft, opening up the throttle prior to a slam decelĕration caused severe engine damage and the pilot made a dead-stick landing on the grass at Thorney Island. Merewether deserved all due commendation for this feat which was achieved with total engine failure and a fire in the engine bay, and in conditions of total cloud cover; the aircraft, though damaged, was repaired only to be written off ten years later in a landing accident at the RAE, Bedford.*

Chapter 5

The supersonic red herring

In Chapter 2 the origins of NATO interest in the V/STOL concept during 1958-59 were outlined, together with the progress of reasoning behind Hawker's decision not to become diverted by demands for operational sophistication even before the principle of thrust vectoring had been successfully demonstrated in the air.

That such an unrealistic attitude of impatience has always existed in Service planning staffs, justifiable in their own narrow aims to achieve operational superiority over potential enemies, may be the result of a lack of technical knowledge but more likely to an absence of experience in the demands of commerce and industry. (It is certainly not alleviated by the relatively short 'tours of duty' by Service officers in such positions as the Operational Requirements Branches, resulting in a lack of continuity and the need to educate new incumbents.)

In the atmosphere of incoherent crystal-gazing being enjoyed in Whitehall and Paris during 1959 Service officers were under an implied political restraint to equate their deliberations between a choice of modest, and therefore inexpensive advances in military aircraft performance, or of leapfrogging time-consuming fundamentals to reach advanced operational targets. In their eventual choice of the more cautious approach—for which Hawker could take much credit—the British Air Staff was unquestionably infinitely wiser than the NATO planners.

Nevertheless *XP831*'s lift-off from the Dunsfold grid on October 21 1960 was the signal to Hawker to start advancing the P 1127 concept. Within a week both the Air Staff and the Ministry of Aviation were stressing the aircraft's lack of operational potential! Despite reassurances from Dr Hooker that a new version of the engine (the BS 53/6) with plenum chamber burning (PCB)—that is with fuel burning in the bypass flow to the 'cold' nozzles—Camm and Hooper were stung by criticism of the P 1127 as a 'dead end', and it was natural that, as detailed design development of this aircraft passed to the specialist departments at Kingston, the Project Office should now embark on an examination of more radical V/STOL demands.

Although the tactical 'hawks' in the RAF had constantly pressed for supersonic performance, no such formal Requirement had materialised. Since it was as yet by no means certain that even a subsonic P 1127 would achieve substantial production for the RAF, Hawker now turned its attention to the NATO requirement—now emerging as NBMR-3, NATO Basic Military Requirement 3—albeit still in a draft form.

Lest it should be thought that the Hawker project designers had always closed their eyes to possible benefits of the lift-jet principle, it must be emphasised that numerous lift-jet configurations had been evolved and studied by the Project Office ever since June 1957, but none had demonstrated the operational potential or flexibility of the basic P 1127 vectored-thrust concept. (The various Hawker V/STOL projects initiated between June 1957 and October 1961 are described in Appendix 3.)

Tunnel half-model of the Hawker P 1150/1 (Hawker Aircraft Ltd, Neg No PROJ36/61).

Once more it fell to Ralph Hooper to spend a weekend scheming up a new design (this time prior to a skiing holiday) which employed the proposed BS 53/6 with PCB. Performance estimates with either 800°K or 1,200°K PCB mean temperatures confirmed a useful supersonic performance, the clean aircraft—designated P 1150/1—being calculated to achieve Mach 2 at 50,000 ft with 1,200°K PCB. Care was, however, taken not to broadcast these forecasts too widely lest interest by the RAF in the P 1127 should slacken!

While the PCB engine was now re-designated the BS 100 (and the BS 53 was named the Pegasus), it soon became evident that the P 1150/1 would not be able to meet NBMR-3, the NATO demands having been further increased early in 1961. This was confirmed by General Bill Chapman, who had returned to the States on promotion but who paid a visit to Kingston on May 24. The General persisted in his view that the vectored-thrust system was the *only* realistic V/STOL configuration and pressed Hawker to persevere with further development of the P 1150.

By mid-1961 NBMR-3 assumed the status of a major international defence competition with countless political, economic and industrial influences at work. Apart from the Rolls-Royce/Dassault/Sud Mirage IIIV entry (with eight RB.162 lift engines and an Atar cruise engine), designs were submitted by Fokker/Republic (with BS 100/3 vectored-thrust engine), and by Breguet and Fiat (the G.95/4). Hawker was urged to join forces with a German consortium and studied an adaptation of the P 1150 (the P 1150/2) with two lift-jet engines in addition to the BS 100.* However, to some extent encouraged by the achievement of successful two-way flight transitions by the first P 1127 prototypes, Hawker persisted in its application of 'pure' vectored-thrust and went on to evolve the P 1150/3, now powered by a 33,000-lb thrust BS 100/9—a scaled down version of the BS 100/3.

* *Such German collaboration did not materialise. Design collaboration between the German Ministry of Defence and Fiat (whose G.95/4A had been designed as a G.91 replacement) resulted in the* Vertikal-Aufklärungs-und-Kampfflugzeug *(VAK) 191B.*

VAK191B

So as to avoid unfavourable association with the P 1150, the Hawker project now became the P 1154 (identical to the P 1150/3) and, in January 1962, was formally tendered to NBMR-3, the brochure (in English and French) demonstrating that all facets of the performance and load demands could be met or exceeded. As a bonus, Hawker could point to solid experience in operation of the P 1127—including the vertical take-offs from grass surfaces. Undoubtedly this practical employment of V/STOL aircraft led to the P 1154 being declared the outright technical winner of the competition.

This 'technical' qualification, however, resulted from the political weakness of Hawker's tender. Once more the 'internationalists' in Paris had imposed their influence. Though the P 1154 had beaten the other finalist, the Mirage IIIV (the Mirage 'Balzac' had already suffered two accidents, one of them fatal), the latter was a multi-national project with development agreements signed with Rolls-Royce, the British Aircraft Corporation and Boeing, and was thus politically favoured. Hawker Siddeley attempted to retrieve an unqualified verdict by negotiating multilateral development agreements with Focke-Wulf of Germany, Breguet of France, Avions Fairey of Belgium, Fokker of Holland and Republic of the USA. However, nationalist sentiments were also in evidence and France

Left *The Dassault Mirage III-001 prototype was converted to VTOL configuration by inclusion of eight Rolls-Royce RB 108 lift engines and a Bristol Siddeley Orpheus cruise engine. Known as the Balzac V-001, it made its first transition on March 18 1963 but crashed a year later* (Rolls-Royce Ltd, Neg No MPC1610).

Below left *Designed to meet the German Requirement VAK 191 for a subsonic V/STOL tactical reconnaissance fighter, the VFW 191B was powered by a Bristol Siddeley vectored thrust engine and two Rolls-Royce RB 162 lift jets* (Rolls-Royce Ltd, Neg No RC295/5).

Below *The German companies of Bölkow, Heinkel and Messerschmitt formed a consortium,* Entwicklungsring-Süd, *to develop a Mach 2 interceptor VTOL fighter. The VJ 101C X-1 prototype, employing four Rolls-Royce-MAN RB 145s in rotating wingtip pods, and two more in the fuselage aft of the cockpit, was destroyed in a crash on September 14 1964* (Rolls-Royce Ltd, Neg No MPC1788).

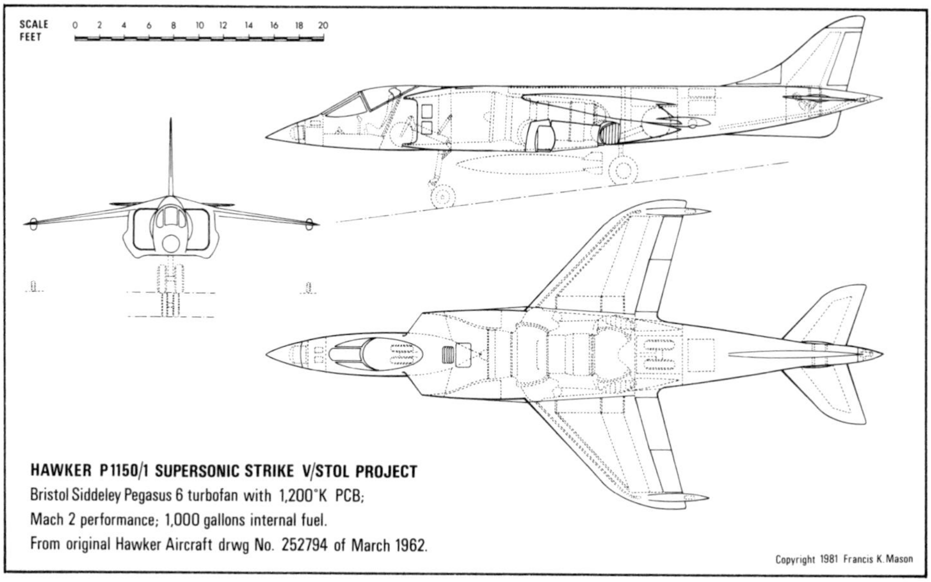

announced that whatever the outcome of this massive international alignment of industrial resources, she would pursue a unilateral course with the Mirage IIIV. Such an impasse could have but one result: NATO withdrew its entire Requirement.

SCALE FEET
0 2 4 6 8 10 12 14 16 18 20
HAWKER P1150/1 SUPERSONIC STRIKE V/STOL PROJECT
Bristol Siddeley Pegasus 6 turbofan with 1,200°K PCB;
Mach 2 performance; 1,000 gallons internal fuel.
From original Hawker Aircraft drwg No. 252794 of March 1962.
Copyright 1981 Francis K. Mason

As the 'European authority' bowed out with its NBMR-3 (and soon after with the NBMR-4 for a V/STOL freighter, and the NBMR-22 for a light V/STOL transport), the British were finally convinced by the technical bouquets bestowed on the vectored-thrust principle. However the Air Staff had maintained a frosty disinterest in the progress of the NATO design contest in 1962, possibly believing that the successful contender would

French contender for the NBMR-3 design competition was the Marcel Dassault Mirage IIIV powered by eight Rolls-Royce RB 162 lift engines and a 20,500-lb thrust afterburning Atar turbofan.

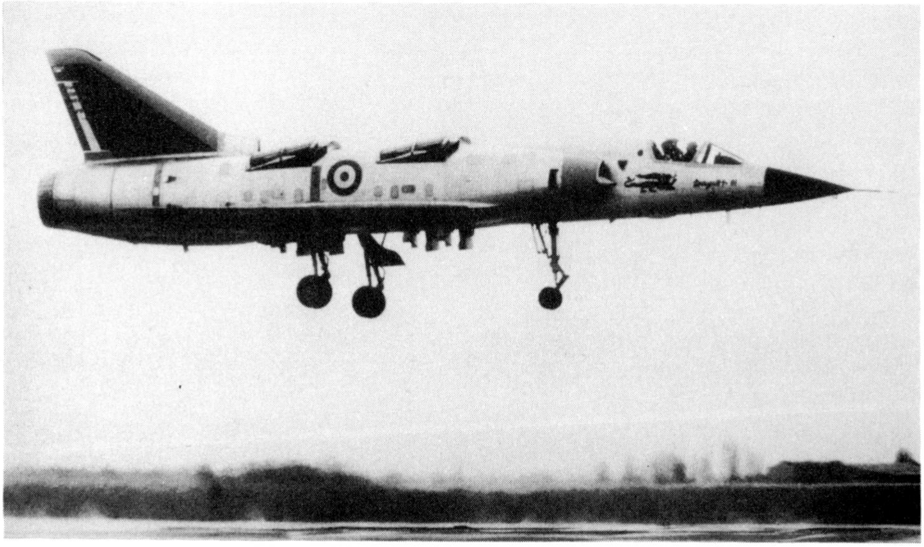

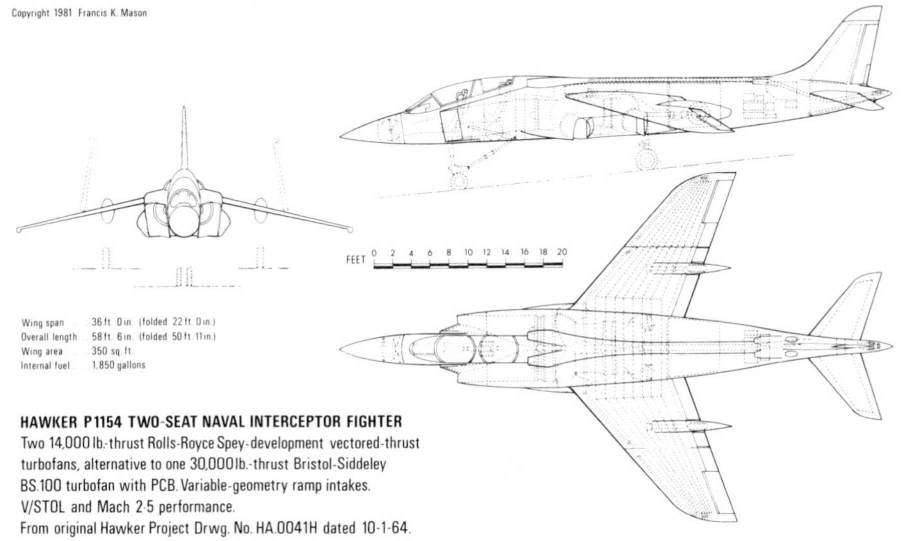

HAWKER P1154 TWO-SEAT NAVAL INTERCEPTOR FIGHTER
Two 14,000 lb.-thrust Rolls-Royce Spey-development vectored-thrust turbofans, alternative to one 30,000 lb.-thrust Bristol-Siddeley BS.100 turbofan with PCB. Variable-geometry ramp intakes. V/STOL and Mach 2·5 performance.
From original Hawker Project Drwg. No. HA.0041H dated 10-1-64.

have little relevance to a purely British Requirement. To 'Europeans' this apparently insular attitude, so often manifest, has been mistaken for a selfish, national stance, yet who is to say that the defence requirements of land-locked nations are in any way similar to those of a sea-girt island?

At the same time the British Admiralty, also aloof from the NBMR—which was regarded as wholly irrelevant—had been evolving a Requirement for a carrier-borne two-seat interceptor.

Thus in mid-1962, in a misjudged effort to achieve substantial cost savings, the Air Staff and Admiralty attempted to draft a joint RAF/Naval Requirement for an aircraft similar in general concept to the P 1154. However, the RAF was demanding a single-seat strike aircraft with supersonic dash capability and sophisticated terrain-following radar, whereas the Navy required a two-seat carrier-borne interceptor capable of sustained supersonic flight at altitude and carrying advanced air-to-air missile systems. Such widely differing requirements posed almost insuperable design problems, but Hawker prepared draft proposals for submission in August 1962.

Meanwhile politics and industrial economics had been playing their parts elsewhere. Rolls-Royce, having relinquished the manufacturing rights on their lift engines to France, could get little support from the British Treasury, nor was any other project being pursued with sufficient firmness to warrant much expenditure on these engines other than that required by the French project. Rolls-Royce civil engine production began running down and by 1963 some 16,000 of the company's workers had been placed on short-time working. This coincided with a new peak in unemployment, particularly in the North. Bristol had, moreover, won a Contract to develop a supersonic version of the Olympus both for the TSR 2 and the Anglo-French supersonic airliner (later to become the Concorde). Again, American funds had been made available through MWDT for the continued development of PCB and the BS 100 engine.

The situation thus at the end of 1962 was that Hawker was in possession of a study Contract for the P 1154 and was engaged in preparing a final project development plan to meet the supposed joint RAF/RN Requirement. Now adopting the BS 100/8 engine (as an outcome of representations made by Bristol), it was proposed to submit the plan in March 1963 and that a development Contract would be forthcoming around the middle of that year; such was essential to meet a target for first prototype flight in mid-1965 and in-Service status by January 1968. With some reluctance this programme (demanded in any case by the Services) was agreed to by Bristol.

In order to be able to submit any coherent plan at all it was necessary to freeze the single-seat design by February at the latest, while the naval two-seater might remain fairly fluid for a few further weeks. Nevertheless it appeared that the joint requirements had at long last stabilised and the design seemed to be progressing moderately smoothly. (Moreover, resulting from very powerful representations by Hawker Siddeley Group senior Directors to Government Ministers, it was tentatively proposed that the development Contract, or at least some limited authority to proceed with preparations for manufacture, might be forthcoming rather earlier than mid-1963, so important was the project considered for the continued existence of the nation's military aircraft industry.)

Then, during the first fortnight of 1963, senior Rolls-Royce design executives visited Hawker to submit a proposal that the P 1154 should use two Spey engines in place of the BS 100; it was claimed by Rolls-Royce that, while performance would remain roughly the same, the Spey already existed in its civil form and that the vectored-thrust version could be made available sooner and could build up in production faster than the Bristol Siddeley engine. These proposals were met with polite interest at Hawker, but this seems to have been wrongly interpreted by Rolls-Royce whose management then informed the Naval Staff that Hawker was prepared to re-examine the whole P 1154 design using vectored-thrust Speys. This was further complicated by Bristol who, far from arguing against the twin-engine concept, went far to agreeing that two smaller engines would appeal to the Navy who, having operated Sea Vixens, Scimitars and Buccaneers, would be eager to accept the traditional twin-engine advantages, especially in carrier-borne operations.

These complications struck at the very roots of the whole P 1154 project. Doubts

Right *Bristol Siddeley BS 100 vectored-thrust turbofan (No 1001); this was the engine intended to power the ill-fated P 1154* (Rolls-Royce Ltd (Aero Division), Bristol, Neg No E88821).

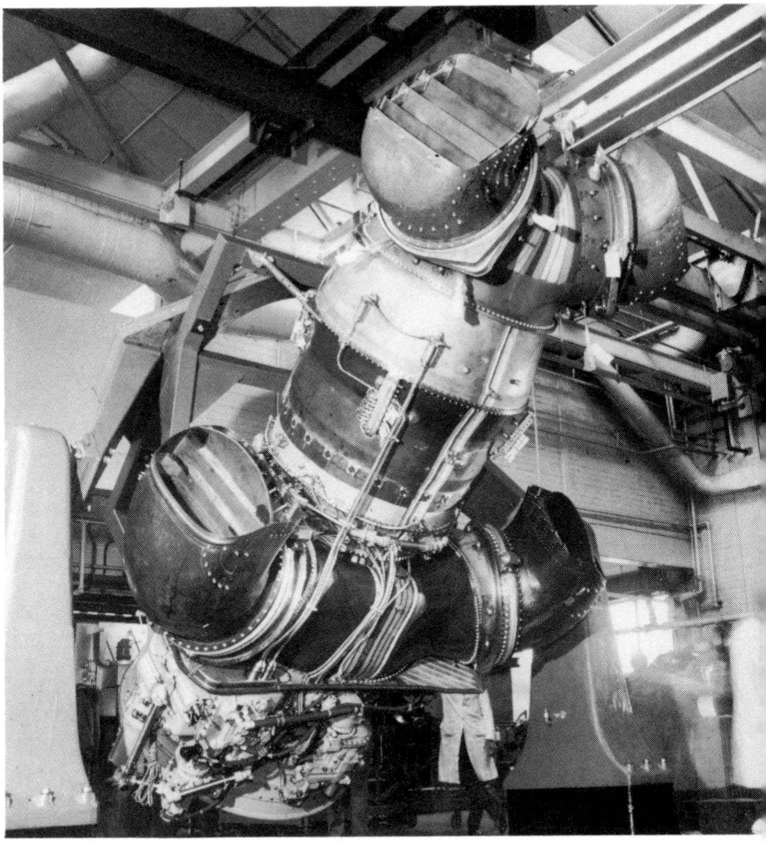

Below left *High-speed tunnel model of the Hawker P 1154 whose design was adjudged the winner of the NBMR-3 competition* (Author's collection).

Below *Display model of the P 1154/RAF. Note single-seat cockpit and P 1127-type outrigger undercarriage* (Hawker Siddeley Neg No 740136).

Display model of the P 1154/Royal Navy. Note wing undercarriage and fairings and two-seat cockpit (Hawker Siddeley, Neg No 740138).

immediately arose in the minds of the Hawker Siddeley management. Were the Rolls-Royce proposals influenced by motives of technical superiority or on other grounds? What would the American reaction be if the Bristol BS 100/PCB programme were abandoned after so much funding had been provided through MWDT? What would the cost and timescale be to produce handed (ie, counter-rotating) Speys and their associated 'cold' ducting? And what would be the effect on the flight test schedule of single-engine failure clearance (asymmetric thrust was totally unknown in the P 1127/P 1154 concept)?

It is not intended to pursue the whole unhappy saga of the P 1154 here. Hawker's representations to retain the Bristol engine were accepted, and the massive development plan (involving a number of development aircraft followed by several hundred production aircraft for the RAF and Fleet Air Arm at a total cost of some £750m) was given the go-ahead in 1963. Work started on the first single-seat and two-seat prototypes early in 1964.

In 1964 the Admiralty, undoubtedly worried by a likely five-year delay before receiving its first operational aircraft and by unit costs of around £1½m per aircraft, opted out of the P 1154 programme altogether and chose instead to purchase McDonnell F-4K Phantoms from America. In the event these aircraft—powered by Rolls-Royce Speys—arrived in service only slightly sooner than the planned P 1154s, cost almost as much and, without V/STOL capability, represented a far less flexible weapon with no significant performance advantage.

The arrival in office on October 15 1964 of a Labour administration heralded doom for the British aircraft industry. Committed to its policy of swingeing defence expenditure limitation, the new Government looked unsympathetically upon the three major military aircraft commitments being undertaken in Britain, the Hawker Siddeley P 1154, the Hawker Siddeley AW 681 and the British Aircraft Corporation TSR 2. As early as November the Air Staff was informed that two of these projects would have to go and, in a bid to save the TSR 2 (on which so many professional and Service reputations had been staked), the two Hawker Siddeley projects were sacrificed—an announcement to this effect being made by Mr Denis Healey, the Minister of Defence, on January 2 1965.

As is now well known, the TSR 2 was also felled by the same political axe soon afterwards, the loss of these three projects advancing the nation's unemployment figures by an estimated 70,000 over the following two years. As an expedient to provide the RAF with its necessary equipment the British Government decided to purchase American General Dynamics F-111 aircraft—and then invoked huge compensation payments by cancellation of its Contract, ending up by transferring old-generation subsonic Buccaneers from the Fleet Air Arm to the RAF!

For Hawker at Kingston the loss of the P 1154 was a terrible blow, although in fact little hardship resulted from unemployment. Mercifully the P 1127 (RAF)—soon to become the Harrier—at last succeeded in gaining the Air Staff's favour. After all, the disappearance overnight of almost every major RAF future project left a yawning absence of work in the offices of the Operational Requirements Branch.

One is only left to ponder the ramifications of the P 1154's cancellation. Certainly it was an exceptionally advanced and exciting concept—in its widest sense further advanced even than that of the TSR 2. Yet one is bound to question whether the resources of Britain's aircraft industry were ever adequate to accommodate the P 1154, TSR 2 *and* Concorde in the late 1960s. Although the P 1154 represented a considerable advance in operational concept over the McDonnell F-4 Phantom (arguably the most efficient 'two-Service' tactical aircraft during the Vietnam War era), it *had* been dogged by design compromise until the Admiralty withdrew from the project in 1964. And one is inevitably faced with the nebulous question regarding the P 1154's long-term development prospects. Better perhaps that the programme was cancelled in 1965 than, say, three years later when it might have been too late to resurrect a 'meaningful' Harrier programme. The very high cost and complexity of the P 1154, even by the standards of the mid-1960s, would have precluded any export potential, save to a tiny market, effectively strangling the whole concept of V/STOL operation.

The final epitaph on the grave of the P 1154 appears to uphold Sir Sydney Camm's own design philosophies: it anathematized the very essence of V/STOL's tactical flexibility in reaching new extremes of complexity and cost.

Chapter 6

The RAF goes V/STOL at last

The fortunes of the Harrier proper effectively started at the moment the Labour Government took the decision to cancel the Hawker P 1154, a decision that was announced in the House of Commons on the afternoon of February 2 1965. Implicit in this announcement was the decision by the Air Staff, at a stroke deprived of two major future projects and soon to suffer a third deprivation, to revert in effect to the long-defunct GOR 345, to meet which so much had been thrashed out back in 1960-61. In this vein the Ministry of Aviation was advocating a critical low-low sortie radius of 160 nautical miles—still a fairly stringent demand. The aircraft would of course remain firmly subsonic in level flight.

It was perhaps significant that at the very moment the P 1154 received its death blow, the West Raynham evaluation of the Kestrel was just beginning, thereby lending added significance to the findings of the trials. Events now moved quickly. The Air Staff issued a new Requirement, ASR 384, specifically for a P 1127 development—henceforth referred to as the P 1127 (RAF).

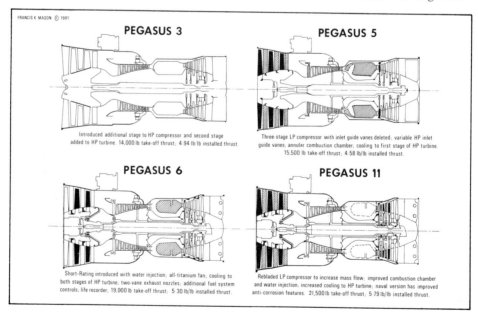

At the same time as authority was given to go ahead with the airframe development, Bristol was making final preparations to bench run their latest engine development, the Pegasus 6—destined to become the first full-production status version. This high-mass-

PEGASUS 3

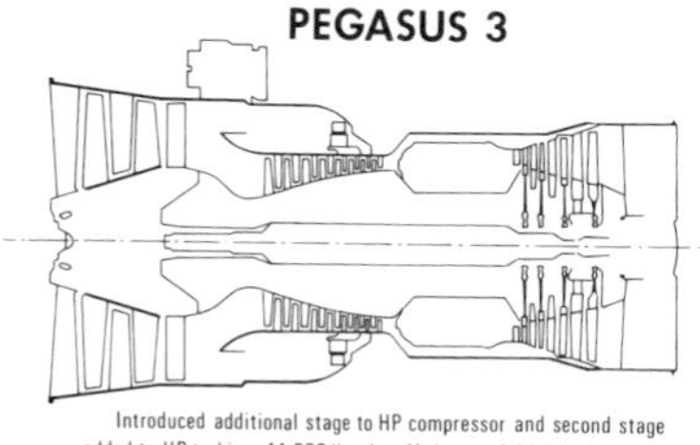

Introduced additional stage to HP compressor and second stage added to HP turbine. 14,000 lb take-off thrust; 4·94 lb/lb installed thrust.

PEGASUS 5

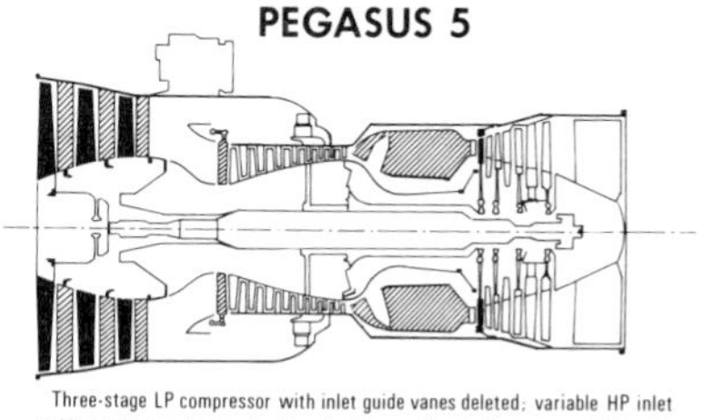

Three-stage LP compressor with inlet guide vanes deleted; variable HP inlet guide vanes; annular combustion chamber; cooling to first stage of HP turbine. 15,500 lb take-off thrust; 4·58 lb/lb installed thrust.

PEGASUS 6

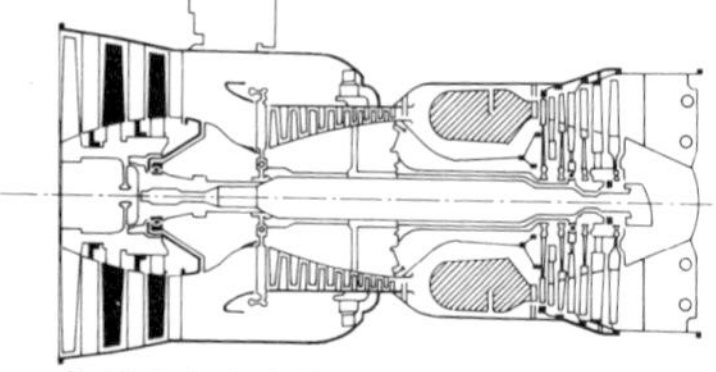

Short-Rating introduced with water injection; all-titanium fan; cooling to both stages of HP turbine; two-vane exhaust nozzles; additional fuel system controls; life recorder; 19,000 lb take-off thrust; 5·30 lb/lb installed thrust.

PEGASUS 11

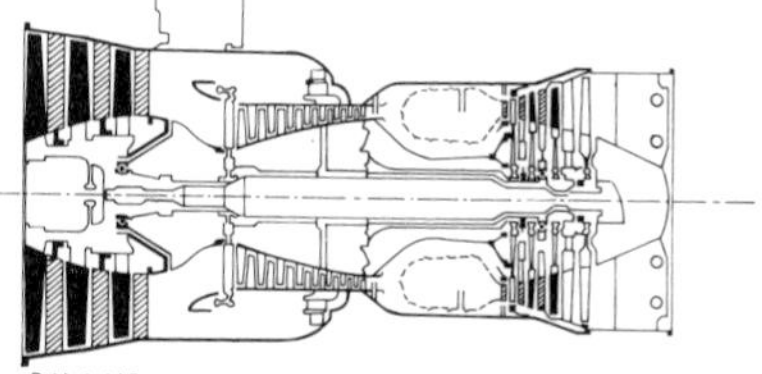

Rebladed LP compressor to increase mass flow; improved combustion chamber and water injection; increased cooling to HP turbine; naval version has improved anti-corrosion features. 21,500 lb take-off thrust; 5·79 lb/lb installed thrust.

Bristol Pegasus vectored-thrust turbofans in No 2 Assembly Shop at Bristol (Rolls-Royce Ltd (Aero Division), Bristol, Neg No E144622).

flow engine introduced water injection for thrust restoration, all-titanium low-pressure fan, cooling to both stages of the high-pressure turbine, two-vane exhaust nozzles, additional fuel system controls for high pressure temperature and pressure ratio limitation and engine life recorder for creep monitoring. In due course the engine, which also introduced the Short-Rating concept (short-time high-thrust), developed 19,000 lb thrust at the significantly improved thrust/weight ratio of 5.30 lb thrust per lb installed weight (an improvement of 15.7 per cent over the Pegasus 5).

It will be recalled that an attempt had been made to achieve variable-geometry intake lips on the Kestrel by use of inflatable bags, but that these had given continued trouble and were dispensed with in favour of the fixed bell-mouth lip fairing. Such a compromise would be totally inadequate to satisfy the high mass flow of the Pegasus 6, so that Hawker embarked on mechanically-variable geometry intakes with multiple blow-in doors arranged circumferentially in the intake walls.

Apart from the alterations to the airframe brought about by the engine requirements, the remainder of the aircraft—as a result of some millions of engineering manhours invested in the development of the P 1127/Kestrel/P 1150/P 1154, as well as three years of study by the Ministry of Aviation—underwent roughly 90 per cent redesign to meet ASR 384.

Airframe

Although the basic airframe configuration remained unchanged, dictated as it was by the fundamental single vectored-thrust Pegasus, the structure itself underwent complete redesign. It retained the ground attack load factors and included the 3,000-hour fatigue life specified in the P 1154, but the design diving speed limitation was increased beyond that of the Kestrel. The undercarriage design was required to withstand increased vertical landing velocity at higher landing weights than those of the Kestrel, and birdstrike resistance, specified for the P 1154, had to be provided.

With the greater thrust of the Pegasus 6 engine, the thrust centre was further aft than previously, but this in itself proved insufficient to require relocation of the engine. However, the centre of gravity could not be allowed to move back on the mean wing chord owing to concern over retaining longitudinal stability in conventional flight, and the main aerodynamic problem was therefore to retain adequate c.g margins with various external stores by providing a more rearward aerodynamic centre.

The Kestrel wing leading edge was redesigned—maintaining the geometry of the interspar integral box—additional span and area being added outboard of the outriggers. The tailplane remained unchanged from that of the Kestrel except that the trim range occupied a larger fraction of the total tailplane movement. A light bobweight was added to the pitch control system.

Undercarriage

Demands were made in the new Requirement for greatly increased energy-absorbing capacity in the landing gear. This was provided by increasing the oleo strokes while maintaining the peak reaction loads, thereby avoiding excessive structural alteration.

The undercarriage geometry was designed to allow the outriggers to give appropriate roll support (roll stiffness to allow about one degree of bank per unit lateral g) at all all-up weights. Thus when the aircraft was just off the ground—that is to say, all legs fully extended—there was more roll freedom from mainwheels to outriggers than with the Kestrel because of longer oleo travel.

Also introduced in the new aircraft were undercarriage door closing sequences after the landing gear had been selected down to minimise debris congestion in the wheel bays during take-off and landing.

Reaction control system

In the early P 1127s a 'constant bleed' reaction system was employed; in this, pilot control movements merely redistributed the constant total thrust from the RCVs to achieve the desired trimming and righting moments. This system was very extravagant of engine thrust as each pound of high pressure air taken represented a considerable energy input from the Pegasus compressors without any compensating energy release from this airflow through the turbines.

In the development of the P 1127 (RAF), a change was made to a 'demand' system so that bleed air is taken from the engine only when the pilot's control movements open the appropriate RCVs.

Water injection

The development of the Pegasus 6 introduced water injection. The maximum take-off thrust available from the engine is limited, particularly at high ambient temperatures, by the turbine blade temperature. As this temperature cannot be reliably measured, the operating limits are determined by jet pipe temperature (JPT). To enable the engine speed and hence thrust to be increased for take-off, water is sprayed into the combustion chamber to keep the blade temperature down to an acceptable level; normally distilled water or de-mineralised water is used to avoid fouling the turbine blades with carbonates and sulphates.

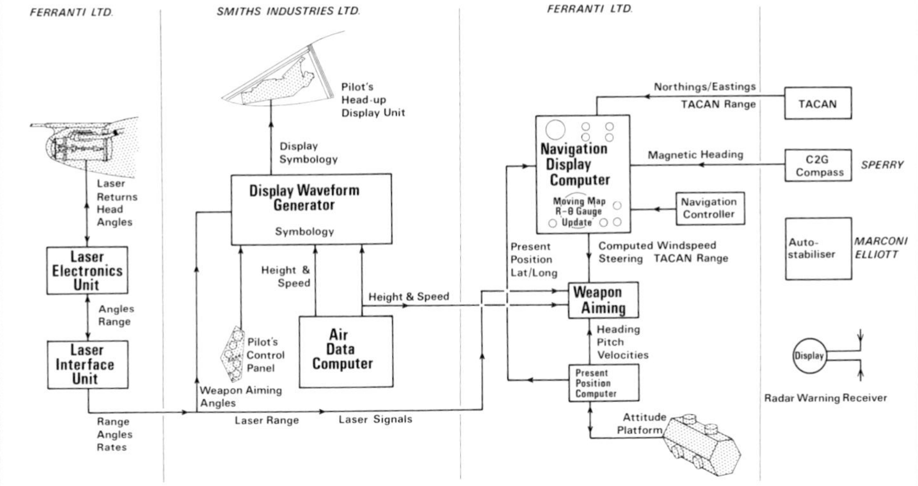

HARRIER G.R.3 OPERATIONAL EQUIPMENT

Francis K. Mason © 1981

Operational equipment

The Kestrel evaluation aircraft, by the nature of their short Service use, featured only very limited operational equipment, confined in effect to a nose camera—although space was provided for such items as inertial platform components. The ASR 384 called for inclusion of an inertial navigation-attack system to be wholly independent of external radio references, and the Ferranti 541 system was developed to provide flight information to a Smiths Industries head-up display (HUD). The system also included a head-down optically-projected moving-map display. In line with RAF requirements the navigational accuracy—without *en-route* update—was to be, typically, 1.5 nautical miles after one hour's flying time.

ASR 384 also called for internal accommodation of a 70-mm oblique camera and a HUD recording camera. A five-camera pod was required to be carried under the fuselage when used in the full reconnaissance rôle; this pod gave horizon-to-horizon photo cover, and data on the aircraft's position and heading was printed automatically on each negative as it was exposed.

Weapon carriage

Although the P 1127 (RAF) was not designed to include any internal gun armament, special single-gun pods each accommodating a 30 mm Aden gun with 150 rounds of ammunition were designed for attachment at the 'five and seven o'clock' positions of the lower fuselage centre-section; by the nature of their design and location, these pods enhanced the deflected-efflux containment otherwise effected by the longitudinal fuselage strakes developed on the P 1127 prototypes and provided considerable lift improvement in the VTO mode.

In addition to the centreline store attachment (stressed for a 1,000-lb store), two stations for underwing pylons were to be provided under each wing for weapons and drop tanks.

The P 1127 (RAF) Development Batch

Although obviously displaying a marked similarity to the Kestrel, the P 1127 (RAF) had in fact undergone a 90 per cent redesign, and had therefore to be regarded as a new aircraft. So as to meet ASR 384's delivery timescale of four years from Requirement-issue,

Harrier

Harrier

Above left *DB Harrier* XV277 *carrying eight Lepus flares on the underwing pylons* (British Aerospace (Experimental), Neg No 3460).

Centre left *DB Harrier* XV277 *with two 1,000-lb bombs on inboard wing pylons and two 1,197-lb cluster bombs outboard* (British Aerospace (Experimental), Neg No 3755).

Below left *Heavily loaded, fully updated Harrier GR Mark 3 carrying six 1,197-lb cluster bombs and centreline reconnaissance pod* (British Aerospace (Experimental), Neg No 7062).

Above *The weapons TI development aircraft,* XV277, *carrying five 1,000-lb bombs, two 1,197-lb cluster bombs, gun pods and full ammunition* (British Aerospace (Experimental), Neg No 3920).

a Development Batch (DB) of six pre-production aircraft *(XV276-XV281)* was ordered in 1965, the first being flown on August 31 1966.*

This and the following aircraft were employed on handling, performance and store-clearance trials during 1966 and 1967, individual aircraft being delivered to Bristol for engine development and to Boscombe Down for initial Service reaction and preliminary preparation of Pilot's Notes.

Principal external distinguishing feature of the DB aircraft was the wholly redesigned engine intake reshaped for the increased mass flow of the Pegasus 6. To meet hover pressure recovery demands mechanically-variable geometry was introduced with six blow-in doors located round the intake cowl; the cowl lip had been designed to minimise spillage drag, employing the same 'peaky' pressure distribution aerofoil section as used in the wing. Early tests, combined with forecast higher mass flows in future Pegasus engines, brought about further redesign of the intake early in 1967 to increase the number of blow-in doors to eight just as the production drawing schedules were being finalised.

* *This aircraft continued on development flying until written off in an accident at Dunsfold in 1973. Owing to an engine-stop maladjustment, the pilot suffered a flame-out in the airfield circuit, but ejected safely.*

Above left *First of the P 1127(RAF) development batch,* XV276, *in natural metal finish; a photo taken prior to engine starting* (Hawker Siddeley Aviation, Neg No K46/66).

Centre left XV276 *after engine start-up; the six blow-in doors opened (production Harriers featured eight doors on each intake)* (Hawker Siddeley Aviation, Neg No K44/66).

Below left *Fourth DB Harrier,* XV279, *at Dunsfold; in the background are pairs of 100- and 230-gallon drop tanks and rocket pods; and in the foreground a 1,000-lb bomb* (Hawker Siddeley Aviation, Neg No 7/174).

Above *Last of the six DB Harriers,* XV281 *in hover at Dunsfold. Although regarded as fully representative of the production Harrier GR Mark 1 (note eight blow-in doors), only four of the ultimate 12 wing vortex generators are fitted* (Hawker Siddeley Aviation, Neg No 112677).

Below *Six blow-in doors identify this as a DB Harrier, modified to Mark 3 standard and fitted with bolt-on ferry wingtips* (British Aerospace (Experimental), Neg No 7279/9, dated January 30 1978).

Initial fuselage assembly of early Harrier GR Mark 1s at Kingston in 1968 showing mating of the nose and rear sections to the centre fuselage prior to locating in the walk-round scaffolding for system installation (Hawker Siddeley Aviation, Neg No 43529).

Early in 1967 Hawker Siddeley was formally notified that the P 1127 (RAF) had been named the Harrier GR Mark 1 (GR = Ground Attack/Reconnaissance)*, and a Contract, drafted the previous year, was confirmed for 60 production aircraft *(XV738-XV762* and *XV776-XV810)* to be produced at Kingston powered by 19,000-lb thrust Pegasus 6 (Mark 101) engines.

The first production Harrier GR Mark 1, *XV738,* was flown by Duncan Simpson on December 28 1967, this and the following five aircraft—which flew during 1968—joining the DB aircraft at Dunsfold, Bristol and Boscombe Down for Service clearance flying. (The provision of a dozen specifically-designated development Harriers contrasted sharply with Hawker's experience with the Hunter, of which a marked lack of development examples resulted in lengthy delays before the aircraft could be introduced to service; the Harrier joined the RAF exactly on schedule.)

By late summer of 1968 five Harriers were being flown from Boscombe Down, engaged in Service evaluation and the CA Release programme; two other aircraft flew from Dunsfold on store trials with drop tanks, bombs and SNEB-Matra rocket pods, all of which underwent carriage and jettison clearance throughout the flight envelope.

At the outset Royal Air Force deployment of the Harrier was announced as being two

* *The name Harrier originated in correspondence between Camm and the author in September 1961. In reply to a request for suggested names for a possible 'RAF P 1127', the author put forward the names Hawk, Heron, Harrier and Kestrel. Camm favoured 'Harrier' (albeit with suspicion that his leg was being pulled—vis-a-vis a possible 'Marsh Harrier' connotating with his Chief Project Engineer, Bob Marsh), having expressed his likely confusion between Hawk and Sea Hawk, the latter still in service. The name Heron—applied to a Hawker aircraft more than 30 years previously—evidently fostered embarrassing personal recollections; and Camm felt that Kestrel was traditionally in the Rolls-Royce province while Hawker was at that time 'in the enemy camp'. Camm had evidently forgotten that his previous Harrier (of 1928 vintage) was a markedly underpowered aeroplane possessed of truly horizontal and apparently unwilling take-off characteristics. In the event 'Harrier', 'Hawk' and 'Kestrel' were all adopted as names of Kingston-designed aircraft between 1963 and 1973.*

Above *Second production Harrier GR Mark 1,* XV739; *note the full array of vortex generators on the wing* (Hawker Siddeley Aviation, Neg No 136058).

Below *The very first production Harrier,* XV738 *(originally a Mark 1), seen here as a fully modified GR Mark 3 in the markings of No 3 (F) Squadron during Exercise 'Heath Fir' in 1976* (Ministry of Defence, Neg No 1721-47).

Right *Harrier* XV744, *which participated in the Transatlantic Air Race of 1969; a view showing the inflight refuelling probe, bolt-on ferry wingtips and underwing 100-gallon drop tanks* (Hawker Siddeley Aviation, Neg No 1149/69).

Below right *The Transatlantic Air Race, 1969. Harrier* XV741 *over its operating site near St Pancras Station, London* (Hawker Siddeley Aviation, Neg No 124049).

squadrons—one based in the United Kingdom in RAF Strike Command and one in Germany with the Second Tactical Air Force—plus a Harrier Conversion Unit whose aircraft would be available for operational deployment with the front line units in times of necessity.

First RAF squadron scheduled to receive the Harrier was No 1 (Fighter) Squadron based at Wittering, Cambridgeshire, and its first aircraft, *XV746,* was delivered on April 18 1969, followed by three further aircraft during the remainder of that month. This squadron thus became the world's first operational unit to fly combat V/STOL aircraft.

In order to centralise Harrier maintenance facilities and to simplify interchange of aircraft with No 1 Squadron, the Harrier Conversion Unit, No 233, was also located at Wittering and this unit took delivery of its first aircraft, *XV747,* early the following year.

The Harrier, however, first leapt into public prominence during the Transatlantic Air Race held between May 4 and 11 1969. Two aircraft of No 1 Squadron, *XV741* and *XV744,* were flown to Boscombe Down on April 9 prior to delivery to Wittering for clearance of the inflight refuelling probe and bolt-on ferry wingtips (both of which features were standard optional fits on production aircraft). Flying between downtown New York and a site near London's St Pancras Station, and being refuelled in flight several times *en route,* the Harriers were adjudged winners of the race—although the supersonic Phantoms of the Fleet Air Arm returned the faster in-flight times. It was the RAF's ability to operate out of confined spaces within the city limits that emphasised the Harrier's unique concept.

During the first nine months of Harrier service with the RAF all pilots of No 1 Squadron were second-tour officers who were adequately experienced to achieve full conversion to type with their unit. By mid-1970, however, first-tour pilots, who had received training with No 233 OCU, started to assume full operational duties with the squadron.

By July 1970 No 1 Squadron had worked up to its full complement of 18 aircraft (a process retarded by accidents, of which those resulting from bird strikes assumed the majority*) and preparations were well advanced to start equipping the German-based Squadron, No 4 (Fighter) Squadron, at Wildenrath. The first Harrier, *XV779,* was delivered the following month and by the end of the year had been joined by 14 further aircraft. As with No 1 Squadron, the nucleus of Harrier flying experience was provided by a small number of jet Qualified Flying Instructors (QFI) who had originally converted to the aircraft at Dunsfold early in 1969. Thereafter first-tour pilots started arriving on the squadron from the OCU. (As shown in Chapter 7, two-seat Harrier trainers began delivery to the RAF in mid-1970.)

In the meantime No 1 Squadron had taken its Harriers (with 16 pilots, plus two from No 233 OCU) to Akrotiri in Cyprus for its armament practice camp between March 3

* *The problem of bird strikes had long been foreseen and featured significantly in strike-resistance requirements in ASR 384. Not only was the aircraft naturally prone to high-speed strikes owing to the Harrier's low-level operating rôle but, during hovering manoeuvres over rural sites, the aircraft was particularly vulnerable to bird ingestion. For some years the RAF employed a number of expedients to discourage bird assembly near airfields. A total of 11 bird-strike accidents to Harriers was reported between 1969 and 1978.*

V741

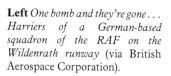

Left *One bomb and they're gone . . . Harriers of a German-based squadron of the RAF on the Wildenrath runway* (via British Aerospace Corporation).

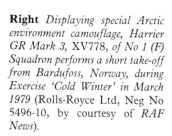

Right *Displaying special Arctic environment camouflage, Harrier GR Mark 3,* XV778, *of No 1 (F) Squadron performs a short take-off from Bardufoss, Norway, during Exercise 'Cold Winter' in March 1979* (Rolls-Royce Ltd, Neg No 5496-10, by courtesy of *RAF News*).

Below *The meaning of concealed-site operation. Harrier GR Mark 1s of No 1 (F) Squadron* (via Bruce Quarrie).

and 25 1970. No attempt was made to extend operations away from the established runway environment on this occasion, the opportunity being used simply to gain pilot proficiency in weapon delivery with the Harrier.

During the autumn of 1970 a second Wildenrath-based unit, No 20 (Fighter) Squadron, started converting to Harriers, and to support deliveries to a third squadron a further production order for 17 aircraft was placed with Hawker Siddeley.*

In 1971 two pilots from No 1 Squadron flew their Harriers aboard HMS *Ark Royal* to perform trials to gain type shipboard clearance in pursuance of a plan to deploy RAF Harriers at sea and to assist in deployment of Harriers for overseas reinforcement purposes. (It should be explained that at that time future Royal Navy requirements for a maritime version of the Harrier had yet to be announced, although design of a new limited-deck anti-submarine class of ship was in hand. See Chapter 9).

Deployment from dispersed sites

Although Harrier squadrons of the Royal Air Force are assigned to, and normally located on fixed airfield bases in peacetime, each unit periodically disperses to temporary sites—usually for week-long periods. The latter would be the operational environment in times and theatres of war in which it has to be assumed that permanent sites would be zeroed-in by hostile missile and strike forces.

* *These aircraft were* XW763-XW770 *and* XW916-XW924. *An 18th aircraft,* XW630, *had been built as a replacement aircraft, additional to the first production batch, to replace* XV743 *which had been destroyed in an accident at Dunsfold before delivery to the RAF.*

Left *Harriers of No 1 (F) Squadron at Bardufoss. It was from this airfield that Hawker Hurricanes of the RAF fought during the Norwegian campaign in 1940* (via Bruce Quarrie).

Below left *No 1 (F) Squadron Harrier temporarily based in Belize during 1975. In the background is an inflatable hangarette* (Ministry of Defence, Neg No PRB4447/149).

It is perhaps significant that in 1978 the Director of Operational Requirements (RAF) reflected the RAF's concern for the vulnerability of airfield-deployed combat aircraft, citing the 'almost total destruction of the Egyptian Air Force by Israeli aircraft in the first hours of the 1967 Middle East war'.*

Although the Wittering-based No 1 Squadron has performed numerous dispersed-site operations during the past ten years, it has fallen to the German-based squadrons to engage more frequently in such exercises—often in support of NATO ground forces based on the Continent. Exercises involving Harriers have ranged from the north of Norway to Sardinia, from detachments to Belize in Central America to Cyprus in the Eastern Mediterranean.

One of the most obvious attributes of the Harrier in the dispersed-site environment is its relative simplicity (reflecting Sir Sydney Camm's original concept). An important factor for the RAF is the constant examination of expedients to reduce the amount of equipment that has to be taken into the field to support the aircraft. Apart from such materiel as camouflage software, landing pads and tracking hardware, inventories of fuel, ammunition, bombs and servicing equipment have to be provided. Normally the aircraft are dispersed radially around a centralised logistics area, but routine 'tween-flight servicing must be carried out at the isolated dispersal.

Already large portable, flexible fuel bags have been introduced to offset difficulties in bulk-liquid handling in the field, and improved integral power sources were specified in the mid-1970s as a Harrier up-date to provide independent ground stand-by and servicing power to reduce dependence upon unwieldly ground generators.

Some indication of the extraordinary success achieved by RAF Harriers in recent off-base exercises may be gained by the following figures†:

Exercise	**Location**	**Duration**	**No of missions**
'Big Tee'—12 Harriers (one aircraft flew 41 sorties)	England, 1974 (No 1 (F) Sqn)	Three days	364
'Oak Stroll'—28 Harriers	West Germany, 1974	Nine days	1,120
On-base, without runways—31 Harriers	Wildenrath, 1974	Eight days	888
'Cold Winter'—10 Harriers	Norway, 1979 (No 1 (F) Sqn)	Seven days	343

If full weapon delivery had been involved in Exercise 'Big Tee', the 12 Harriers would have discharged 550 tons of ordnance and 77,000 rounds of 30 mm ammunition, a substantial logistic task.

* *Cf* The Royal Air Force View on Vectored Thrust, *Air Commodore H.A. Merriman, CBE, AFC, FRAeS. See Bibliography. Air Commodore Merriman, however, suggests that this concern for the RAF's vulnerability dates from the 1950s, whereas this book has suggested that his predecessors at that time were somewhat deaf to proposals to overcome the 'concrete runway' philosophy!*

† *Op cit, Merriman.*

HAWKER SIDDELEY (BAe) HARRIER G.R. MARK 3
21,500-lb thrust Rolls-Royce (Bristol) Pegasus 103 turbofan
Aircraft 'K' (XW922) of No. 233 O.C.U., Wittering, 1980

COLOUR SCHEME

Upper surfaces, Dark Green BS381C/641
and Dark Sea Grey BS381C/638
Lower surfaces (extending as shown)
Light Aircraft Grey BS381C/627
National markings
Roundel Blue BS381C/110
and Post Office Red BS381C/538
Walkway and inspection panel outlines
Signal Red BS381C/537
Fin identity letter Light Blue
Undercarriage oleos, jacks and hubs
Light Silver Grey BS381C/631

PRINCIPAL GEOMETRIC DATA

Wing Span (Combat) ...	25 ft 3 in
Wing Span (Ferry) ...	29 ft 8 in
Overall Length ...	45 ft 8 in
Wing Area (Combat) ...	201·1 sq ft
Wing Area (Ferry) ...	215·9 sq ft
Quarter-Chord Sweepback	34 degrees

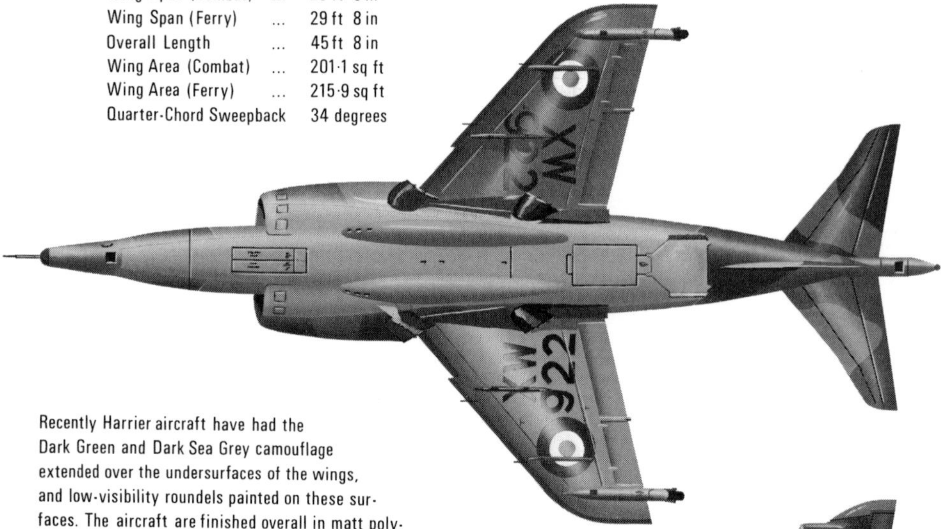

Recently Harrier aircraft have had the Dark Green and Dark Sea Grey camouflage extended over the undersurfaces of the wings, and low-visibility roundels painted on these surfaces. The aircraft are finished overall in matt polyurethane paint.

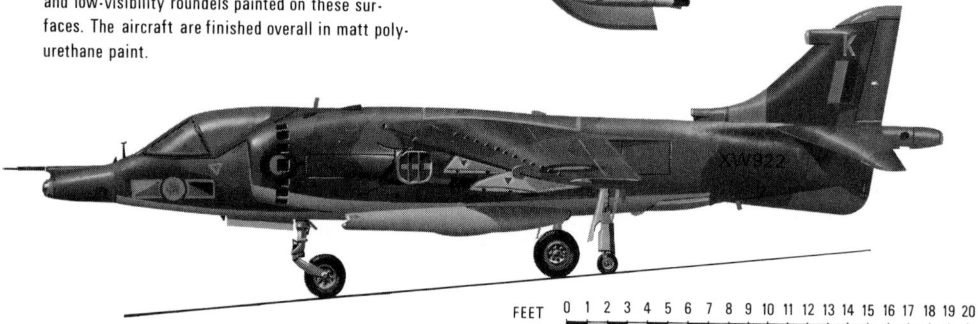

Hawker Siddeley Harrier Mark 1

Manufacturers' Demonstration Aircraft G-VSTO

Aircraft finished in high gloss epoxy paint overall

HAWKER SIDDELEY HARRIER G.R. MARK 3
Aircraft '20' of No. 1 (Fighter) Squadron finished in temporary Dark Sea Grey and White arctic camouflage overall for NATO Exercise 'Cold Winter', Bardufoss, Northern Norway, 1979.

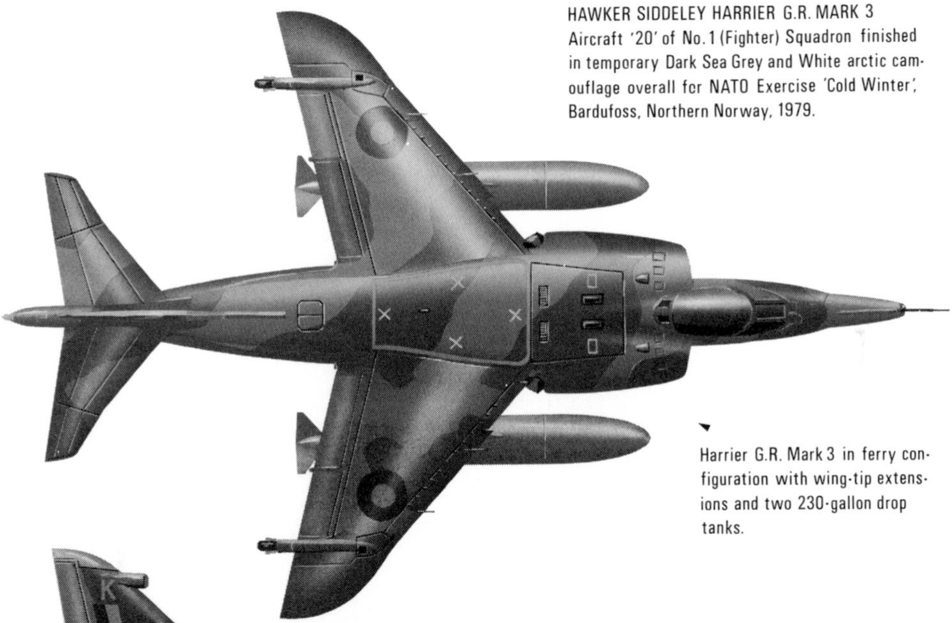

Harrier G.R. Mark 3 in ferry configuration with wing-tip extensions and two 230-gallon drop tanks.

Above *Fine study of a No 3 (F) Squadron Harrier GR 3 landing vertically on its steel mat in Germany during 1977* (Ministry of Defence, Neg No 2036-41, by courtesy of *RAF News).*

Below *Harrier GR 3s (before fitting of the laser nose) of No 3 (F) Squadron operating from a dispersed site in Germany during Exercise 'Oak Stroll' in 1974* (Ministry of Defence, Neg No PRB3437/42).

Harrier updating: the Marks 1A and 3

Last of the squadrons scheduled to receive Harriers was No 3 (Fighter) Squadron at Wildenrath, which took delivery of its aircraft early in 1972. By that time all squadrons were being issued with a single two-seat Harrier T Mark 2 for instrument rating and on-unit conversion.

Meanwhile Rolls-Royce (Bristol) had further developed the Pegasus engine by uprating the thrust output to 20,000 lb and, to permit a 1,000-lb increase in VTO all-up weight, this engine (the Pegasus Mark 102) was progressively retrofitted in all existing RAF Harrier single-seaters—whose designation was now changed to GR Mark 1A—as engine life expired and the aircraft became due for engine change.

A more significant update of the Harrier was initiated when the Pegasus Mark 103 became available for RAF aircraft. This version of the Pegasus 11, producing 21,500-lb thrust and featuring a re-bladed fan to increase mass flow, improved combustion and increased cooling to the high pressure turbine blades, had been specified by the US Marine Corps for their AV-8As and in late 1973 the production rate of the new engine allowed progressive retrofit to all Harrier GR Mark 1As (and T Mark 2As).

At the same time that Harriers underwent this new engine update, the opportunity was taken to incorporate new operational equipment. Stemming from a major avionics programme, a new laser rangefinder had been developed and was now integrated into the Ferranti 541 system.

The Ferranti laser ranging and marked target seeking (LRMTS) equipment was accommodated in a new nose cone. Not only could this device provide laser-pulse-derived range to the ground target—either along boresight or along a depressed or offset mark provided by the FE 541—but also provided a search capability; in the latter mode it could seek IR radiation originating ahead of the Harrier, scattered by the target from a coded IR designator laser operated by a Forward Air Controller on the ground. The integrated LRMTS/FE 541 was fitted in all single-seat Harriers during 1973-76, their designation being changed to GR Mark 3. Bomb delivery accuracy was much improved, with target acquisition in single-pass, low-level, lay-down attacks being considerably facilitated.

In the mid-1970s a further modification was introduced, that of a passive radar warning system, into the laser-equipped Harriers. The radar warning receiver (RWR) antennae are located in a fairing on the leading edge of the fin, for the forward hemisphere, and in the rear tail cone for the rear hemisphere. Incoming radar signals—indicating that the Harrier is being illuminated on hostile radar—are processed in the receiver system and presented in the cockpit as direction and type of radar (emission band, pulse/track-while-scan/CW, etc) so that the pilot may take the necessary evasive action.

Typical utilisation of the Harrier is about 250 hours per annum, and some aircraft are approaching 3,000 hours' flying time. Normal operational attrition reduced the number of early production aircraft, so that in 1976-77 15 new Harrier GR Mark 3s were built and delivered to the RAF, followed by 24 in 1979-80.

The Falkland Islands, 1982

In May 1982 Royal Air Force Harriers were flown in full-scale combat for the first time during the major operation to recover the Falkland Islands after their illegal seizure by Argentine armed forces. Although this operation was largely fought by the Royal Navy and its Sea Harriers (and is more fully described in Chapter 9), the RAF was called on to give support to the land forces in ground attack, long-range bombing and in logistic supply.

Above *A No 20 (F) Squadron Harrier performs a short take-off in the Borken area of West Germany during Exercise 'Heath Fir' in 1976* (Ministry of Defence, Neg No 1721-90).

Below *A Harrier GR Mark 3, complete with laser nose and RWR, of No 4 (F) Squadron during Exercise 'Heath Fir'* (Ministry of Defence, Neg No 1721-8).

Top *Developed jointly by Hawker Siddeley Dynamics and SA Engins Matra, the AS.37/AJ.168 Martel (Missile Anti-Radar and TELevision) guided air-to-surface missile is shown here as an early trial installation on DB Harrier* XV277 (Hawker Siddeley Aviation, Neg No 723723).

Above *Martel-equipped DB Harrier,* XV277, *modified with associated nose radar and tail-mounted RWR antennae* (British Aerospace (Experimental), Neg No 4829).

Below *In its camouflaged dispersal, a Harrier GR 3 undergoes servicing of its electronic equipment* (via British Aerospace Corporation).

From the outset it was realised that the very small complement of Sea Harriers might be fully stretched in providing air defence cover for the Task Force, and it was therefore decided to deploy the RAF Harrier GR 3s of No 1 (Fighter) Squadron to the South Atlantic in the ground-attack rôle, giving them a secondary air combat rôle by adapting their outboard wing pylons to mount Sidewinders. In the event, however, this latter expedient was not required and the Harriers were employed exclusively for ground attack, delivering gun, rocket and bomb strikes against the Argentine positions on the Islands.

Among the lesser-realised aspects of the campaign was the fact that the Harriers were called upon to operate in salt-air conditions, an environment for which the Sea Harrier (with its corrosion-resistant Pegasus 104 engine) was specially prepared—but for which the RAF Harriers were not; moreover, when the *Atlantic Conveyor* was sunk, all spare Pegasus engines were lost. Nevertheless the Harriers maintained a serviceability rate of more than 90 per cent throughout the operation.

It only remains here to point to the superb manner in which, at exceptionally short notice, an RAF squadron of Harriers could be deployed in severe weather conditions to a war zone 8,000 miles distant, and be cross-operated with the Royal Navy from ramp-equipped carrier decks. If anything was needed to justify all the previous trials, training and exercises with the Harrier, the Falkland Islands campaign provided the reward.

The Harrier GR 5 and the future

Current plans are for the Harrier GR 3 to remain in service at least until the mid-1980s, for it has already been suggested that a further production batch may be undertaken to offset attrition (including the losses incurred in the South Atlantic).

However, for a number of years plans have been studied to introduce a second-generation version of the Harrier by increasing its load-carrying capacity (and hence its range) with a given take-off performance. Although this aspect of improved load/STO performance has already been to some extent achieved in the Sea Harrier with ramp-equipped decks on the Royal Navy's carriers, the ski-launch has not yet been seriously considered by the RAF for land operations.

Moreover, while the United States has opted for a total re-design of the AV-8A to incorporate super-critical wing, improved lift devices and carbon-fibre epoxy-based construction, the British policy has been to pursue a more modest (and less costly) approach based on a 'big wing' with leading-edge root extensions (LERX). This expedient, however, did not fully satisfy the performance requirements being suggested by the British Ministry of Defence, and in 1981 it was decided that considerable amortisation benefits would accrue from design and production collaboration with McDonnell Douglas in America. As outlined in Chapter 10, the American AV-8B will provide the basis for the proposed Harrier GR Mark 5, scheduled to enter service during the later 1980s, and an order for 60 such aircraft by the British Government was forecast in 1981.

Chapter 7

Harriers made for two

Long before the British Air Staff's GOR 345 specification had been finalised, but in anticipation of Hawker being invited to tender the P 1127, Camm directed his project designers to investigate the design alterations likely to be required to suit the design for the training rôle. In the past, adaptation of single-seat fighters to accommodate an instructor's cockpit had proved a fairly straightforward exercise in airframe engineering with limited aerodynamic compensation. In a V/STOL aircraft not only is the all-up weight increase of critical importance but any significant alteration of centre of gravity in relation to centre of thrust has to be carefully controlled. Moreover, there was already in 1960 a trend in military requirements for the two-seat 'trainer' version of any combat single-seater to be capable of reproducing exactly similar combat sorties and weapon carriage and delivery, a particularly stringent requirement for an aircraft whose engine thrust would seldom—if ever—be sufficient for vertical take-off under maximum load conditions.

It was with these considerations (not exactly defined as the P 1127 had yet to fly) in mind that Richard Cox-Abel schemed up the four theoretical two-seat configurations available for the P 1127. While these were by no stretch of the imagination regarded as specific design studies, they served to demonstrate the various structural and weight penalties that would accrue. Obviously the most attractive layouts for maximum commonality with the single-seater were the conventional side-by-side and tandem seating arrangements, and Hawker possessed recent experience of developing the Hunter trainer with side-by-side seating. Such a layout would, however, demand an entirely new front (and possibly centre) fuselage with consequential lateral 'spreading' of the engine intakes; this would be unacceptable owing to the sharp bend (already probably near its efficiency limit) required immediately forward of the engine face. Thus there could never be any debate on the Service's preference for side-by-side or tandem seating, and by elimination the tandem layout was adopted as the only possible configuration. The first detailed project drawings were produced of such an aircraft in March 1960.

In the absence of a specific requirement the general arrangement drawings were put aside pending development of GOR 345 which, it will be recalled, underwent constant change at this time. As the Requirement approached finality, Camm was notified on February 10 1961 by Air Commodore Ian Esplin (the newly appointed Director of Operational Requirements (A) at the Air Ministry) of the broad requirement for a two-seat version of the P 1127 capable of performing the same weapon delivery tasks as the GOR 345 single-seater as well as the flying training rôle.

With the withdrawal of GOR 345 at the end of 1961 and the Air Staff's shift of interest to the supersonic V/STOL strike fighter concept, virtually all work on the two-seat P 1127 at Kingston came to an end, the design staff becoming preoccupied not only with the P 1150/P 1154 but with the development of the P 1127 prototypes and the Kestrel.

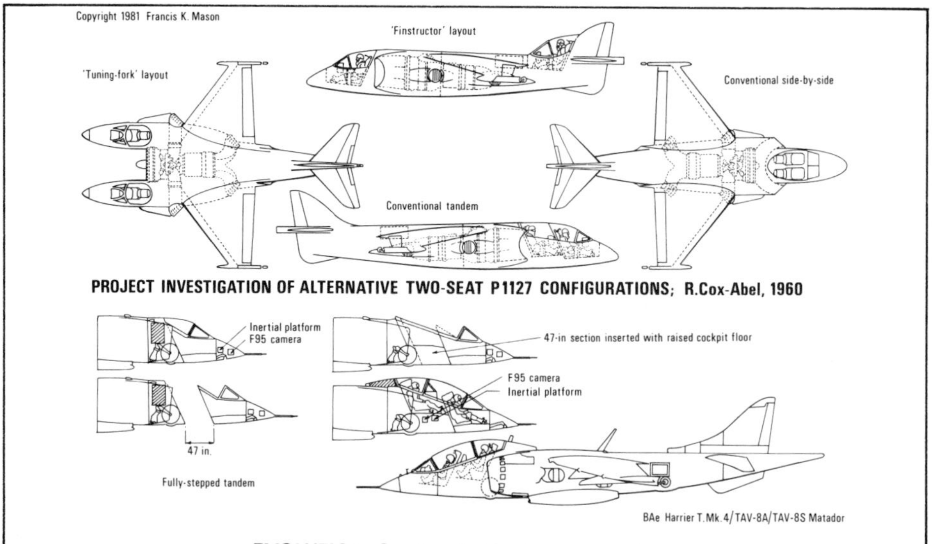

EVOLUTION OF THE TWO-SEAT HARRIER

As the first Kestrels approached completion in 1964 and manufacture of the first RAF P 1154 prototype commenced, renewed interest was being shown in a P 1127 two-seater—as a possible preliminary to development of a P 1154 trainer. It was originally intended to modify one of the P 1127 prototypes (*XP976* was suggested) to two-seat configuration and in July 1964 it was decided that a feasibility study would be undertaken at the Hawker Siddeley Hamble design facility; on the 30th Mr R.K. Page, the Chief Project Engineer at Hamble, paid the first of a number of visits to Kingston to discuss the likely design alterations. Foremost in his mind was the perennial production designer's doctrine—maximum commonality.*

It should be explained here that with experience in practical operation of V/STOL aeroplanes confined to the P 1127 prototypes—and none by the RAF—the Air Staff was in a difficult position with regard to formulating a Service V/STOL trainer requirement and therefore was anxious to read the Hamble feasibility study before committing itself to a specific Requirement. By the end of the year the two-seat P 1127 study was complete and on January 4 1965 this was submitted to the Ministry of Aviation.

However, cancellation of the P 1154 and reversion to the GOR 345 concept for a subsonic P 1127 (RAF) resulted in delays at the MoA, and on June 22 Squadron Leader A.R. Keys, DFC (of the new Ministry of Defence's OR 16 department), visited Kingston to see if some sort of direct liaison could be initiated with the MoD to speed the preparation of a P 1127 (RAF) two-seater Requirement (ASR 386). In the event it was not until the following year that a Contract for two prototype two-seaters was signed with Hawker Siddeley.

Design development of the two-seater took place in parallel with the single-seater, it being intended to provide an exactly similar weapon system for operational training and to provide proficiency in the use of the nav-attack system—as well as conversion training in V/STOL techniques. The Air Staff Requirement also demanded that the aircraft be capable of being flown from the front seat as a single-seater in combat conditions as part of the front-line operational Harrier force. The aircraft was therefore designed to the full

* *Fix It, But Don't Alter (many of) The Drawings (FIBDATD).*

fighter/strike strength envelope as the RAF's GR Mark 1 and was eventually to be cleared for an identical weapon carriage capability. Ballast would be carried in a lengthened tail cone in order to maintain the correct relation between centre of gravity and engine thrust centre, this ballast being removed—together with the rear seat—when the aircraft would be flown as a combat single-seater.

Inclusion of the rear cockpit necessitated movement forward of all the single-seater's cockpit and nose structure ahead of the seat frame and insertion of a 47-in structure containing the rear cockpit. The cabin conditioning system immediately aft of the GR Mark 1's seat was removed, increased in capacity (for the enlarged cabin) and repackaged in the two-seater's canopy fairing immediately aft of the rear occupant's head. Owing to the position of the nosewheel bay the new rear cockpit frame was moved aft *over* the bay so that the rear occupant's seat line was raised some 18 in above that of the front; this had the beneficial effect of providing the rear pilot with an excellent view over the head of the front pilot, facilitating short landing approach, weapon aiming and other manoeuvres. A pair of side-hinged manually-operated canopies enclosed the cockpits which accommodated a pair of Martin Baker Type 9 Mark 1D ejection seats. The new seating arrangement became known as 'stepped-tandem.'

In order to limit the nose moment about the aircraft's centre of gravity, both the F 95 camera and inertial platform—previously located in the extreme nose of the single-seater—were moved to positions below the rear cockpit, the camera, as before, directed obliquely to port.

To offset the destabilising effect of the nose extension (which reduced 'weathercock stability', or the tendency to point into wind without sideslip), additional rear keel area was provided by moving aft the tail fin and rudder unit by 33 in and raising it 11 in by insertion of a fixed fin structure; at the same time a new enlarged ventral fin was included. In the pitching plane, tunnel tests indicated that flight stability and control requirements would be met without movement aft of the tailplane. Moreover the movement forward by 56 in of the nose reaction control valve (and balancing movement of the aft RCV) demanded little increase in reaction control bleed air despite the large increase in pitch and yaw inertias.

The wing of the GR Mark 1 remained wholly unchanged in the two-seater and the centre fuselage was almost identical. The all-moving tailplane was also structurally unaltered but embodied one minor addition—vibration dampers consisting of four steel, grit-filled 3-in tubes in each tailplane tip—found necessary to eliminate tailplane 'buzz' during engine running on the ground; this phenomenon accompanied the interaction between tailplane and rear fuselage pitching moment resonant frequencies. (The single-seater's fuselage natural frequency is not a sub-harmonic of that of the tailplane.)

The first two-seat Harrier, *XW174* (although strictly a prototype, it was generally referred to as a development aircraft, being entirely representative of the proposed production version), was first flown by Duncan Simpson on April 22 1969, but six weeks later on June 4 this aircraft was destroyed in a crash at Larkhill, near Boscombe Down, following a fuel system fault. Duncan Simpson, who was flying the aircraft alone, ejected safely but was badly injured; happily, he recovered and resumed test flying some weeks later.

The second development aircraft, *XW175,* was completed and flown for the first time on July 14, being initially identical to *XW174.* Development flying continued and demonstrated inheritance of the single-seater's superlative handling qualities. However, despite all the attention afforded to achieving weathercock stability, it was discovered that in deep buffet at extreme angles of attack (over 15 degrees) over a narrow Mach number

Above *The first ill-fated Harrier two-seat development aircraft,* XW174. *Rows of unpainted flush rivets on the fin bear testimony to the increased fin area of the two-seater, but the extended tail cone, which carried a brake/anti-spin parachute during development flying, was not a standard fit in production aircraft* (Hawker Siddeley Aviation, Neg No 109549).

Below *An early in-hover photo of* XW175, *the second development two-seater, with low-visibility markings on fuselage and tail. The fin-tip extension has not yet been fitted* (Author's collection).

Above *The second development Harrier T Mark 2,* XW175, *during the trials to restore weathercock stability, showing the greatly extended fin (unpainted)* (Author's collection).
Below XW175 *in low hover. Note the traditional national markings and the F95 camera port immediately forward of the engine intake* (Hawker Siddeley Aviation, Neg No 700363).

Above *The second Harrier two-seat prototype,* XW175, *temporarily fitted with a rearward fin extension during weathercock stability trials* (British Aerospace (Experimental), Neg No 3732).

Below *Harrier T2 two-seater (probably* XW264) *in ferry configuration; 330-gallon underwing tanks, refuelling probe and ferry wingtips. The black rectangle forward of the engine intake was for photo definition during wool-tufting, probably in the course of weathercock stability trials* (British Aerospace (Experimental) Neg No 3796).

The first production Harrier T Mark 2, XW264, *equipped with an RWR antenna on the fin, extensively wool-tufted over the centre fuselage and wing during weathercock stability trials* (British Aerospace (Experimental), Neg No 3742).

band pilots had to apply excessively coarse stick movement to counter rolling moments generated by unusual sideslip angles.

This resulted in an intensive search for an aerodynamic remedy which would ensure that the aircraft pointed into wind under *all* flight conditions. As the only major alteration in the Harrier's aerodynamic shape lay in the cockpit profile it was thought likely that airflow breakaway aft of the canopy was reducing fin effectiveness and causing the aircraft to wander directionally. This was soon ruled out and attention turned to increasing the fin area. An interim extension, increasing the fin height by 18 in, was produced and fitted on *XW175,* and during flight test the pilots reported some improvement, but advocated further extension; an extension of 23 in was produced—with serious misgivings by the stressmen who demanded strict limitation of airspeed and sideslip angles—and this was greeted by the pilots as an unqualified success. However, as such an extension was regarded as too drastic a remedy, the pilots were asked to re-examine the flight characteristics of the 18-in extension and it was now discovered that, in fact, full weathercock stability had been restored, and it was the smaller extension that was applied to the Harrier two-seater in production as the T Mark 2. Early aircraft, which were completed before the modification was finally resolved, were retroactively fitted with the extended fin.

Another temporary remedy adopted during the weathercock stability investigations involved the ventral airbrake. It had been discovered that extending the airbrake in flight above the critical angle of attack, when weathercock stability deteriorated, contributed a measure of stability, so the airbrake operating circuit was linked to the tailplane; thus with the control column pulled back to attain high angles of attack (beyond the normal cruise flight range of movement) the airbrake was automatically actuated to 26 degrees OUT, and retracted on release of the stick when the tailplane returned to the cruise flight range. This proved a simple expedient to adopt and so the 'flipping airbrake' was retained in production aircraft.

Into service

A total of 12 production Harrier T Mark 2s was ordered in 1967 (increased later by a further five), and these commenced manufacture the following year. A couple of aircraft joined the development programme to assist with weapon carriage clearance in 1969 (one of these being lost in an accident at Boscombe Down following a fuel system failure on July 11 1970), and on gaining CA Release the first deliveries were made to the Harrier Operational Conversion Unit—No 233 OCU— at Wittering, Northants, in July 1970. Within a year three other aircraft had been delivered to the front line Harrier squadrons at Wittering and in Germany; apart from representing a potential back-up for the operational strength of the squadrons, these Harrier two-seaters served as Instrument Rating trainers, weapon delivery instruction aircraft and as pilot technique and proficiency vehicles.

Prior to the arrival of the two-seaters at Wittering, the front-line Harrier squadrons had had to undertake their own conversion training in V/STOL operations without the benefit of prior two-seat experience—in itself a remarkable testimony to the relatively straightforward flight characteristics of the Harrier. However, most of the 'first-generation'

First production Harrier T Mark 2, XW264, *during store clearance trials, seen here with 1,000-lb bombs on inboard and centreline pylons, and cluster bombs on outboard pylons. The aircraft later crashed at Boscombe Down* (Hawker Siddeley Aviation, Neg No 702082).

First installation of LRMTS/FE541 and RWR equipment in a Harrier T Mark 4 two-seater (British Aerospace (Experimental), Neg No 7286/3, dated February 1 1978).

Harrier squadron pilots were at least on their second operational tour and were thus fairly experienced. The myth had therefore been put about by the sceptics—and there were still a few about—that only highly-experienced pilots could fly the Harrier. With the arrival in service of the T Mark 2 it proved entirely feasible to route first-tour pilots to the front-line squadrons with no more than 500 total flying hours behind them.

Service development of the two-seater followed that of the single-seater. With the clearance of the up-rated Pegasus 102 engine to 20,000-lb thrust, this engine was retrofitted in the existing T Mark 2s (11 aircraft in 1973), thereby introducing the T Mark 2A designation. Later on, with three further aircraft produced in 1976, the 21,500-lb thrust Pegasus 103 was retrofitted in the RAF two-seaters, resulting in the designation change to T Mark 4. More recently, Harrier T 4s have been retrofitted with the RWR antenna installation in the fin and tail cone for passive radar warning that the aircraft is being 'illuminated' by hostile radar. The Ferranti LRMTS FE 541 has also been fitted in the Harrier T Mark 4.

The two-seat demonstrator, *G-VTOL*

The Chief of the British Air Staff during the Harrier two-seater's development period, Air Chief Marshal Sir John Grandy*, made the following observation after flying in a T Mark 2: 'There are many milestones in a pilot's life and this first flight in the Harrier is the greatest I have ever achieved. It is a truly remarkable machine, with tremendous potential in air operations'.

* *Sir John Grandy, GCB, KBE, DSO, who had commanded a fighter squadron during the Battle of Britain, subsequently led the first Hawker Typhoon Wing at Duxford during the war, commanded the British Nuclear Test Task Force on Christmas Island in 1957-58, and was Assistant Chief of the Air Staff (Ops) in 1958-61.*

Left *Pending the preparation of the two-seat Harrier demonstrator,* G-VTOL, *Hawker Siddeley Aviation employed a single-seater,* G-VSTO, *as a temporary expedient* (Hawker Siddeley Aviation, Neg No 713007, dated 1971).

Below left *An early picture of the Harrier two-seat demonstrator,* G-VTOL, *in its red, white and blue colour scheme* (Hawker Siddeley Aviation, Neg No 714647).

Above *The two-seat Harrier demonstrator shown carrying Matra F.1 rocket pods (each containing 36 rockets)* (British Aerospace (Experimental), Neg No 5285, dated September 4 1974).

Below G-VTOL *fitted with two 230-gallon drop tanks inboard and four flight mock-ups of the Hawker Siddeley Dynamics SRAAM 75 (Short Range Air-to-Air Missile) outboard. Originally named Taildog, SRAAM was a third-generation solid-propellant infra-red missile with folding fins* (British Aerospace (Experimental), Neg No 4838).

Harrier two-seat demonstrator, G-VTOL, *landing aboard the amphibious assault cruiser, HMS* Fearless *(12,120 tons) in June 1975* (Hawker Siddeley Aviation, Neg No 751426).

Not that the manufacturer required any such espousal. Yet it was clear that not only was it necessary to see in order to believe; there was no real substitute for seat-of-the-pants experience. The fire of enthusiasm by the United States Marine Corps had been sparked by practical, first-hand knowledge gained by experienced line pilots (see Chapter 8). It was clear that, having now evolved a two-seat Harrier—wholly representative of the combat single-seater—this version could be employed to good effect not only to demonstrate all facets of V/STOL techniques but to give 'instant' experience of such techniques to influential Service Staff members who might not be qualified pilots; as such it would provide an efficient sales tool as well as representing a prime gospel platform. 'One minute in jet-borne flight has more impact than hours of brochure-reading.'

So it was in 1970 that the Hawker Siddeley Aviation management decided to build and operate its own two-seat Harrier demonstrator. The aircraft, designated the Harrier Mark 52, was completed the following year—appropriately registered *G-VTOL* by the Department of Trade and Industry—and was granted a Special-Category Civil Certificate of Airworthiness by the Air Registration Board in September 1971. Although capable of carrying the full range of external stores, being a civil-registered aircraft *G-VTOL* (usually referred to in speech as 'Veetol'), did not as a matter of course carry the Aden gun packs, recourse being made to the longitudinal underfuselage strakes.

The aircraft itself was manufactured at private expense and all Harrier component and equipment suppliers provided their relevant parts on an embodiment loan basis. *G-VTOL* was the first two-seat Harrier to fly with the Pegasus 102 engine (which had received civil certification), and later gained the same distinction with the 21,500-lb thrust Pegasus 103. So as to be cleared for worldwide demonstration work the aircraft was fitted with a larger range of radio/navigation aids, such as ILS and ADF, than the standard RAF versions.

G-VTOL has given numerous demonstrations at home and overseas, including ski-ramp take-offs (see Chapter 9) and shipboard operation. The first carrier operation was, in fact, a demonstration exercise aboard the Indian Navy's 19,500-ton carrier *Vikrant* (ex-

Interesting study of the Harrier Mark 52 carrying both registration marks ZA250 *and* G-VTOL, *and resplendent in grey and white colour scheme. Nearest to the camera is the British Aerospace Hawk,* ZA101/G-HAWK, *also a demonstration aircraft* (British Aerospace Corporation, Neg No 792805, dated 1979).

Royal Navy HMS *Hercules*) in July 1972. John Farley, then Deputy Chief Test Pilot at Dunsfold, flew the two-seater out to Bombay via Naples, Akrotiri, Teheran, Kuwait and Masirah, equipped with two 330-gallon ferry tanks. In two days Farley flew 21 sorties from the carrier, giving second-seat flying experience to a number of senior Indian Navy pilots (including the commanding officer of a Hawker Sea Hawk squadron, this being the aircraft for which the customer was seeking a replacement). One of the outstanding features of these demonstrations was the steamy heat of the monsoon season which produced an ambient temperature of 30°C (86°F) but, despite these severe conditions, *G-VTOL* gave a convincing demonstration which unquestionably sparked Indian determination to acquire Harriers as future maritime air equipment. In 1980 an order for six Sea Harrier FRS Mark 51s and two two-seat Harrier T 60s was placed by the Indian Government for delivery in 1983, the aircraft being scheduled for operation from the *Vikrant*.

HAWKER SIDDELEY (BAe) HARRIER T. MARK 4
21,500-lb thrust Rolls-Royce (Bristol) Pegasus 103 turbofan
Aircraft XW269 of No. 4 (Fighter) Squadron, Wildenrath, 1979
(Fitted with LRMTS/FE541 and RWR equipment)

Leading Particulars as for Harrier G.R. Mark 3 except...

Overall Length ... 56 ft 0·2 in

Colour specification as for Harrier G.R. Mark 3 except that Dark Green and Medium Sea Grey extend to all under surfaces, and red/blue roundels are applied under the wings.

Aircraft insignia of No. 4 (Fighter) Squadron. Black, red and yellow; drawn 4 x page scale.

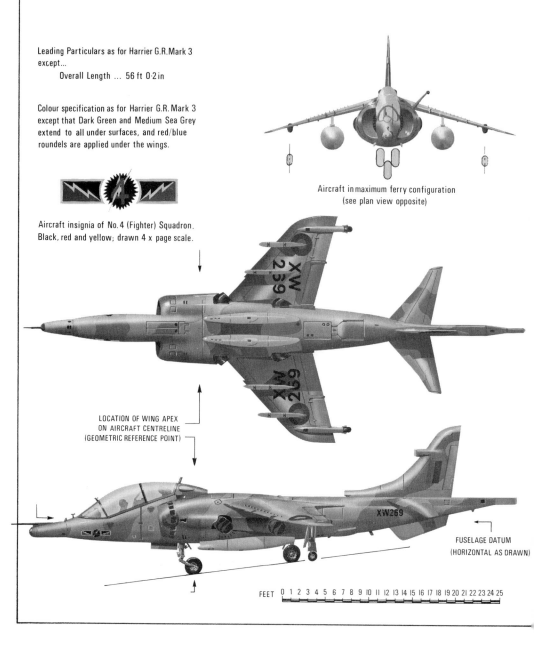

Aircraft in maximum ferry configuration (see plan view opposite)

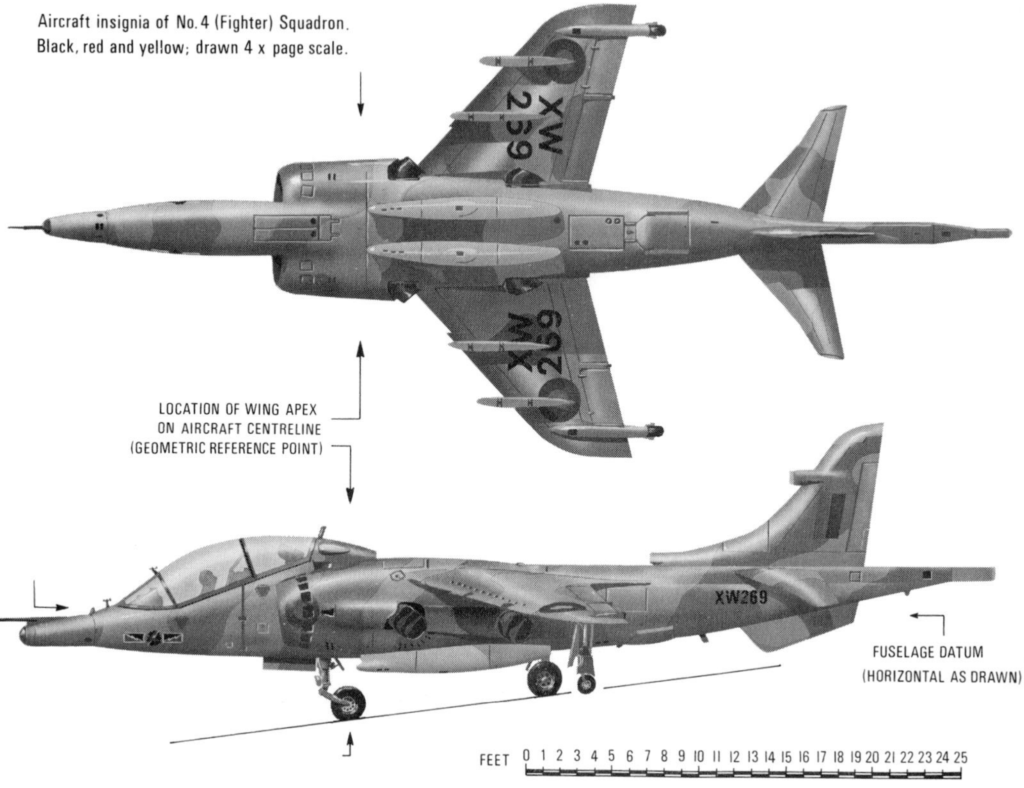

Hawker Siddeley Harrier Mark 52

Manufacturers' Demonstration Aircraft G-VTOL
Shown in 1971 paint scheme

(Dark blue fuselage, wing borders and tailplane; red wing panels, nose and flash; white fin, cockpit sills, fuselage upper surface and panel fimbriations; Union flag on fin.)

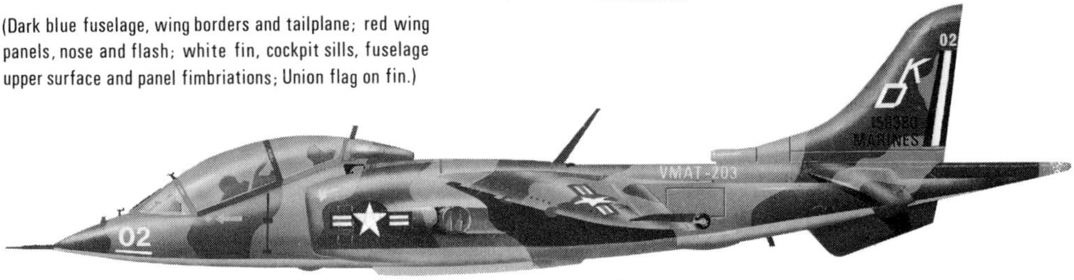

Hawker Siddeley TAV-8A Harrier Mark 54, 71-59380, of U.S. Marine Corps Attack Training Squadron VMA(T)-203, during ski-ramp trials, NAS Patuxent River, 1979.

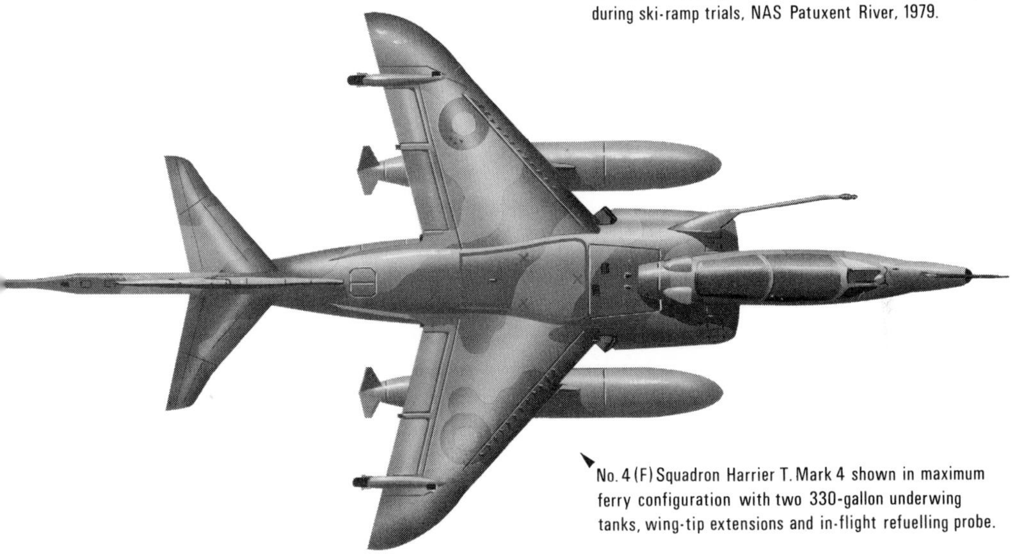

No. 4 (F) Squadron Harrier T. Mark 4 shown in maximum ferry configuration with two 330-gallon underwing tanks, wing-tip extensions and in-flight refuelling probe.

Chapter 8

The American partnership

One is perhaps apt to lose sight of the fact that, in all probability, had there been no participation by the United States in the original Bristol vectored-thrust engine development programme there would have been no Hawker P 1127 and no Harrier. As outlined in Chapter 2 it was the continued support and enthusiasm of Colonel Bill Chapman and the MWDT that resulted in roughly three-quarters of all engine development costs being subscribed by US Offshore funding.

Throughout the period 1958-63 American interest in the P 1127 continued, and was manifest particularly in NASA aerodynamic research, dating from Mr John Stack's initiation of model testing. From mid-1960 onwards countless visits to Hawker were paid by members of the US Department of Defense and American commercial organisations, undoubtedly with some specific military collaboration in mind for the future; in September that year General Schreiver, Chief of the USAF's Research and Development Command, and the Hon Courtland Perkins, Assistant Secretary of the USAF (R & D), were given a full briefing on the state of the P 1127.

Leaving aside the supersonic distractions, associated with Hawker's design tenders to NBMR-3—which do not appear to have attracted 'domestic' American interest, apart from the funding of the advanced BS 100 engine with PCB—US Armed Forces interest gradually crystallised in a subsonic ground support aircraft; such a proposal was put forward by NASA to the Pentagon in mid-1961. It was with this possible application in mind that American participation in the Tripartite Evaluation programme came about in 1964-65. As already shown in Chapter 4 the Americans, however, came to regard the evaluation as little more than applied research rather than an operational exercise.

In the meantime a more radical approach had been pursued in America following a visit to Kingston by Dr Larsen, Assistant Secretary to the US Army, on May 8 1962, and a proposal was formulated during the following six months for an American aircraft manufacturer to enter negotiations with Hawker to develop the P 1127 for use by the US Army. In due course the Northrop Corporation of Beverley Hills, California, emerged as the interested party, and in January 1963 an instrument of collaboration was signed by Northrop and Hawker Siddeley by which Hawker would provide design information and research experience for the development of the P 1127 in the USA. During July that year a Northrop team, headed by Mr G.C. Grogan (the Director leading the project)*, worked at Kingston to learn of progress to date on the P 1127/Kestrel, and later carried out a survey of US Army support operations in Germany. Grogan was a convinced vectored-thrust disciple and went to great lengths to campaign for a P 1127-development to replace

* *And including S.L. Shaw (Director of Advanced Aircraft Systems), H. Asdurian (Propulsion Specialist), G.A. Schnug (Manufacturing and Materials), H.R. Pink (Chief of Flight Test Group) and J. Patierno (Technical Management).*

Line-up of XV-6A Kestrels on arrival at Patuxent River on May 5 1966 prior to the American Tri-Service trials (US Navy Department).

the Grumman OV-1 Mohawk reconnaissance aircraft with the US Army. There is no doubt that many influential US Army Generals were won over by his arguments, although no-one was confident that a foreign design using a radically new operating technique would be simple to 'sell' to the Armed Forces administrators in Washington.

In the end the 'US Army P 1127' fell victim of the American inter-Service 'Rôles and Missions' wrangling which eventually resolved the demarcation dispute by limiting the weight of fixed-wing aircraft to be flown by the US Army; this was substantially lighter than that of the P 1127 in operational guise. Notwithstanding the cancellation of the US Army-Northrop project, the collaboration was of some benefit to Hawker in providing experience which proved valuable in the company's approach to the Harrier during 1965-66.

★ ★ ★

With the benefit of hindsight it can be appreciated that the strictly limited approach by the Americans to the Operational Evaluation trials with the Kestrel in England probably set the United States behind several years in the operational use of a V/STOL combat aircraft.

As it was, six of the Kestrels were shipped to the United States for trials by the US Air Force, US Navy and US Marine Corps (the latter had not even participated in the West Raynham evaluation). From the moment of their arrival the six aircraft (designated XV-6As in America) embarked on a continuing series of evaluations, individual aircraft being assigned to Edwards Air Force Base, the US Navy and Marine Corps. A series of Tri-Service Trials, initiated at Patuxent River Naval Air Station, included deck operation from the large attack carrier USS *Independence* (CVA-62, 60,000 tons) and the assault ship USS *Raleigh* (LPD, 13,900 tons) during May 1966—some weeks ahead of the first British trials with a Kestrel aboard the Commando carrier HMS *Bulwark*.

The XV-6A trials in America continued for more than three years and while any conclusive opinions were avoided by the USAF and US Navy, enthusiasm was

Above *One of the XV-6A Kestrels aboard USS* Independence *(CVA-62), here flown by Commander J.J. Tyson, US Navy, previously one of the West Raynham evaluation pilots* (US Navy Department).

Below *Another XV-6A aboard USS* Independence *during the Tri-Service trials on May 15 1966. The pilot of this aircraft was Lieutenant-Colonel J.K. Campbell, USAF* (US Navy Department).

An early Harrier GR Mark 1, XV742 *(a TI aircraft retained by the manufacturers), temporarily repainted in US Marine Corps colours for demonstration purposes in 1969. The aircraft is seen here carrying five 1,000-lb bombs during a slow fly-by at Dunsfold* (Hawker Siddeley Aviation).

immediately apparent among the pilots of the Marine Corps. This elite and prestigious Service is charged by the President of the United States—as Commander-in-Chief of the Armed Services—with the amphibious delivery of attack forces to hostile territory and with air support of these forces until reinforced by the other Services. It is, however, a factor limiting these operations that the USMC depends entirely upon the US Navy for the sailing of the ships in which it is embarked. An aircraft possessed of conventional combat performance and weapon delivery, yet capable of helicopter-style launch and recovery, appeared to match the Marine Corps' task ideally.

Thus it was—with little prior notice—that two USMC pilots, Colonel Tom Miller (later General, Chief of Staff (Air), USMC) and Lieutenant-Colonel Bud Baker, USMC*, presented themselves at the Hawker chalet during the September 1968 SBAC Display at Farnborough, stating that they were in Britain to fly the Harrier and asking to be given copies of the Pilot's Notes. Within a fortnight they were flying Harriers at Dunsfold and at once confirmed that here indeed was the ideal USMC weapon. They returned to the USA with a glowing report of their experience for their Chief of Staff, General K. McCutcheon, USMC, in Washington.

By January 1969 a US Navy test pilot team was in Britain, carrying out a Navy Preliminary Evaluation of the Harrier, and their findings enabled the Marine Corps to obtain funding approval in June for 12 Harriers in the 1970 Fiscal Year appropriations—as part of a declared intent to purchase 114 Harriers† for Marine Air by the mid-1970s.

The following year, despite conservative misgivings by the US Navy, the USMC purchase plans were approved. USMC procurement limitations were, however, imposed by the US Government and Navy Department such that the Marine Corps Harrier was to

* *Colonel Bud Baker was to command the first Marine Corps Harrier squadron, VMA-513, at Beaufort MCAS, South Carolina, in April 1971 but, sadly, lost his life the following year.*
† *Reduced to 110 as related later.*

HAWKER SIDDELEY AV-8A (HARRIER MARK 50)
21,500-lb thrust Rolls-Royce (Bristol) Pegasus 103 turbofan
Aircraft 71-58390 of U.S. Marine Corps Attack Squadron VMA-231, U.S.S. Guam (LPH-9), 1973

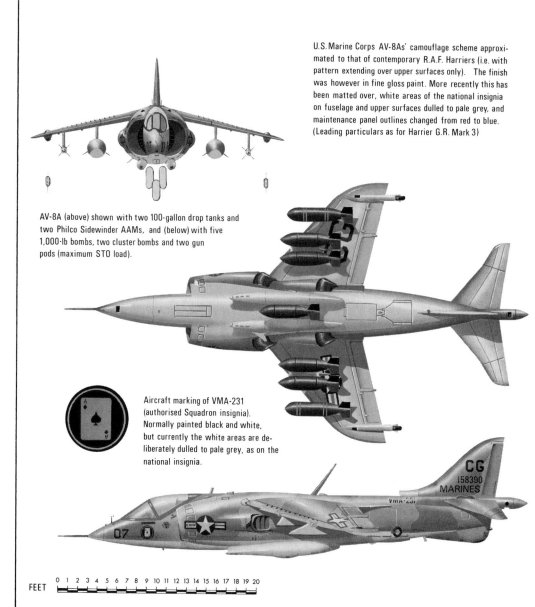

U.S. Marine Corps AV-8As' camouflage scheme approximated to that of contemporary R.A.F. Harriers (i.e. with pattern extending over upper surfaces only). The finish was however in fine gloss paint. More recently this has been matted over, white areas of the national insignia on fuselage and upper surfaces dulled to pale grey, and maintenance panel outlines changed from red to blue. (Leading particulars as for Harrier G.R. Mark 3)

AV-8A (above) shown with two 100-gallon drop tanks and two Philco Sidewinder AAMs, and (below) with five 1,000-lb bombs, two cluster bombs and two gun pods (maximum STO load).

Aircraft marking of VMA-231 (authorised Squadron insignia). Normally painted black and white, but currently the white areas are deliberately dulled to pale grey, as on the national insignia.

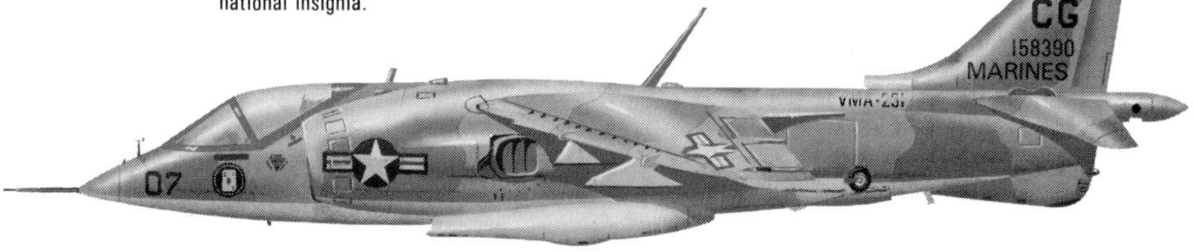

FEET 0 1 2 3 4 5 6 7 8 9 10 11 12 13 14 15 16 17 18 19 20

Hawker Siddeley AV-8S Matador (Harrier Mark 55)

No.008-10 (BuAer No.71-61175) of Escuadrilla 008, Spanish Naval Air Arm, SNS Dédalo, 1981. High-gloss pale grey and white finish.

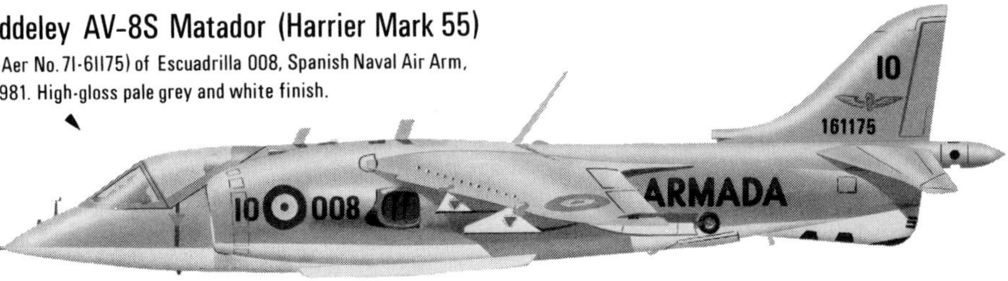

McDonnell Douglas YAV-8B (Second Aircraft, 71-58395)

Colour scheme. Aircraft glossy white with dark blue upper fuselage decking and tailcone; black anti-glare panel, edged blue. Red cheat line, propulsion nozzles, wing tips and bands on tail surfaces. American flag on fin bordered by two blue bars. Windscreen and canopy frames blue. Gun pods, LIDs and pylons white.

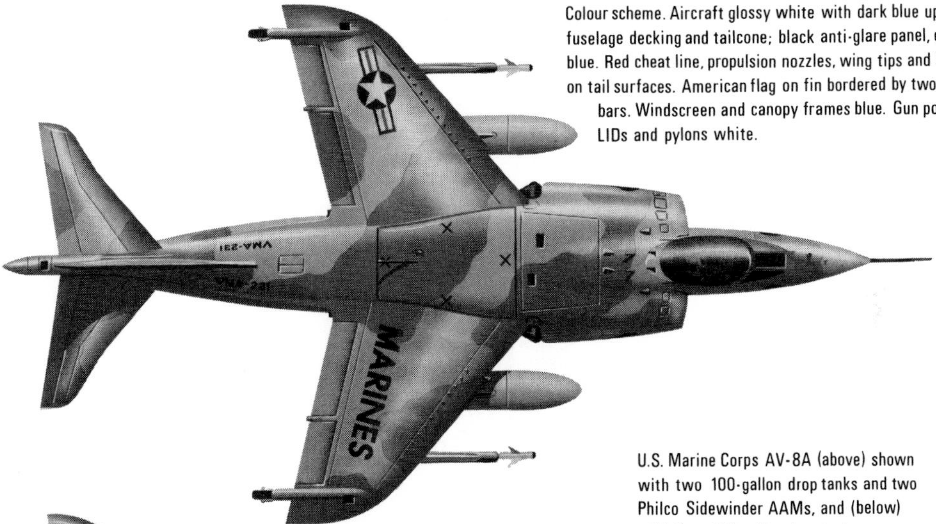

U.S. Marine Corps AV-8A (above) shown with two 100-gallon drop tanks and two Philco Sidewinder AAMs, and (below) with four 100-gallon drop tanks.

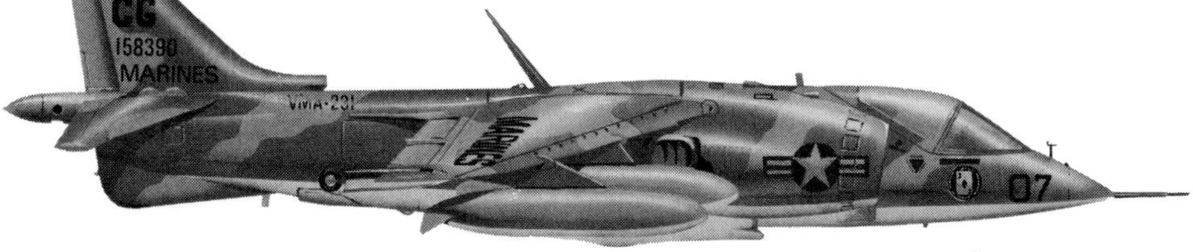

be an 'in-production, off-the-shelf' aircraft incorporating the smallest number of alterations needed to meet the USMC task, and was to be subject of US Navy Board of Inspection and Survey Trials (BIS) at Patuxent River.

Moreover, conditional on the purchase of further aircraft—beyond the initial dozen—was that a substantial production content would be undertaken in the USA. So it was that towards the end of 1969 Hawker Siddeley Aviation entered a 15 year licence agreement with McDonnell-Douglas, 'assigning to the American Company exclusive rights for the sale and manufacture of the Harrier and its derivatives in the USA, and agreeing to the mutual exchange of data and drawings on vectored-thrust V/STOL configurations stemming from the Harrier during the same period'.

However, during the FY 1971 budgetary debates, Congress decided against meeting the costs of transferring Harrier production to America; as progressively fewer Harriers remained to amortise these costs the penalty of transfer appeared less and less attractive and, to Hawker's astonishment, it transpired that the entire USMC fleet procurement of Harriers was manufactured in England.

Despite US Navy misgivings, their demands for alterations proved minimal: an in-service Navy radio in place of the RAF equipment, a weight-on-wheels switch to make-safe all weapon circuits, and checklist cockpit placards. Carriage of US Navy ordnance—including Philco Sidewinder air-to-air missiles on the outboard wing pylons—required contractor flight testing, firing and release clearance, and this was undertaken by Hawker under the UK authority of the A&AEE.

The Marine Corps required their aircraft to be powered by the Pegasus Mark 103, but delivery of this engine was inconsistent with airframe completion; the first ten aircraft,

An early AV-8A, 71-58384, *of Marine Attack Squadron 513, being refuelled in flight by a Marine Corps Douglas A-4M* (US Navy Department).

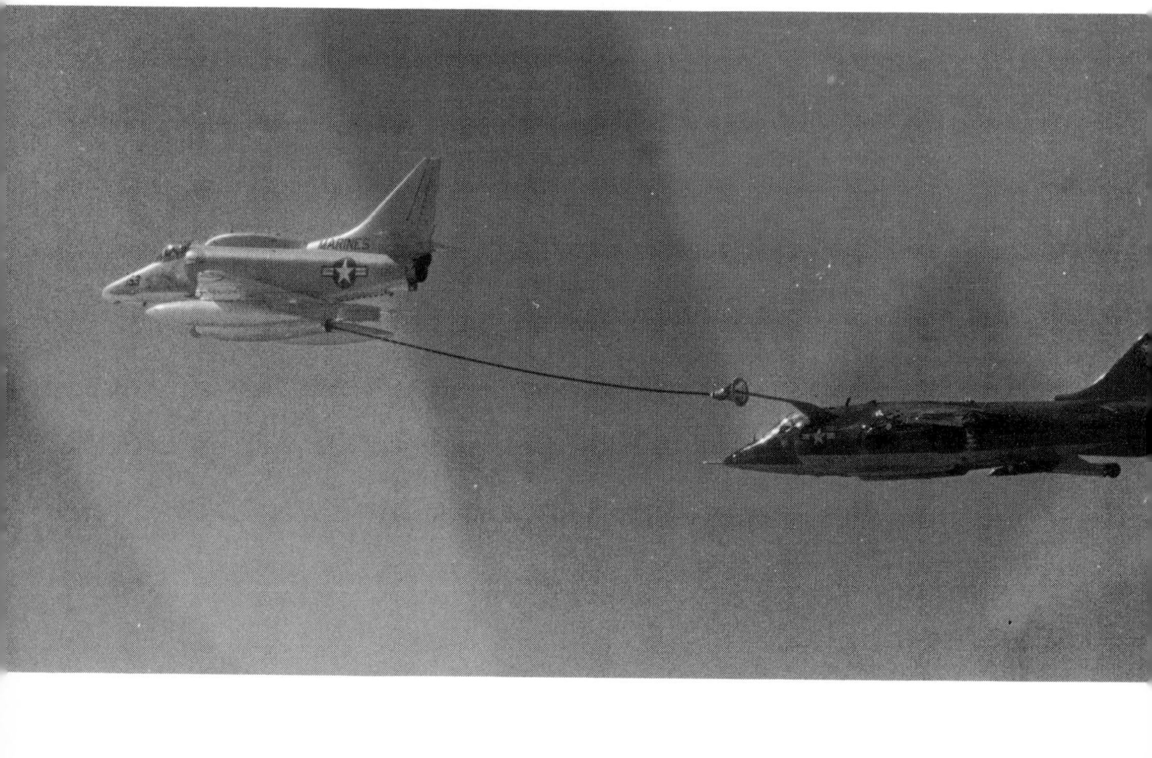

Removing the Pegasus turbofan from a US Marine Corps AV-8A at Cherry Point (Rolls-Royce Ltd (Bristol)).

delivered in January 1971, were therefore delivered with Mark 102 engines but were later retroactively fitted with Mk 103s.

The first AV-8As underwent BIS trials at Patuxent River in February 1971 and included ship compatibility flying aboard USS *Guadalcanal* (LPH) and USS *Coronado* (LPD), leading to US Navy approval to operate from these classes. The Harrier was the world's first jet fighter to be thus cleared.*

The following month Marine Attack Squadron 513 (VMA-513) was equipped with ten AV-8As at Beaufort MCAS under Colonel Bud Baker, the squadron's initial effort being given to land-based operation.

As deliveries continued in 1972 and operating experience was accumulated by VMA-513, two major alterations to the AV-8A were recommended by Navair on behalf of the Marine Corps. The first was to remove the Ferranti 541 inertial nav-attack system, equipment which had not proved popular with the Marines, being too complex and requiring lengthy pre-take-off alignment time, thereby compromising rapid operational reaction which was regarded as the AV-8A's prime asset in the Marine task. Thus, from the 60th aircraft, delivered in the FY 1973 batch, all FE 541 components were omitted;

* *The RAF Harrier ship release at this time was confined only to the Royal Navy's attack carriers (CVA), stemming from the trials aboard HMS* Eagle *in March 1970.*

the Smiths Head-up Display (HUD) was retained, and a new item of avionics—the Smiths Interface/Weapons Aiming Computer (I/WAC)—incorporated. Known as the Baseline System, this solved the ballistic equations and generated the necessary attack information in the HUD; possessing no navigation outputs and being strictly limited in the weapon aiming modes, it met the reduced mission requirements of the Marine Corps compared with those of the NATO Harriers. The cockpit alterations thus necessitated were also extended to include a fully aerobatic attitude reference system—this being retro-fitted to AV-8As delivered previously.

A second major alteration to the AV-8A was the replacement of the Martin Baker Type 9 Mark 1 ejection seat. Although the US Navy had used Martin Baker seats for 15 years without complaint, American policy was to develop an indigenous model and the Harrier was selected as the vehicle. The Stencel S IIIS-3 seat satisfied the Navair specification and, although qualification trials were not without their setbacks, this version was introduced in the 90th AV-8A.

The Stencel seat achieved faster parachute deployment after clearing the aircraft by incorporating both high- and low-speed operating modes, as well as a relative-wind-seeking extraction rocket for the parachute and a ballistic spreader. The American seat was lighter than the MBA Type 9, but the success rates on ejection by the two seats has proved to be roughly the same.*

Among other relatively minor changes that have been introduced in Marine Corps AV-8As (the engineering task being undertaken by McDonnell-Douglas) during the past seven years have included the removal of the ram-air turbine. Some problems were encountered with the aircraft's hydraulic system (particularly during shore-based operations from rough strips), and Hawker was asked to introduce additional filters in the system. The ram-air turbine was omitted from the final AV-8A before delivery and the modified system is being introduced retrospectively as aircraft are updated by McDonnell-Douglas.

The progressive development costs of the above alterations, together with clearance of additional weapon system demands and their associated attack modes, caused the original Marine requirement for 114 aircraft to be reduced to 110 in the FY 1974 appropriations, although the total purchase funding remained the same as originally contracted. Moreover, because of the possibility of the US Congress further cutting short the Contract funding before the 110 Harriers had been delivered, the US Marine Corps deliberately delayed ordering two-seat TAV-8A trainers until the FY 1975 appropriations were under consideration.

The TAV-8A is related to the AV-8A in exactly the same manner as the RAF's two-seater is to its single-seat counterpart. It was evolved from the standard two-seater to include the Baseline attack system and Stencel seats as well as all electrical, mechanical and weapon carriage modifications introduced in the AV-8A. In addition, on account of the USMC requiring the TAV-8A to be capable of performing the Tactical Air Commander (Airborne) combat rôle, a full range of TAC VHF to UHF (with front and rear cockpit operation) was included.

The first TAV-8As were delivered during the summer of 1976 and underwent an abbreviated BIS trial before entering service with Marine Attack Training Squadron 203 (VMA(T)-203) at Cherry Point in August that year. The aircraft underwent deck qualification aboard the attack carrier USS *Franklin D Roosevelt*.

* *It was intended to introduce the Stencel seat in the F-14 and F-18 naval fighters, but this plan has not yet materialised.*

Above *An AV-8A of VMA-513 in formation with an F-4 Phantom of VMFA-251 and an A-4M of the US Marine Corps* (McAir Neg No D4C-86045, dated September 1971).

Below *The first US Marine Corps TAV-8A (Harrier T Mark 54),* 71-59378, *at Dunsfold in 1975* (Hawker Siddeley Aviation, Neg No 751866).

GUAM

US Marine Corps experience

The United States Marine Corps can justifiably claim that its entire adventure with the Harrier has been an outstanding success, so much so that, having achieved—and in many areas surpassed—all its original objectives, it has publicly stated its aim of becoming an all-V/STOL attack force during the next two decades.

Following VMA-513 into service in 1971, the Marine Corps Attack Squadrons 231 and 542 (VMA-231 and VMA-542) were equipped with AV-8As. In January 1972 VMA-513 embarked in the helicopter assault ship USS *Guam* (18,300 tons) and commenced operations in the North Atlantic to investigate the feasibility of employing a mixed complement of helicopters and Harriers aboard a 'Sea Control Ship'.

The evolution of the Sea Control Ship had been advocated by Admiral Elmo R. Zumwalt, Chief of Naval Operations, US Navy, as an alternative to the leviathan CVA, of which the USA possessed 14 examples. He theorised that such carriers, each costing upwards of $1.5 billion to build and with a complement of about 5,000 men, constituted an impossible burden besides respresenting a relatively vulnerable and inflexible weapon. He suggested that, in performing the primary Navy tasks of applying military power overseas and keeping open the seas for international traffic, more numerous smaller carrier units represented greater flexibility at lower operating costs. It was pointed out that the future problem lay not so much in a deficiency in seaborne airpower capability but more in an insufficiency of units: the CVA would be available only in very small numbers and could therefore not maintain a presence—for sea control purposes—in all areas in a global conflict. Furthermore, in the relatively commonplace low-key hostile confrontations, the presence of a CVA could be considered over-provocative, besides offering an unnecessarily tempting target for suicidally-inclined extremist regimes.

Thus was the concept of the Sea Control Ship—of which perhaps seven or eight could be built for the cost of a single CVA—born, and the USS *Guam* was regarded as the 'feasibility vessel' during its commission with mixed Harrier/helicopter complement. VMA-513 went far to demonstrate the Harrier's ability to operate from the *Guam*'s restricted deck space, and in a period of ten days during 1972 three Harriers completed more than 170 sorties. The following year, in severe weather conditions which restricted operation of the helicopters, four Harriers performed over 130 sorties in 18 days.

While VMA-231 and -542 flew Harrier detachments at Iwakuni and Kadena, Okinawa, in the Far East during 1976 and 1977, 14 AV-8As of VMA-231 were deployed aboard USS *Franklin D. Roosevelt* with the American Sixth Fleet in the Mediterranean between September 1976 and April 1977, completing about 2,000 sorties, of which some 400 were carried out at night. Between 1971 and December 1978 the USMC AV-8A squadrons operated from 18 naval ships ranging from the 94,400-ton CVN USS *Eisenhower* down to the 16,800-ton LPD-class. During the course of 88,000 operational hours their best achievements included sustained sortie rates of over six missions per aircraft per day, STOL sorties with 8,000-lb payload over 225-nautical mile radius, average of 11.4 minutes from request to bombs-on-target and one and a half minutes for lift-off from alert.

No one could minimise the outstanding significance of the AV-8A/*Guam* demonstrations, yet on Admiral Zumwalt's retirement from the US Navy, the Sea Control Ship programme was shelved. It had represented the concept of the 'Harrier Carrier', which had come to be actively pursued outside America. Nevertheless, the US Navy has

Left *US Marine Corps AV-8As of VMA-513 aboard USS* Guam, *showing the very restricted deck space when ranging a full complement of helicopters* (British Aerospace, Neg No 743527).

AV-8As of VMA-342 (fitted with flight refuelling probes) aboard a US Navy carrier, identity unknown (British Aerospace, Neg No 741287).

renewed its interest in maritime V/STOL operation, and a new flat-deck ship for the Sea Control task, the Vertical Support Ship (VSS), is currently being proposed.

Not confined to the air-to-ground support rôle, USMC Harrier squadrons have also been responsible for air defence over surface forces—being equipped with such weapons as the Sidewinder AIM-9—yet it might be thought likely that in the presence of sophisticated hostile combat aircraft the strictly subsonic Harrier would be outclassed.

It was with this in mind that in 1971 NASA initiated a flight programme employing one of the surviving XV-6A Kestrels to explore the possibility of improving the manoeuvrability of an aircraft by vectoring thrust (VIFF, vectoring in forward flight). Despite the relatively low thrust rating of the Pegasus 5 and certain airframe limitations in the Kestrel, the initial investigations demonstrated that VIFF considerably enhanced the aircraft's potential in air combat. The test programme was then extended to involve joint studies with Britain's RAE using full-status Harriers.

To begin with, pilots were introduced to a large number of combat situations using the differential manoeuvring simulator at Langley, 'flying' a Harrier using VIFF against another with nozzles fixed aft. The former almost invariably 'won' the encounter, even when starting from an inferior situation. These demonstrations were confirmed in flight trials with Harrier versus Hunter and Phantom fighters, the Harrier kills being attributed to the additional lift, deceleration and nose-up pitch associated with VIFF.*

* *Hugh Merewether had performed some attempts at Viffing in the first DB Harrier* XV276 *before the US Marine Corps entered the arena.*

A further series of trials—pursued by the USMC AV-8A squadrons—involved extension of the VIFF flight envelope and carrying out survivability trials against a supersonic interceptor and a low wing-loading air defence fighter. In almost every instance the Harrier pilot was capable of holding his own and on numerous occasions 'victories' were demonstrated against F-14, F-15 and F-18 opponents.

★ ★ ★

By way of ending this brief summary of the AV-8A's service with the US Marine Corps, it is perhaps worth quoting the most extraordinary single statistic relating to the operation of Harriers from naval vessels—of which by far the greater proportion has to date been undertaken by the US Marine Corps. It is that in ten years of operational deck sorties, such missions have exceeded 10,000 without so much as a single deck accident, much less an aircraft loss. No other aircraft in the history of naval aviation has come near to approaching this astonishing record.

BRITISH AEROSPACE SEA HARRIER F.R.S. MARK 1
21,500-lb thrust Rolls-Royce (Bristol) Pegasus 104 turbofan
Aircraft XZ460 of No. 800 Squadron, Fleet Air Arm, 1980

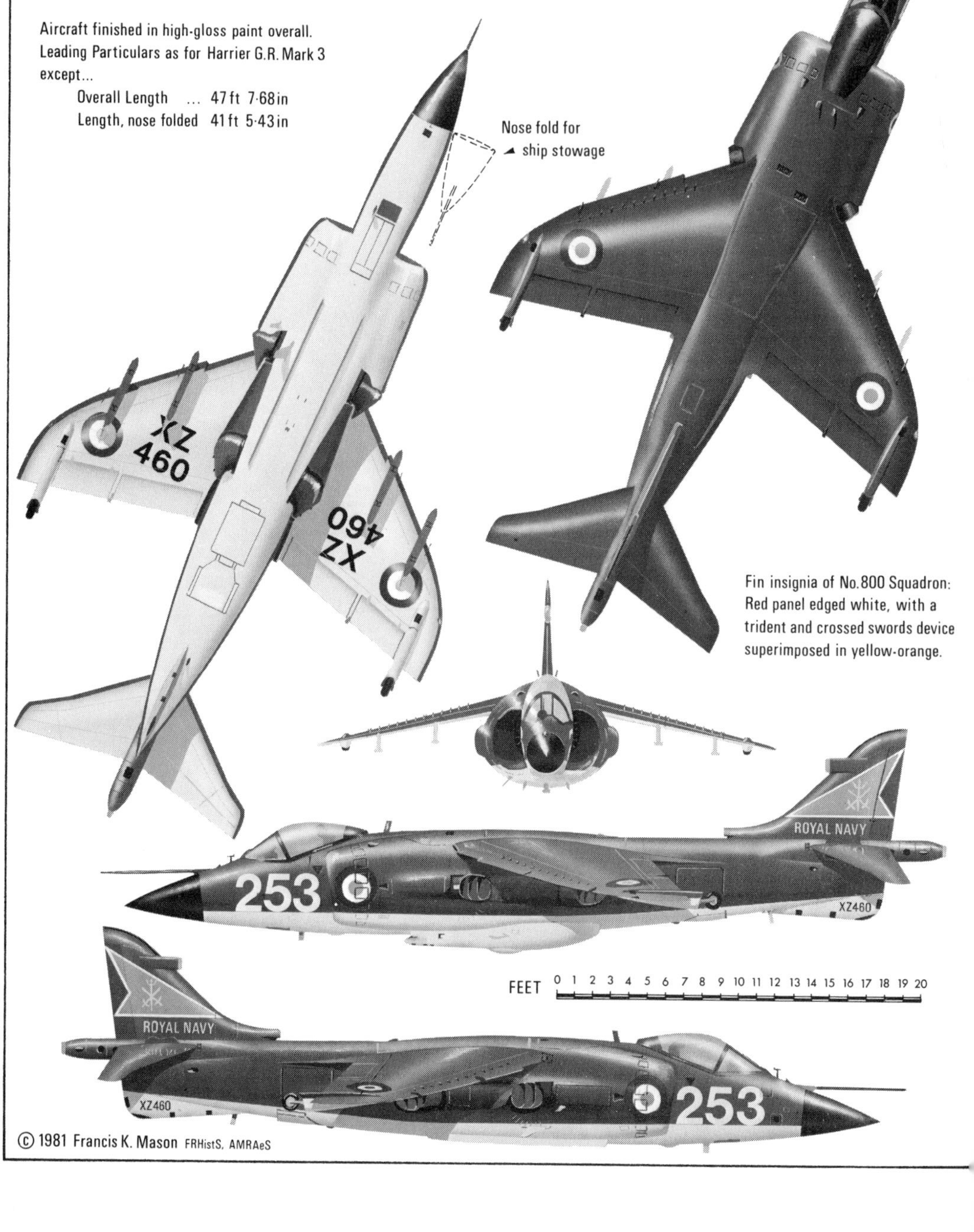

Chapter 9

Sea Control by the Royal Navy

Since the demise of the shipborne floatplane in the 1940s (apart from the sponson-equipped helicopter) all fleet defence aircraft at sea have depended solely upon operation from the aircraft carrier and from the 'helicopter platform'. The aircraft carrier assumed the rôle of capital ship after the Second World War, only the United States, Great Britain and France possessing the building facilities—and motivation—to produce these large and expensive vessels. During the past 20 years the Soviet Union has also emerged as a major maritime power and has introduced a new class of dual-purpose aircraft-carrying heavy cruiser.

As mentioned in Chapter 1, it was the US Navy Department that, shortly after the Second World War, started investigating means by which fleet air defence might be undertaken by vertical take-off interceptors, implicit in the tentative requirement being the ability of the aircraft to operate from small ship platforms or restricted deck areas. There is no evidence to suggest that at that time the United States Navy considered abandoning the aircraft carrier as such, but that VTOL fighters might *complement* the fleet's air defence arsenal.

Although the various VTOL aircraft designs produced during the 1950s proved workable in the very limited 'laboratory' conditions appropriate to the prototypes, they were soon seen to be unwieldy and tactically inflexible. Moreover, the emerging pattern of sea power after the Second World War confirmed the United States as the world's most powerful maritime power, centred as it was on its ability to perform its two major tasks, those of delivering worldwide military power and influence and of ensuring free passage of the world's shipping. As had been so convincingly demonstrated during the savage Pacific campaign in the war against Japan, America's primary maritime weapon had been the carrier task force; nothing occurred after the war to suggest that the pattern of operation by the aircraft carrier and its associated complement of specialist aircraft would be radically altered.

Elsewhere, however, the war's economic depredations focused attention upon the high cost, manpower demands and potential vulnerability of the aircraft carrier, and although Britain continued in its brave attempt to retain some semblance of maritime air power by means of a small seaborne air force, such a force—with its swiftly contracting Imperial defence responsibilities—must inevitably come to represent no more than a component part of the West's maritime strength.

From the earliest days of the Hawker P 1127 project it was clear to those at Kingston that in this aircraft lay one answer to the problem of providing air cover for amphibious operations without sole dependence upon helicopter services or the presence of an expensive and vulnerable aircraft carrier, of which Britain in the early 1960s possessed but three, plus a 'Commando carrier'. The Suez operation of late 1956 had demonstrated the extent of Britain's dependence upon land bases to launch a very modest amphibious operation, while its seaborne air power was shown to be of only limited value in the short term.

Not surprisingly, therefore, neither the US Navy Department nor the British Admiralty was receptive with any marked enthusiasm to radical proposals that might diminish the continuing dependence upon the aircraft carrier. Rather the opposite. Constant lobbying continued to secure appropriations to support further carrier construction.

In due course, however, the British Admiralty came to acknowledge—some two years after the first demonstration of successful vertical take-off by *XP831*—the possibility of maritime application of V/STOL. After pursuing a detached interest in the NBMR-3 fiasco during 1961, the Admiralty evolved a ship-borne two-seat interceptor fighter requirement in an attempt to benefit from cost-saving commonality with the RAF's P 1154 but, as already related in Chapter 5, the widely differing naval and RAF requirements effectively compromised the entire project and in 1964 the Admiralty pulled out of the enterprise altogether; instead preference was expressed for the perpetuation of conventional shipboard operation by aircraft such as the demonstrably-excellent McDonnell Douglas F-4 Phantom.

In truth it must be suggested that in all probability, at the time when the Admiralty planners were evolving the P 1154 Requirement, no one really possessed either the experience nor the real authority to express operating parameters for a first-generation naval V/STOL combat aircraft of such advanced concept as the Mach 2+ P 1154. In so saying it must also be recognised that had the naval P 1154 gone ahead in 1964 without serious development problems, the entire concept of naval V/STOL operations must have become stultified by continued operation of the aircraft carrier as being expressed in the mid-1960s. The inevitable demise of the British aircraft carrier would have resulted in the P 1154 being transferred to the RAF (as were the Fleet Air Arm's Phantoms and Buccaneers in any case). It is most unlikely that the naval P 1154 would have been capable of following a subsequent development course that would have permitted the flexibility of operation about to be demonstrated by the Sea Harrier. Indeed, it has been the nature of the less sophisticated Sea Harrier—and its greater operational flexibility—that has broken the entrenched philosophy of 'ship dictating aircraft design'. The Sea Harrier has indeed brought about the evolution of an entirely new naval ship design philosophy and engendered the survival of ship-borne high performance combat aircraft, especially in the world's smaller maritime forces.

* * *

The first significant event in the development of ideas for maritime operation of the P 1127 was the demonstration by *XP831* aboard HMS *Ark Royal* in February 1963—after the Admiralty had committed itself to paper with the naval P 1154 Requirement! Between the 8th and 13th of that month Bill Bedford and Hugh Merewether—neither of whom possessed any previous carrier-flying experience whatsoever—flew *XP831* through a full range of vertical and short take-offs and vertical landings without the slightest difficulty, even expressing their opinion that carrier operation was simpler than airfield operation.

Such a convincing demonstration clearly encouraged both Hawker and the Admiralty, and further deck trials would certainly have followed during 1964-65 had not the naval P 1154 programme been abandoned. As it was, the preponderance of deck operation experience was gained by the US Navy and Marine Corps with the evaluation Kestrels (XV-6As) aboard USS *Independence* and *Raleigh* in 1966 (as related in Chapter 8), while

Above XV758, *an early Harrier GR Mark 1, undergoing trials aboard the Commando carrier, HMS* Bulwark *(27,300 tons)* (Hawker Siddeley Aviation, Neg No 417199).
Below XV758 *in hover over HMS* Bulwark*'s flight deck* (Hawker Siddeley Aviation, Neg No 418499).

Harrier GR 1s of No 1 (F) Squadron, RAF, undergoing type shipboard clearance trials aboard HMS Ark Royal *in March 1970* (Hawker Siddeley Aviation, Neg No 711923).

British experience in June that year was limited to trials with a Kestrel aboard the Commando carrier, HMS *Bulwark* (27,300 tons); the latter were conducted in pursuance of a plan to employ future RAF Harriers in the rôle of amphibious assault support alongside the vessel's helicopter complement. The trial was later repeated by a production Harrier GR Mark 1, *XV758,* (fully equipped with wing drop tanks and rocket pods) aboard HMS *Bulwark.*

In August 1969 a Harrier was operated from the aft-situated helicopter platform aboard the cruiser HMS *Blake* (12,100 tons), thereby demonstrating the small landing space requirements of the aircraft and its lack of dependence upon specific wind-over-deck (WOD) requirements. The flying trials on HMS *Blake* were performed while the ship was rolling up to ±6 degrees with WOD up to 35 knots. (There was, incidentally, no other operational motive for this demonstration; it was not, for instance, at any time suggested that the Harrier would assume the operational rôles of the cruiser's anti-submarine helicopter.)

Pursuing the operational plan to deploy RAF Harriers aboard the two remaining British fleet carriers, two Harriers were flown aboard HMS *Eagle* (50,000 tons) in March 1970, the outcome of which was the issue of a Service Release for deck operations by RAF squadron pilots, the first such unqualified clearance ever formally issued in any world air force. The following year No 1 (Fighter) Squadron took its Harriers to sea for the first time in HMS *Ark Royal* off the Scottish coast. None of the RAF pilots had ever flown from a ship before.

Against the continuing successful operation of Harriers (both of the RAF and the US Marine Corps) from ships—they have performed more than 10,000 ship sorties from 39 ships of nine navies without so much as a single deck accident, much less an aircraft loss—the Royal Navy in the late 1960s embarked on a re-appraisal of its maritime air tasks, a re-appraisal rendered all the more vital by the cancellation in 1966 of its large

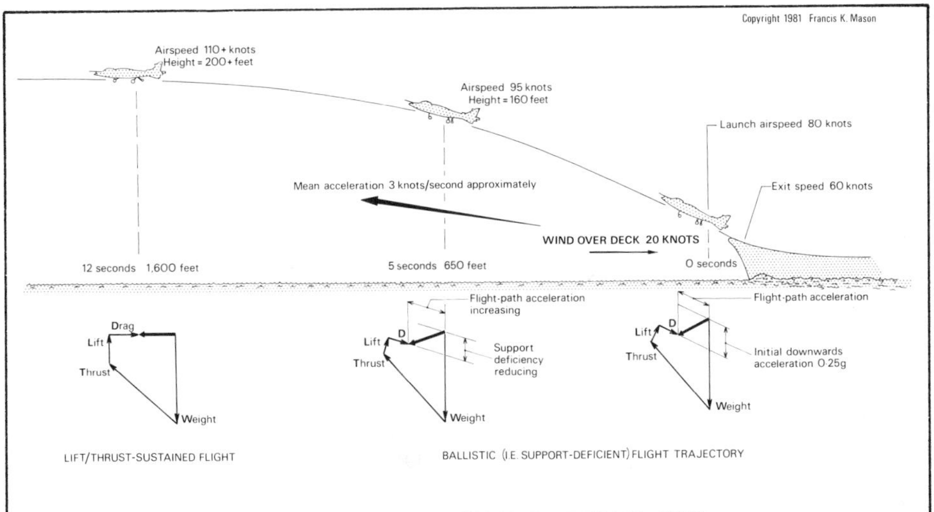

THE PRINCIPLES OF SKI-LAUNCH SHORT TAKE-OFF
TYPICAL RAMP ANGLE, LAUNCH WEIGHT, EXIT SPEED AND WIND CONDITIONS

conventional carrier project, the CVA-01. At this time the Royal Navy possessed two fleet carriers, HMS *Ark Royal* and HMS *Eagle,* both of which would end their useful sea life during the 1970s without an extensive and costly re-fit; HMS *Bulwark* and *Albion,* the two Commando carriers, would be joined by a third, HMS *Hermes,* in 1973. The transfer of a large proportion of the Phantoms and Buccaneers to the RAF would, moreover, render the large fleet carriers superfluous, and without a seaborne air combat aircraft element the Royal Navy would be capable of maritime operation only under air protection provided by land-based aircraft or aircraft of the US Navy.

In the late 1960s the Admiralty started planning a new class of ship, then termed the Through-deck or Anti-submarine Cruiser, intended solely for helicopter operation. Construction of the first vessel in this class, HMS *Invincible* (19,810 tons)* started in 1972 and the ship was launched at Barrow-in-Furness in May 1977. In the meantime, however, the Admiralty had gained Treasury sanction for the development of a naval version of the RAF's Harrier, it being intended to embark an Air Group of five or six Sea Harriers and up to ten Sea King helicopters in each of the three *Invincible*-class ships. The Through-deck Cruiser was, therefore, in its originally conceived form, not entirely tailored to the Harrier and, despite its relatively extensive deck space, was incapable of exploiting the aircraft's best short take-off load-carrying capabilities, particularly with large helicopters ranged on deck.

The ski-ramp

It was in 1972 that a Royal Navy engineering officer, Lieutenant-Commander D.R. Taylor, writing a thesis at Southampton University, first showed that by curving up the front end of a ship's flight deck so that a V/STOL aircraft, such as the Harrier with thrust vectoring, may be launched on an upward trajectory, very substantial performance gains become available compared with the conventional flat-deck launch.†

* *The other ships in the class being HMS* Illustrious *and* Ark Royal.

† The Operation of Fixed-Wing V/STOL Aircraft from Confined Spaces, *D.R. Taylor, Lieutenant-Commander, RN, MBE, MRAeS, MIMechE, University of Southampton, 1973. Thesis leading to award of MPhil, 1974.*

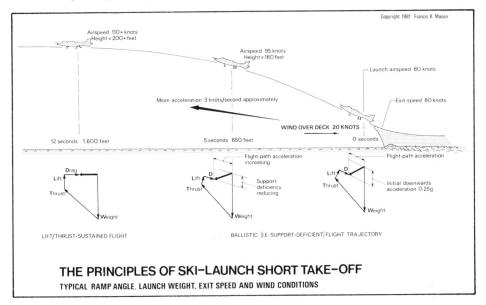

Right *DB Harrier* XV281 *ski-launching from the Bedford ramp, set at six degrees, on August 23 1977, carrying two 100-gallon drop tanks and two BL755 cluster bombs* (Hawker Siddeley Aviation, Neg No 771818).

Centre right *The first ramp launch by a Harrier two-seater.* XW175, *then a Mark 2A, being flown from six-degree ramp setting by an RAF pilot on August 23 1977* (Hawker Siddeley Aviation, Neg No 771823).

Below right *Two-seat Harrier demonstrator* G-VTOL *flying from the RAE ski ramp set at 15 degrees in May 1978* (British Aerospace Corporation).

Because of the upward momentum imparted by the ramp, it was shown that the Harrier could be launched with less speed than from a flat deck. Immediately after leaving the ramp the Harrier would not, in fact, be truly flying; there would be a deficiency in vertical support, and this would curve the flight path towards the horizontal. However, due to the high thrust/weight ratio of the Harrier, there would still be a thrust component sufficient to accelerate the aircraft along the upward inclined velocity vector. After a part-ballistic trajectory occupying some ten seconds, therefore, the Harrier would have acquired about 30 knots additional airspeed and would then be fully sustained in 1 g flight, still accelerating longitudinally; transition to wingborne flight with jets aft could commence at the top of the trajectory so that transition would be complete some 15 seconds later—exactly as in a flat-deck short take-off.

The Hawker Siddeley engineers at Kingston, who had been involved with Doug Taylor's original thesis studies in 1972, continued their ski-ramp studies using knowledge and computer aids outside the scope of the thesis work. Considerable company funding was invested in these studies which, during 1974 and 1975, confirmed that the 'ski-jump' launch bestowed very important performance gains.

Until mid-1975 official support had been difficult to enlist. At that point the go-ahead with Sea Harrier production plans was obtained, and what had previously been regarded as superfluous 'boat rocking' was now cautiously encouraged. 'Nevertheless the Flat Deck Preservation Society still appeared to view with alarm and suspicion the prospect of steel hills on flight decks.'*

Notwithstanding these reservations, the Ministry of Defence late in 1976 secured for Hawker Siddeley a Contract to design and build a ski-ramp for practical flight testing, and this ramp was designed to incorporate variable launch angles from six to 20 degrees.† It comprised 40 steel channels each 30 in wide and 40 ft long carried on an adjustable support structure such that a range of circular arc ramps could be set, each tangential to the ground at ramp entry.

The first Harrier ski-launch test was carried out on August 5 1977 with the ramp set at six degrees, and further launches continued until September 7; 73 launches were performed using the DB Harrier *XV281* single-seater, and 43 launches with a Harrier two-seater, the launch speeds varying between 53 and 113 knots. This series was followed by tests at nine, 12, 15 and 20 degree ramp angles between October 1977 and June 1979, during which 251 launches were performed at exit speeds ranging from 42 to 90 knots.

In September 1977, as a result of the six-degree ramp testing, the Admiralty decided that HMS *Invincible* (now re-classified as a Command Cruiser, probably to avoid any politically offensive connotation with 'aircraft carriers' or flat decks) should feature a ski ramp, and by mid-1978 the ship had been retrofitted with a seven-degree ramp at the forward end of her Harrier runway. To avoid interference with the firing arc of her Sea

* *Cf* Ski-Jump: A Great Leap for Tactical Air Power, *John W. Fozard, British Aerospace, 1979.*

† *The ramp was fabricated and erected by British Steel (Redpath Dorman Long, Scunthorpe) at the RAE, Bedford, in only five months, and was ready for use in July 1977.*

A Sea Harrier launching from the Farnborough 15-degree ramp at the time of the 1978 International Air Show (British Aerospace Corporation, Neg No 792427).

Dart missile launcher the ship's ramp height was limited, and this factor restricted the ramp angle.

In the second quarter of 1978 British Aerospace (the State-owned conglomerate which now embraced the Hawker Siddeley facility at Kingston and Dunsfold) started work on plans to exhibit a ski-jump at the Farnborough International Air Show in September that year. The 15-degree ramp was constructed from British Army Medium Girder Bridge (MGB) components and every day during the show Harriers gave public demonstrations of this unique operating technique. During September 1978 a total of 71 ramp launches was performed at Farnborough.

Such were the proven benefits of the ski-launch techniques seen to be in 1978 that it was decided to equip HMS *Hermes* (the Royal Navy's ASW helicopter-only carrier) with a 12-degree ramp during her 1979 dockyard refit prior to embarking the first Sea Harrier squadron in 1980.

HMS *Illustrious,* the second Command Cruiser, was launched by HRH Princess Margaret into the River Tyne on November 30 1978 equipped with a seven-degree ramp; it is likely, however, that when the third ship, HMS *Ark Royal,* is completed, relocation of the Sea Dart launcher may permit a ramp with significantly greater ramp exit angle.

Before going on to describe the Sea Harrier and its entry into service, it is worthwhile mentioning here another class of naval vessel which was conceived at the time that ski-ramp calculations confirmed the outstanding benefits bestowed. This was the Vosper Thornycroft 'Harrier Carrier', specifically designed as the result of discussions between Hawker Siddeley and VT. Capable of embarking up to 12 Sea Harriers and about six helicopters, the design of this class of vessel was dictated throughout by the maximum-load six-degree ramp-launch performance of the Sea Harrier, possessing a 420-ft deck length, a rear-located turntable and a maximum design speed of 25 knots. Propulsion was to be provided by eight 5,000-hp gas turbine-driven generators. Although the numerous benefits (not least of which are the vessel's low costs of construction and manning) have been canvassed during the past five years, the future of the project continues in doubt.

The 500th ski-launch, performed by a full-standard Harrier GR Mark 3, XZ136, *carrying two 100-gallon drop tanks and two cluster bombs; ramp angle, 20 degrees* (British Aerospace Corporation, Neg No 792163).

The Sea Harrier

In 1971 the Royal Navy obtained sanction to pursue a Naval Staff target for a version of the Harrier to operate at sea from the *Invincible*-class Command Cruisers alongside their helicopter Air Group. The aircraft was to be developed—as usual—on the basis of minimum cost, time and efficiency risk, with only essential and cost-effective changes from the Pegasus 103-powered Harrier GR Mark 3 (at that time yet to enter service with the RAF). The naval Harrier's rôles were to be threefold:

a) Air interception and fighter rôle against long-range maritime patrol and ship-based fighter-attack aircraft. Radius of action, 400 nautical miles at altitude.

b) Reconnaissance rôle with sea-search capability over 20,000 square miles in one hour at low altitude.

c) Strike and ground attack rôle against ships, fast patrol boats and shore targets. Radius of action, at least 250 nautical miles depending on sortie profile.

The essential changes from the RAF's Harrier were divided between those required to meet the combat mission demands and those needed to suit 'ship-at-sea' compatibility. The former was limited to the following: revision of the weapons system which now included a larger Smiths Industries Head-Up Display driven by a 20,000-word digital computer, not only generating display symbology but also functioning as a very flexible air-to-air and air-to-surface weapon-aiming computer; inclusion of a Ferranti self-aligning attitude-reference platform; and Ferranti Blue Fox radar.

The Ferranti attitude-reference platform is not truly inertial (so as to avoid alignment problems at sea) but still achieves previous-generation inertial navigation accuracy; it is controlled by an 8,000-word digital computer which also performs all the navigation and endurance functions, and is cross-referenced to a Doppler radar from Decca.

The Blue Fox radar is the primary external sensor and is derived from the Seaspray radar used in the naval Lynx helicopter, but much modified for the air-to-air and air-to-surface modes required for the naval Harrier's operational tasks; the radar display is a TV-

The Royal Navy's new Command Cruiser, HMS Invincible (Ministry of Defence).

raster daylight-viewing tube which presents flight information, together with radar data, to the pilot.

All the new equipment was designed with sea deployment in mind, the electronic units being self-checking and monitoring; fault diagnosis is possible in most cases without external test gear, with rectification achieved by module replacement.

Radio navigation aids—in addition to the digital nav-attack system—include UHF Homing, TACAN with offset facility and an I-Band radar transponder to assist ground control guidance. Passive electronic surveillance and warning of external radar illumination is provided by a radar warning receiver (RWR) with forward and rear hemisphere antennae in the fin and tailcone.

The five weapon pylons have been redesigned from those on the RAF's Harrier, now including stronger ejector release units. The entire range of RAF and US Marine Corps stores can be carried, but a new missile control panel in the cockpit allows for carriage and firing of the Philco Sidewinder missile from the outboard pylons, and Martel and Harpoon air-to-surface missiles from the inboard pylons.

To achieve maximum ship-at-sea compatibility, as many magnesium components as possible have been eliminated from the airframe and engine to avoid sea-air corrosion. Only four such components remain: the engine gearbox (oil washed inside and non-air-scrubbed outside), the nosewheel and outrigger wheels.

Cost-effective alterations in the naval Harrier are mainly confined to the cockpit which has been entirely revised to provide the pilot with the best operating efficiency from his multi-mode weapons system. During the course of the naval design definition studies it was realised that the RAF Harrier's cockpit space was ergonomically limiting, having remained essentially unchanged since the original design of the P 1127 in 1959. The RAF's equipment fit severely taxes the available space, and the additional multi-mode naval equipment could only be accommodated—without costly miniaturisation—in an enlarged cockpit. By raising the pilot by some 11 in, the new cockpit provides more panel space and console width, although the overall cabin width remains unchanged (to avoid the risk of engine intake complications). Much greater volume is now available beneath

Sea Harrier XZ457 *at Yeovilton in 1980* (British Aerospace, Kingston, Neg No 801758).

the cockpit floor and a larger nose cone becomes available to accommodate the Blue Fox radar.

The cockpit layout has been entirely revised with new instruments arranged to minimise pilot workload, including miniaturised warning caption modules and so on. Pilot view is improved by the raised cockpit, not only rearwards but also forwards and downwards.

The latest Martin Baker Type 10 zero-zero rocket ejector seat is employed; this version includes a 1.5-second sequence from initiation to parachute deployment, compared with 2.25 seconds in the RAF's Type 9 seat. The RAF Harrier's canopy-fragmenting system, using explosive cord, is retained.

Minimum cost, minimum change philosophy extends to the naval Harrier's powerplant which remains the 21,500-lb thrust Pegasus 11, although the in-service designation has been altered to the Mark 104 to differentiate the naval version; in this the major casings have been changed from magnesium-zirconium to aluminium, while all ferrous components have been coated with a sacrificial aluminium paint. In order to accommodate the higher electrical generating load the HP drive shaft has been strengthened.

It is important to emphasise here that the total weight penalty for 'navalisation' of the Harrier is less than 100 lb—an extraordinary achievement unequalled by any other modern aeroplane transposed from land to maritime operation.

* * *

Initial project design studies for the naval Harrier were completed early in 1972—including the scheming of the raised cockpit—and preparations were undertaken for detail design to commence the following year. However, it was not until May 1975 that Government sanction was obtained by the Ministry of Defence to go ahead with production plans, on the basis of 34 production aircraft, designated the Sea Harrier FRS Mark 1.*

* *FRS = Fighter/Reconnaissance/Strike.*

Above *The first Sea Harrier during manufacture at Kingston in 1977, identifiable by the larger nose cross-section and radome hinge recess* (Hawker Siddeley Aviation, Neg No 770103).

Above right *Sea Harrier FRS Mark 1,* XZ451, *in flight over the Surrey countryside* (British Aerospace Corporation).

Below XZ450, *the first Sea Harrier FRS Mark 1, during early test flying at Dunsfold, prior to application of Service paint finish* (British Aerospace Corporation, Neg No 782970).

Meanwhile, two Hawker Hunter two-seaters* were ordered to be converted to accommodate the entire Sea Harrier's operational equipment, including the Blue Fox radar. Used for nav-attack system development trials these aircraft—one based at British Aerospace's Dunsfold facility and the other at the Royal Signals and Radar Establishment (RSRE) at Bedford—would later be handed over to the Fleet Air Arm as airborne weapons system trainers. The first aircraft flew on January 9 1978.

The first of four Sea Harrier development aircraft, *XZ439,* was flown to Dunsfold on August 20 1978, this aircraft being employed on performance and handling programmes, followed later by store clearance trials. *XZ440* was delivered to the A&AEE at Boscombe Down for systems trials, followed by 1979 by *XZ450.*

On March 26 1979 HMS *Invincible,* complete with seven-degree ski ramp, commenced her sea trials, and on September 19 that year the first Sea Harrier squadron, No 700A Squadron of the Fleet Air Arm, was commissioned at RNAS Yeovilton, taking delivery of the Royal Navy's first aircraft, *XZ451.* Between October 24 and November 8 *XZ439, '40, '50, '51* and *'52* completed type operational trials aboard HMS *Hermes* in the Irish Sea (being joined by the Harrier Mark 52 two-seater, temporarily registered *ZA250*).

No 700A Squadron, otherwise termed the Sea Harrier Intensive Flying Trials Unit, took delivery of the first five production Sea Harriers before being disbanded and effectively re-formed as No 899 Headquarters Squadron of the Fleet Air Arm. No 800 Squadron, formed at Yeovilton in 1980, was destined to become the first carrier-deployed Sea Harrier squadron, followed by Nos 801 and 802 Squadrons.

The Royal Navy did not order any two-seat Harriers (perhaps surprisingly), it being considered from experience that specialist deck landing training in V/STOL techniques was superfluous. Moreover the existence of the two Hunter two-seater systems trainers sufficed for operational training purposes. A single Harrier T Mark 4, *XW927,* was, however, based at Yeovilton from late 1979 for use by No 899 Squadron, although it was on charge to the Fleet Requirements Air Development Unit (FRADU).

* *Designated the Hunter T Mark 8M; the two trials aircraft were* XL580 *and* XL602; *later a reserve aircraft, XL603, was added to the Contract.*

Above *Early production Sea Harriers undergoing type operational trials aboard HMS* Hermes *in October 1979* (British Aerospace Corporation, Neg No 79539A).
Below *Sea Harrier XZ451 aboard HMS* Hermes (British Aerospace Corporation, Neg No 795657).
Bottom *Sea Harrier FRS 1,* XZ453, *flies slowly past HMS* Invincible (Ministry of Defence).
Above right *Air-to-air view of Sea Harrier FRS Mark 1,* XZ451 (British Aerospace Corporation, Neg No 792830).

The Sea Harrier represents a remarkable achievement in wholly updating a land-based counterpart at low cost, high cost-effectiveness. The operating technique and dimensions of the Harrier are such that traditional deck paraphernalia—such as fuselage stressing for catapulting, arrester hook and wing folding—have been rendered superfluous, enabling the ship-borne variation to retain all the performance attributes of the land-based version, yet still considerably extend its operational task capabilities.

Harrier and Sea Harrier operations in the South Atlantic, 1982

By January 1982, 29* Sea Harrier FRS Mark 1s had been delivered to the Royal Navy, although one of these, *XZ454*, had been lost at sea in an accident on December 1 1980, the pilot being saved after ejection. The majority of these aircraft constituted the equipment of Nos 800, 801 and 899 Squadrons (commanded by Lieutenant Commander A.D. Auld RN,† Commander N.D. Ward AFC, RN,‡ and Lieutenant Commander N.W. Thomas RN** respectively), at that time shore-based at RNAS Yeovilton. The balance of aircraft was being used either for trials at various UK establishments or for training at Yeovilton.

The situation regarding aircraft carriers in the Royal Navy at the time was something of a transient matter. The last of the old fleet carriers, HMS *Hermes* (after having been converted from an ASW helicopter-only carrier to operate a single squadron of Sea Harriers from the 12-degree ramp on her deck) was already scheduled for scrapping under a Government Defence Review published in 1981, it being decided to replace her by HMS *Illustrious* late in 1982. HMS *Invincible*, now re-styled an Anti-Submarine Command Carrier, was herself already due to be sold to Australia in 1983, her place being taken by HMS *Ark Royal* on completion in 1984. Thus had the Royal Navy—by now

**It was generally stated at the beginning of the Falkland Islands operations that all 34 Sea Harriers had been delivered to the Royal Navy; reference to Appendix 5 shows that this was not so. Indeed, at the time of writing one such aircraft still remains to fly, having been delayed by the need for additional instrumentation required for a trials programme.*

† *Lieutenant Commander Andrew Donaldson Auld, RN, was awarded the Distinguished Service Cross,* vide *Supplement to* The London Gazette, *No 49134, October 8 1982, p 12836.*

‡ *Commander Nigel David Ward, AFC, RN, was awarded the Distinguished Service Cross,* op cit, *p 12835.*

** *Lieutenant Commander Neil Wynell Thomas, RN, was awarded the Distinguished Service Cross,* op cit, *p 12836.*

almost wholly equipped and orientated for North Atlantic (ie, NATO) responsibilities—dropped its sights from four carriers to just two.

When, on April 2 1982, the Argentine forces carried out a full-scale military invasion of the Falkland Islands the Royal Navy was thus scarcely equipped to mount a powerful, well-balanced and air defended fleet with which to sail to a war zone 8,000 miles distant, especially when opposed by an enemy land-based air force comprising more than 200 aircraft of fairly modern vintage. The risks attendant upon such an adventure must have concentrated naval minds wonderfully.

Yet, between April 3, when Prime Minister Margaret Thatcher announced the assembly of a British naval task force, and April 5—when it sailed from Portsmouth—HMS *Hermes* (equipped and staffed as flagship) and HMS *Invincible* had assembled their ships' companies, a force of Royal Marine Commandos, 20 Sea King helicopters (of Nos 820 and 826 Squadrons), 20 Sea Harriers of Nos 800, 801 and 899 Squadrons, together with all their crews, weapons and stores. In addition to the naval Sea Harrier pilots a small number of RAF Harrier pilots also took passage in the carriers.

Shortly afterwards four further Sea Harriers and six Harrier GR 3s of No 1 (Fighter) Squadron, RAF, together with spare Pegasus engines (as well as 11 Wessex, Chinook and Lynx helicopters), were taken aboard the requisitioned merchant container ship, MV *Atlantic Conveyor*, for subsequent passage to the South Atlantic. The Harriers and Sea Harriers were thus the only British fixed-wing aircraft to be employed by the Task Force during the Falklands operation (codenamed 'Operation Corporate').

While the Task Force and its following stream of troop transports, supply vessels, assault craft and auxiliaries made their way south—pausing at Ascension Island to take on further weapons and supplies—diplomatic efforts to resolve the crisis broke down and it quickly became clear that full-scale military operations were inevitable. During much of the voyage southwards the Sea Harrier pilots carried out frequent training exercises both in the air defence rôle and against surface practice targets in the ground attack rôle, for it should be remembered that although the Sea Harrier was perfectly capable of delivering bombs and rockets in the latter rôle it had been as an interceptor for which the majority of naval flying training had been carried out. Moreover, several of the naval pilots were

Above left *Drop tank-equipped Sea Harrier over RNAS Yeovilton in 1982* (Ministry of Defence).

Above *Sea Harrier* ZA176 *at Dunsfold shortly before embarking for the South Atlantic, showing the newly-adopted all-over grey scheme and subdued markings* (British Aerospace Corporation, Neg No 821377).

Below ZA176 *in company with the first development Sea Harrier* XZ438, *showing the contrasting colour schemes* (British Aerospace Corporation, Neg No 821318).

Sea Harriers of one of the Royal Navy squadrons just prior to the Falkland Islands operations. The nearest aircraft is XZ491 (Ministry of Defence).

newly arrived on the squadrons and had done little or no deck flying. Among the weapons embarked in the carriers were Aden gun pods, AIM-9L Sidewinder air-to-air missiles, BL 755 cluster bombs, SNEB rocket packs and 1,000-lb iron bombs.

From the earliest hurried planning stages of the likely operation to recover the Falkland Islands it had been recognised that the Sea Harriers' primary task would be to defend the Task Force from enemy air attack, and secondarily to provide such ground support as was allowed by the availability of aircraft. Once these duties were defined, No 1 (Fighter) Squadron, based at Wittering in the United Kingdom (and with a detachment at Belize), was ordered to readiness for deployment in the South Atlantic. Modifications were put in hand forthwith to allow Sidewinder missiles to be fired from the outboard wing pylons, and pilots immediately undertook a concentrated course in ramp launching at RNAS Yeovilton in their Harrier GR 3s.

The recapture of South Georgia ('Operation Paraquet') did not involve carrier operations or the use of Sea Harriers, and so it was during the first dawn low-level air attack on the Falkland Islands of May 1 that the Sea Harrier gained its baptism of fire. Immediately following the withdrawal of the RAF Vulcan bomber (which had just performed an astonishing night attack on the airport at Port Stanley after an air-refuelled flight of 3,500 miles from Ascension Island), nine Sea Harriers, led by Lieutenant Commander Auld, carried out a gun and bomb attack against the same target in the face of fairly heavy ground fire—which included a number of Short Tigercat SAMs. One aircraft of No 800 Squadron was hit in the tail by a single small-arms bullet, but all returned safely to HMS *Hermes*. Other Sea Harriers carried out an attack on the small airstrip at Goose Green 50 miles to the west.

Meanwhile, warned by a radar post set up by the Argentine forces on East Falkland, enemy fighters were approaching from the mainland and some of these were intercepted by covering Sea Harriers armed with Sidewinders. During the day a Mirage, a Skyhawk and a Canberra were destroyed by the naval fighters without loss; a second Mirage was also shot down—it was thought by Argentine ground fire.*

Although to some extent hampered by deteriorating weather—as winter approached in the South Atlantic—and handicapped by the need for the carriers to remain well to the east of the Islands at the limit of or beyond the range of mainland-based Argentine aircraft, air attacks by the Sea Harriers continued day and night against land targets during the first week in May, most of the pilots being called upon to fly as many as four operational sorties daily. On May 4 the Sea Harrier *XZ450* (the very first Sea Harrier to fly, back in 1978) was shot down by ground fire during a low level attack on Goose Green, the pilot being killed. Two days later two further Sea Harriers (*XZ452* and *XZ453*) were reported missing from patrol while flying from the Task Force, and it must be assumed that they collided in bad weather or cloud.

In the matter of the loss of the Type 42 destroyer, HMS *Sheffield*, sunk by an AS.39 Exocet ASM air-launched by an Argentine Super Etendard IV in daylight on May 4, it was felt in some quarters that the Sea Harriers' air defence screen had been penetrated. It should, however, be emphasised that HMS *Sheffield* was performing radar picket duties beyond the Task Force perimeter and was therefore beyond the immediate patrol area of the Sea Harriers. The incident did lend considerable emphasis to the Royal Navy's total lack of airborne early warning facilities, though, the Gannet aircraft—which had performed this task in former years—having been removed from service with the progressive run-down of British carrier forces ever since the 1960s.

After considerable losses had been inflicted on the Argentine Air Force (principally among Pucará ground support aircraft and helicopters on the ground in the Falklands), the Task Force had now lost 15 per cent of its defending fighter force, and the main assault had yet to be launched. Replacements and reinforcements were, however, on their way. While the *Atlantic Conveyor* had already sailed from England, it would be several days before she reached the South Atlantic and it fell to No 1 (Fighter) Squadron, RAF, commanded by Wing Commander P.T. Squire, AFC†, to provide the reinforcing muscle. Four Harrier GR 3s were flown from Britain to Ascension Island where their pilots spent a short period resting before flying on to join the carriers in the South Atlantic on May 8-9. The first of these legs—on which the aircraft were refuelled in flight several times by Victor K2 tankers of Nos 55 and 57 Squadrons—constituted a nine-hour flight, the longest hitherto accomplished by RAF single-engine fighters, and the flight as a whole, involving pinpoint use of navigation aids for refuelling rendezvous and culminating in deck landings on carriers in the middle of the South Atlantic, represented a masterpiece of planning, skill and endurance by all concerned in the operation. On May 18 six further Harriers of No 1 Squadron joined HMS *Hermes*, having flown off the *Atlantic Conveyor*. (Nine days later this large merchantman was hit and sunk by an air-launched Exocet missile with the loss of all spare Pegasus engines, as well as the 11 helicopters.) Yet at a stroke the striking power of the Task Force had been immeasurably strengthened.

There followed a brief period in mid-May of relatively little activity by the Task Force while the ships carrying the ground forces (notably the SS *Canberra*) assembled, a period

* *After this day it proved impossible to give exact daily losses in aircraft suffered by the Argentine air forces, although independent sources in Argentina consistently (and subsequently) reported higher losses than those claimed by the British Task Force. This tended to be confirmed by the reports of captured Argentine airmen when interrogated.*

† *Wing Commander Peter Ted Squire, AFC, RAF, was awarded the Distinguished Flying Cross,* op cit, *p 12854.*

Amidst a clutter of Sea King helicopters, cluster bombs and Sidewinders, a missile-armed Sea Harrier launches from HMS Hermes *on her way south to the Falkland Islands in April 1982* (Ministry of Defence).

in which the Argentine air forces made a number of attempts to attack the fleet, losing several aircraft to the Sea Harriers in the process, as the RAF Harriers joined in the attacks on the Islands using laser-guided and cluster bombs against dispersed targets around Port Stanley and Darwin, as well as carrying out essential photo reconnaissance sorties over the Islands' defences.

D-day for the main assault landing in San Carlos Bay was May 21. The task allotted to the Sea Harriers was to provide an air defence screen both against fighter-bombers—the Argentine Mirage IIIEAs and A-4P/Q Skyhawks—flying from the mainland, and against Island-based IA-58 Pucará and Aermacchi MB.339 ground support aircraft. The screen was necessarily flown well clear of the assault beaches themselves so as to allow free rein to the ground and ship gun and missile defences. As the assault forces went ashore during May 21 the RAF Harriers were tasked with ground attack missions against neighbouring enemy concentrations, including those at Darwin and Goose Green, to prevent interference by enemy aircraft and the mounting of a significant counter-attack against the beachhead.

This was the most hazardous moment of the entire operation, with a major part of the Task Force concentrated in confined waters, the carriers necessarily some distance away, and with assault forces vulnerable to air attack until covered by deployed SAMs ashore. During the initial landing phase the expected air attacks developed as successive waves of Mirages and Skyhawks made for the beachhead; despite all the Sea Harrier pilots could do (and despite being able to fly only about eight aircraft simultaneously they are reckoned to have destroyed at least seven of the attackers, of which two were shot down by Lieutenant Commander Auld), a number of raiders got through and attacked the ships at anchor. The frigates HMS *Ardent* and *Antrim* were both struck by 1,000-pound bombs and the former, hit by no fewer than nine bombs and several rockets, was lost.

Elsewhere RAF Harriers were attacking the airstrip at Goose Green, and in the course of these attacks *XZ963* was hit by a SAM and shot down, the pilot being wounded and taken prisoner (and later evacuated to the mainland by the Argentine forces). On this day British forces claimed the destruction of a total of 17 Argentine aircraft, while Argentine sources reported the loss of 23 (the balance presumably failing to regain the mainland

Sidewinder-equipped Sea Harrier in the South Atlantic (Ministry of Defence).

The first RAF Harrier of No 1 (Fighter) Squadron arrives on board HMS Hermes *after its marathon flight from Ascension Island early in May 1982* (Ministry of Defence).

either due to battle damage or lack of fuel); British losses amounted to the one Harrier GR 3 and five helicopters (one of these in an accident involving a bird-strike).

On the crucial day following the initial landings in San Carlos Bay, the Argentine air force failed to follow up its initial attacks, and it is generally considered that this failure was a decisive feature of the entire operation; for the assault forces were able to consolidate their positions ashore without interference, having suffered not a single casualty among Army personnel during the initial landing phase. It was during this lull in air activity that armoured vehicles and artillery were brought ashore, and that SS *Canberra* sailed into San Carlos Bay with 3,500 men of the Parachute Regiment and Royal Marines.

It is not intended here to describe the progress of the land operations during the brilliant action to recover the Falkland Islands, but to confine this narrative to those operations by the Harriers and Sea Harriers in their support.

While the RAF Harriers continued to provide support for the ground forces ashore, the Sea Harriers kept up their cover over the carriers as well as making frequent attacks in the Port Stanley area. Squadron Leader J.J. Pook* of No 1 Squadron was nominated mission leader of the Harriers during the invasion phase, leading particularly successful raids on the Goose Green area on May 21 and 27 in which he personally destroyed two Puma helicopters. On May 30, while attacking a gun position on Mount Harriet, his Harrier *XZ972* was hit and he was forced to eject over the sea when still 30 miles from HMS *Hermes*, but was rescued. Another RAF pilot, Flight Lieutenant David Morgan†, had been seconded to fly Sea Harriers with No 899 Squadron from HMS *Hermes* and flew more than 50 sorties; among his air victories was a Puma helicopter shot down with guns,

* *Squadron Leader Jeremy John Pook, RAF, was awarded the Distinguished Flying Cross,* op cit, *p 12854.*

† *Flight Lieutenant David Henry Spencer Morgan, RAF, was awarded the Distinguished Service Cross,* op cit, *p12853 (Air Force Department).*

Operating side-by-side, bomb-, gun- and missile-equipped Harriers and Sea Harriers aboard HMS Hermes *during the latter stages of the Falklands campaign* (Ministry of Defence).

and two Mirages from a formation of four (the other two being destroyed by his wingman). The senior Sea Harrier pilot, Commander Ward, shot down three aircraft—a Mirage, a Pucará and a Hercules (the latter being used as a bomber by the Argentine air force). It was while taking off from HMS *Hermes* for a night low-level strike against Port Stanley airport on May 24 that Lieutenant Commander G.W.J. Batt* crashed in Sea Harrier *ZA192* and was killed; he had already flown 29 combat missions, including five against heavily defended targets, one of them on May 4 when his wingman had been shot down and killed.

On May 27, the eve of the capture of Darwin and Goose Green by the Parachute Regiment, the Harrier *(XZ998)* flown by Squadron Leader R.D. Iveson† was hit by ground fire and the pilot was obliged to bale out behind enemy lines; for 48 hours Iveson evaded capture and was eventually recovered unhurt by a British helicopter. The following day, during an attack in the Port Stanley area, two Sea Harriers (*XZ456* and *ZA174*) were hit by ground fire and once more, rather than risk fouling the aircraft carriers' decks with damaged aircraft, the pilots ejected close to the Task Force and were picked up from the sea.

As the land battle moved away eastwards towards Port Stanley, a temporary forward operating base for the Harriers and Sea Harriers was established at Goose Green for emergency use. On June 9 Wing Commander Squire was leading a strike by Harriers on

* *Lieutenant Commander Gordon Walter James Batt, RN, was posthumously awarded the Distinguished Service Cross,* op cit, *p 12834.*

† *Squadron Leader Robert Douglas Iveson, RAF, was Mentioned in Despatches,* op cit, *p 12856.*

an Argentine field HQ when a bullet from the ground defences passed through his cockpit; temporarily distracted, he turned away and was attacking a secondary target when his engine started losing power. Pulling up, he decided to make for the forward base at Goose Green where he crash landed, without injury to himself; his Harrier, *XZ989* was badly damaged but was later recovered by helicopter. Wing Commander Squire resumed flying from HMS *Hermes* within a couple of days.

Final victory in the Falkland Islands was gained by the British forces when the Argentine commander surrendered in Port Stanley on June 14. The relatively brief, bloody but superbly executed operation had been undertaken to uphold the principle of security of sovereign territory in the face of unprovoked totalitarian aggression. Human and material losses were inflicted upon the invaders far in excess of those suffered by the Task Force, although those among the Royal Navy ships were grievous enough. British losses of aircraft totalled 36, of which six were Sea Harriers and four were Harriers, and five of their pilots were killed.

In practical terms the British fighters had lived up to the highest expectations in every allotted task, in all weathers, day and night, in air combat and ground support, and in conditions of extreme logistic strain. Their pilots had fought a well-trained and determined enemy and succeeded in destroying a significant number of high performance aircraft in air combat. As if to underline the high opinion universally expressed of the Sea Harrier the British Defence Minister, John Nott, immediately announced that HM Government was ordering 14 additional Sea Harriers to replace those lost (including one lost at Yeovilton during training) as well as to increase the strength of the established squadrons.

Figures announced at the end of the campaign showed that 28 Sea Harriers and ten Harriers flew more than 2,000 combat sorties, destroyed at least 28 enemy aircraft in air combat, and achieved an overall serviceability rate of more than 90 per cent. Perhaps most outstanding was the fact that not one Harrier or Sea Harrier was lost in air combat. It can be said without question that had the Royal Navy and the Royal Air Force not possessed these remarkable aircraft the Falkland Islands operation could not have been mounted.

Harriers for export

At the time of writing—apart from the United States—two nations overseas have confirmed their interest in maritime operations by V/STOL aircraft with orders for Harriers: Spain and India. By implication of her intention to purchase the carrier HMS *Invincible*, complete with deck ramp, Australia has presumably considered operating Sea Harriers, although the situation still remains to be made clear.

Following demonstration trials by John Farley in a Harrier aboard the Spanish carrier *Dédalo** in October 1972, the Spanish Government ordered six single-seat Harriers and two two-seaters. Because of political sensitivity (the Franco Government was then still holding office), the Contract was channelled through the United States and the aircraft—built at Kingston—were shipped to America (carrying American BuAer numbers and designated AV-8As and TAV-8As) where the pilots of *Escuadrilla 008* underwent training before embarking in *Dédalo* and sailing for Spain. The aircraft (less one which crashed in America) were delivered in 1976 and were followed by an order for five further aircraft, this time delivered direct to Spain under the designations Harrier Mark 55 (AV-8S) and Mark 58 (TAV-8S). In the Spanish Navy the aircraft are named Matadors, and when based ashore are stationed at Rota.

* *SNS* Dédalo, *previously an American World War 2 carrier, possessed a wooden flight deck but, contrary to some misgivings (not held by the manufacturer) it did not burst into flames under the Pegasus' exhaust blast.*

MARINA
008
5

159563

008
8
6

Top left *Spanish Harrier: an AV-8A Matador,* 008-5, *flying in the United States; this aircraft was lost in an accident before it could be embarked for Spain* (via British Aerospace Corporation).

Centre left *First of two TAV-8A Matador two-seaters, carrying American BuAer No 159563* (British Aerospace Corporation, Neg No 760253).

Bottom left *Second of the Spanish TAV-8A Matadors,* 008-8, *pictured in Spain during 1980. Note* Escuadrilla 008*'s squadron insignia on the nose* (British Aerospace Corporation, Neg No 802915).

Above *Spanish AV-8A Matador,* 008-4, *in hovering flight over the* Dédalo (Courtesy of Rolls-Royce Ltd).

Below *First of the second batch of Spanish AV-8S Matadors (Harrier Mark 55s),* 008-9, *during transition from short take-off in 1980. Changes introduced since the first batch include an additional aerial amidships and the inscription ARMADA in place of MARINA on the fuselage* (British Aerospace Corporation, Neg No 802910).

Left *The first Indian Sea Harrier FRS Mark 51,* IN601, *which was first flown by Heinz Frick at Dunsfold on August 6 1982. Bearing the temporary registration* G-9-478, *the aircraft was shown at the 1982 SBAC Display at Farnborough* (British Aerospace Corporation (Dunsfold), Exp Neg No 8086/6).

It was announced in 1982 that Spain proposes to purchase 12 McDonnell Douglas AV-8B Harrier IIs (see the following Chapter) for her Navy at a cost of $379m. This third-party sale will be completed in the mid-1980s from the American production line with 25 per cent of the airframe being manufactured in Britain. It is expected that the aircraft will be embarked in Spain's new aircraft carrier, SNS *Principe de Asturias* (15,000 tons), which was launched at Bazan on May 22 1982, and is equipped with an integral deck ramp for Harrier operation.

The other nation, India, also opted to purchase Harriers as a result of a company-sponsored demonstration—this time John Farley's trip out to INS *Vikrant* at Bombay in July 1972 with the two-seater *G-VTOL*: as told in Chapter 7, the Indian Government has ordered six Sea Harrier FRS Mark 51s and two Harrier T Mark 60s for delivery in 1983. Despite some speculation that losses incurred during the Falkland Islands operation might be made good by usurping Indian Sea Harriers already on the Kingston production line, the Indian order has gone ahead without interruption, and at the time of writing the first aircraft has flown.

Chapter 10

The American partnership and the future

Due to its very high thrust/weight ratio, the Harrier enjoys many of the characteristics of a supersonic fighter such as rapid climb and high acceleration and, as already stated, by using VIFF the US Marine Corps AV-8As have outfought modern supersonic fighters in close combat. This agility is achieved for a very modest fuel usage, the Pegasus turbofan requiring a full-throttle fuel-flow of about 250 lb/min, compared with at least three times this figure (per engine) for a re-heated conventional fighter.

Notwithstanding these proven attributes, in spite of the past abortive supersonic adventures in the early 1960s, both the British and American Service authorities returned to the supersonic theme in the early 1970s.

Following the partnership negotiations, successfully completed between Hawker Siddeley Aviation and McDonnell Douglas Corporation, joint studies were started in 1973 to exploit the thrust of a new version of the Pegasus turbofan which, with a 2¾-in larger fan diameter, returned a thrust of 24,500 lb during bench running. However, owing to its increased diameter, retrospective application to existing aircraft was economically unattractive, with the result that an entirely new joint British/American project, the AV-16, was initiated on an 'Advanced Harrier' for the US Marine Corps (and possibly eventually for the RAF). The basic AV-16 design was intended to remain subsonic, the excess thrust being employed to enhance take-off performance with increased war-loads; when employing PCB the AV-16-S6 version would be supersonic at altitude, both versions featuring provision to mount a total of seven store pylons.

The project was, however, unfortunately being undertaken against a background of massive worldwide inflation increase—and forecasts of unparalleled economic gloom. The cost tag of $1,000m, being quoted for development (and 'Americanising') of aircraft and engine in 1974, was expected to double by the time in-service status was reached. The AV-16 project was therefore cancelled. Henceforth Hawker Siddeley embarked on investigations to evolve a new wing design which, by retrofitting to existing Service Harriers (and Sea Harriers), might claw back some of the load and performance benefits of the subsonic AV-16 while still exploiting the Pegasus 11 (Mark 103 and 104).

McDonnell Douglas, licensee for the Harrier in the United States, was determined that development should also proceed in the USA and sought means of providing the increased payload-radius demanded in an 'Advanced Harrier' for the US Marine Corps without the need for relatively costly engine performance increases. (It is perhaps worth remarking here that already the first calculations being undertaken in Britain at this time on the ski-ramp launch suggested that, by use of a 12-degree ramp angle, more than 80 per

Left *The Rolls-Royce (Bristol) Pegasus 15 with enlarged fan, intended for the McDonnell Douglas AV-16 supersonic aircraft which was discontinued in the mid-1970s* (Rolls-Royce Ltd (Bristol), Neg No E178767).

The first YAV-8B, 158394, *launching from the ski-ramp at Patuxent River. It was lost in an accident following engine failure during a flight to St Louis to undergo engine change on time expiry. The pilot ejected safely* (McDonnell Douglas Corporation, Neg No C12-8071-9, dated July 1979).

cent of the USMC's increased performance demands could be met by the standard AV-8A!).

By means of a number of airframe changes, McDonnell Aircraft (McAir) was able to demonstrate to the US Navy and US Marine Corps that the payload-radius of the AV-8A could be increased by a factor of at least two (depending on the particular mission) without need to change the Pegasus from its current 21,500-lb V/STOL thrust rating. These changes included the use of a new wing, improved engine intake features and increased lift improvement devices (LIDs).

By use of a supercritical wing aerofoil, with greater area and span, containing 2,000 lb more internal fuel and incorporating six weapon pylon stations, making use of large slotted flaps linked with nozzle deflection at STO unstick, and manufactured largely in carbon fibre composite, it would be possible to limit the weight to that of the AV-8A.

Use of a larger-area engine air intake with a double row of blow-in doors to provide a bigger throat with higher pressure-recovery in V/STOL would provide 600 lb greater VTO weight from the existing Pegasus 103 engine; a new elliptic cowl lip profile would compensate for spillage drag in cruising flight.

Enhanced LIDs would consist of longitudinal fences attached to the underfuselage gun pods together with a retractable cross-dam at the forward end of the pods to capture the ground-reflected jets in V/STOL to provide greater ground cushion and reduce hot gas recirculation; these simple features alone would provide some 1,200 lb greater VTO payload.

The supercritical, composite wing

In 1974 a McAir design team, led by the Harrier Aerodynamics Engineer, Mr T.R. Lacey, working with Mr K. Miller at NAVAIR's Aero-Hydro facility, started work on the development of a mission-tailored wing to meet the US Marine Corps demand to *double* the payload-radius of the AV-8A Harrier.

To begin with, to achieve better cruise performance, the aspect ratio was increased, and to improve longitudinal stability at high angles of attack (always a critical characteristic of the P1127/Kestrel/Harrier) particularly when carrying stores, wing sweepback was

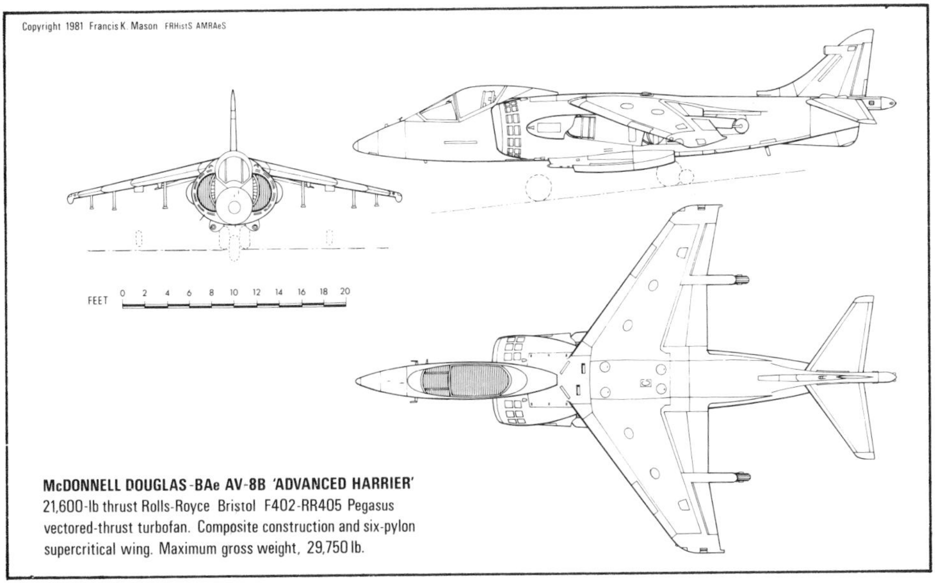
Copyright 1981 Francis K. Mason FRHistS AMRAeS
FEET 0 2 4 6 8 10 12 14 16 18 20
McDONNELL DOUGLAS-BAe AV-8B 'ADVANCED HARRIER'
21,600-lb thrust Rolls-Royce Bristol F402-RR405 Pegasus vectored-thrust turbofan. Composite construction and six-pylon supercritical wing. Maximum gross weight, 29,750 lb.

reduced; to allow increased fuel capacity and permit lighter structure, the wing thickness/chord was increased, as was wing area (the latter improving manoeuvrability at the increased aircraft-loaded weights).

The increased span and aspect ratio permitted the addition of a pair of wing store pylons, and because of the increased internal fuel capacity the inboard pylons—previously used mainly for drop tanks—could be more often made available for weapons.

To permit full turnaround on narrower flight decks the outriggers were moved inboard, while the increased span allowed the roll-control RCVs to be located further outboard, thereby increasing lateral control moment without increasing engine bleed.

Perhaps the most significant alteration to the wing was the extension of the trailing edge inboard of the outriggers to permit a larger trailing edge single-slotted flap with positive airflow circulation to increase wing lift during take-off. The flap, linked to nozzle deflection in the STO mode, induced airflow over the wing, while the rear nozzle efflux

Demonstration mock-up of the McDonnell Douglas AV-8B produced to display the supercritical wing, revised engine intakes, the six pylon configuration, the gun-pod strakes and cross-dam LIDs (McDonnell Douglas, Neg No D4C-116688-11, dated August 7 1975).

would entrain air over the deflected flap, increasing the velocity differential between upper and lower surfaces; such supercirculation would generate more than 6,700 lb extra STO lift.

The deeper flap section allowed improved structure to withstand higher flap airloads, while the reduced flap hingeline sweep provided more forward space for wing fuel.

Multiple sine-wave wing spars provided reserve strength through redundant load paths, and the entire structure was designed to withstand severe battle damage. Carbon fibre composite was widely employed in the wing, only the leading edge, tips, outrigger and pylon attachments, and centreline rib remaining in traditional materials. One-piece upper and lower wing skins were mechanically attached, the upper being detachable for inspection, the lower permanently fixed. The total wing structure weight saving was about 330 lb.

The following summarises the wing specification differences between that of the Harrier (AV-8A) and of the AV-8B*:

	Harrier (AV-8A)	**McAir AV-8B**
Wing area	201 sq ft	230 sq ft
Wing span	25.3 ft	30.3 ft
Leading-edge sweep	40 degrees	36 degrees
Average thickness/chord	8.5 per cent	10.5 per cent
Fuel capacity	2,834 lb	4,950 lb
Trailing-edge flap	Small, 50 degrees, plain	Large, 60 degrees, positive circulation
Outrigger track	22 ft	17 ft
Store stations	Four	Six
Aerofoil section	Peaky	Supercritical

Other changes

The front fuselage has been altered to accommodate a cockpit raised 10½ in to improve pilot visibility and increase avionics capacity. Structure is of composite material, reducing weight in this area by almost 25 per cent. Left and right half shells are composed of 0.149-in moulded sandwich skins with a low-density, epoxy-based core between carbon-fibre sheets with integrally-moulded stiffeners.

To balance the additional weight of the nose-mounted avionics, the rear fuselage (designed at Kingston by Hawker Siddeley) has been extended 18 in and the structure restressed to withstand greater in-flight loads imposed within the enhanced VIFF envelope, the extension providing greater volume for the rear equipment bay; to provide increased fin area to compensate for the larger nose, the taller Sea Harrier fin is incorporated.

The tailplane, like the wing, has been redesigned to make use of carbon-fibre construction. Often subjected to critical harmonic resonance—to which composite material is considered to possess better resistance—the tailplane comprises metal leading edge, carbon-fibre lower skin with bonded-on spars and upper skin, and detachable honeycomb trailing edge.

The engine incorporates all the corrosion-resistant components included in the Sea Harrier's Pegasus 104, but the sub-variant proposed for the McAir AV-8B is matched to the improved intake characteristics and, in line with recent Rolls-Royce (Bristol) efforts, will enjoy a 1,000-hour engine operating limit with hot-end inspection periods of 500 hours. Production engines are designated F402-RR405, and will provide an installed thrust of about 22,100 lb.

* *Cf* The AV-8B Wing: Aerodynamic Concept and Design, *T.R. Lacey and K. Miller.*

Preparing a Pegasus 11 with zero-scarf nozzles for flight in a McAir YAV-8B (Rolls-Royce Ltd (Bristol), Neg No E219949).

Also included in the AV-8B are redesigned exhaust nozzles. The new rectangular titanium, zero-scarf front nozzles constrict the engine's 'cold' efflux better than the original Harrier's shorter nozzles and now exhaust into a space more efficiently bounded by deeper strakes, inboard pylons and the new retractable cross-dam. These improvements generate an estimated additional 200 lb of VTO thrust, and the lighter titanium component weight saves a further 50 lb.

Updated avionics include the Hughes angle-rate bombing system (ARBS) which comprises a laser/TV tracker in the nose to provide all-weather launch capability with iron bombs, laser-guided weapons and Maverick TV-guided air-to-surface missiles; an AYK-14 mission computer (as used in the F-18 Hornet) is also included.

The navigation system comprises an ASN-130 inertial navigator (also from the F-18), TACAN, radar beacon and radar altimeter, and an all-weather approach/landing system is fitted. Radio equipment includes secure voice and electronic warfare (EW) equipment with radar warning receiver (ALR-67), flare/chaff dispenser (ALE-39) and the advanced, self-protection jamming system (ASPJ), the latter carried in a centreline pod. Much of this off-the-shelf equipment was previously developed for the F-18.

The AV-8B cockpit design technology also reflects the substantial advances made in the F-18. The primary instrument is the Smiths dual-combiner HUD, below which is the up-front communication, navigation and ident control panel. All other controls are grouped in accordance with the 'hands-on-throttle-and-stick' (HOTAS) concept; these comprise all engine and flight controls (excluding rudder), radar warning control, ARBS/TV slew control, armament selector, gun trigger and bomb release, Sidewinder target designator and lock-on, SAAHS disengage and manoeuvring flap switch.

Apart from the 50 per cent increase in internal fuel capacity, the new aircraft has a 15 per cent increase in weapon load capability. Both the inboard pairs of wing pylons (2,000 and 1,000 lb load-stressed) are plumbed for fuel tanks and may carry a wide range of weapons, and the two new intermediate pylons (630 lb stressed) are wired for AIM-9H or -9L Sidewinders. Defensive ECM (ASPJ) will normally be carried on the fuselage (1,000-lb) pylon.

With full internal fuel the AV-8B can carry 9,200 lb of external stores, and when equipped with four 300-gallon drop tanks the aircraft possesses a maximum ferry range of 2,500 nautical miles (dropping the tanks when empty).

AV-8B hardware experience

Confidence in the performance of the new supercritical wing prompted McAir to prepare a full-size wind tunnel aircraft employing a crashed AV-8A, repaired and re-engineered to feature an instrumented Pegasus 3 engine, improved LIDs and a wood-and-metal AV-8B mission-tailored wing. Design forecasts were confirmed during the course of 300 tunnel-test hours on this model—as well as more than 4,000 hours on smaller transonic and low-speed models.

In March 1976 the US Defense Systems Acquisition Review Council (DSARC) recommended embarkation on the AV-8B programme and McDonnell Douglas was contracted to prepare two YAV-8B flight prototypes and a structural-test wing. The last two AV-8As from the initial production batch *(158394* and *158395)* were accordingly

Below left *The first YAV-8B ramp-launching at Patuxent River with four underwing bombs; note the open blow-in doors, cross-dam extended and the engine nozzles fully aft* (McDonnell Douglas, Neg No 04C-118801-1, dated September 1979).

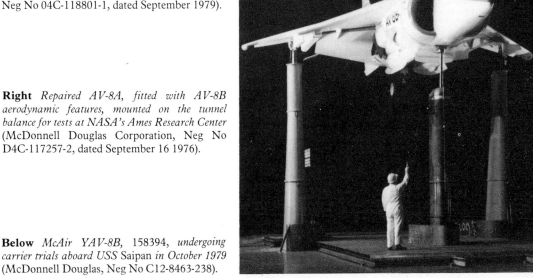

Right *Repaired AV-8A, fitted with AV-8B aerodynamic features, mounted on the tunnel balance for tests at NASA's Ames Research Center* (McDonnell Douglas Corporation, Neg No D4C-117257-2, dated September 16 1976).

Below *McAir YAV-8B,* 158394, *undergoing carrier trials aboard USS* Saipan *in October 1979* (McDonnell Douglas, Neg No C12-8463-238).

modified to feature the supercritical wing, improved LIDs and modified engine intakes and blow-in doors, primarily to demonstrate the improved STO and VTO performance of the new aircraft.

The first YAV-8B was completed 53 days ahead of schedule and proved to be 188 lb lighter than the forecast 12,400 lb operational tare weight. The aircraft was first flown at St Louis on November 9 1978, followed soon after by the second example. During the course of four months' flight testing the YAV-8Bs exceeded the US Marine Corps' performance requirements, in particular returning the astonishingly low fuel-flow figure of 50.7 lb/min at loiter while carrying seven Mark 82 bombs and gun pods; they also comfortably exceeded the tropical V/STO weight and performance demands. One of the aircraft underwent a modification programme investigation at YAV-8C standard to discover to what extent existing AV-8As could be subjected to limited retroactive

Superb air study of the second YAV-8B, 158395, *with one centreline and seven underwing bombs and Sidewinder missiles* (McDonnell Douglas Corporation, Neg No C22-133-3, dated September 1979).

modification and to discover how close performance improvement could thereby come to the AV-8B demands; apart from inclusion of the new LIDs, the YAV-8C included such equipment as the ALR-67 and ALE-39.

During 1979 the US Navy purchased a 12-degree ski-ramp from Fairey Engineering and this was erected at Patuxent River for primary employment by the McAir AV-8Bs (as well as three TAV-8As). One hundred launches were performed between March and June that year at exit speeds between 50 and 73 knots at all-up weights up to maximum AV-8B STO condition.

A further feature to be employed in the AV-8B (and RAF Harrier GR 5, see below) will be a new type of electronic engine control, designed to improve engine acceleration, reduce maintenance and increase the aircraft's operational capability. This Full Authority Digital Electronic Control (FADEC) adjusts the fuel flow to the engine precisely, and replaces the Harrier's hydro-mechanical system. Developed in Britain by Dowty and Smiths Industries Controls, FADEC was first flown in a Harrier by Rolls-Royce test pilot John Fawcett at Bristol in 1982.

In the meantime the structural test wing had withstood 150 per cent of the YAV-8B design in-flight loads, and initially cleared the flight aircraft for 250 hours. Design fatigue life is 6,000 hours, with testing to 12,000 hours to provide a fumble factor of two. This figure was achieved during 1982. (It should be mentioned that carbon-fibre composites possess no known fatigue-limited life.)

In 1979 a full-standard front fuselage was built and approved, and in April 1979 McAir was awarded a long-lead Contract for $35 million to prepare for series production. Four development AV-8B aircraft were ordered, the first being completed in October 1981. This aircraft will extend the flight envelope and perform flutter, handling and performance evaluation tests as well as clearance trials on weapons and systems; the second has been instrumented to measure airloads (particularly in VIFF) and is used for structural and engine testing. The third AV-8B is fully equipped with weapons systems and will undergo shipboard suitability trials, and the fourth aircraft—the first to be a fully-representative production aeroplane—will undergo trials for electro-magnetic compatibility, reliability and maintenance scheduling.

At the time of writing the US Marine Corps has stated a requirement for 340 AV-8Bs (including a number of equivalent two-seaters), and to achieve initial in-squadron status by mid-1985 long-lead funding for production of 12 aircraft was provided in the FY 1981 US Defense Budget, while Congress has already voted $180 million for development funding. If indeed the US Navy (and/or the USAF) expresses determination to 'go V/STOL' with the Harrier, the AV-8B will certainly go ahead with maximum priority. A radar-equipped 'AV-8B-Plus' has been offered to the US Navy and a re-bladed 23,000-lb thrust Pegasus 11-35 turbofan, but it is not yet clear to what extent the Navy will be prepared to sacrifice its 'top-end' fighter inventory (such as the second-generation F-18 programme) to go V/STOL; there are certainly those who believe that the AV-8B represents the thin end of the wedge and constitutes a substantial threat to the traditional super-carrier philosophy. Whether this threat, or that of the 'over-kill syndrome' allied with demand for better carrier cost-effectiveness, will prove to be the critical consideration remains to be seen.

The RAF V/STOL requirement

As part of the partnership agreement between McAir and British Aerospace (as heir to Hawker Siddeley Aviation), roughly half the total AV-8B manufacture will be undertaken in Britain. Approximately 40 per cent of the airframe and 60 per cent of the engine will be produced in the United Kingdom, as will about 50 per cent of the systems components, and a production line will be established to assemble complete aircraft on each side of the Atlantic. These assembly lines will share in the production of any export orders that may be forthcoming.

In the Royal Air Force there was for many years a need, set down in Air Staff Target 403 (AST 403), for a single aircraft to replace both the Harrier (scheduled to remain in service until about 1990) and the SEPECAT Jaguar. The latter supersonic aircraft, product of joint efforts in Britain and France during the 1960s, served in a number of RAF squadrons but failed to measure up to French Service expectations, particularly in the *Aéronavale.* It eventually became clear that a single replacement aircraft, combining V/STOL with supersonic performance (once again) would either constitute an excessively costly project or fail on account of design compromise; moreover the development period

First of the true YAV-8B aircraft in flight during November 1981. Note the camouflage scheme, nose pitot boom, full-depth fuselage strakes and the two wing fences (McDonnell Douglas, Neg No C12-11328-87).

Second US-built YAV-8B development aircraft, showing the LERX and single wing fence on each wing, and absence of nose pitot boom.

for such an aircraft might prove so lengthy that the rate of modern technological progress might outdate the eventual result before the aircraft reached service status. In due course AST 403 was confined to a Jaguar replacement and a new Air Staff Target, AST 409 was drawn up (and updated to a full Requirement, ASR 409) for a Harrier successor. In many ways Hawker Siddeley's proposals to meet this requirement ran parallel to those of McAir's for the US Marine Corps, save that the wing design was confined to mission tailoring to achieve optimum STO weight increase and cruise performance improvement through aerodynamic refinement. By definition a manufacturing compromise, the British 'big wing' design has been evolved to allow retrofit to the existing RAF Harrier GR Mark 3 (resulting in the designation change to GR Mark 5), and features a span increase to 32 ft and area increase to 250 sq ft. The trailing edge geometry has remained unchanged and leading edge sweep reduced marginally, although large leading edge root extensions (LERX) are included. Composite materials were not envisaged but local modifications to engine intakes and LIDs, similar to the USMC AV-8B, would be included. These modifications would also be applicable to the Sea Harrier.

Obviously the decision by the RAF to adopt the AV-8B (with relevant systems changes to meet specific British mission demands) will guarantee the future of this project on a work-shared basis, although the cost to the British Treasury will be substantially higher for the procurement of an effectively new aircraft. In 1981 the British Government announced its intention to order 60 AV-8B-based aircraft to be built jointly in the United States and Britain and termed the Harrier GR 5 for delivery to the Royal Air Force from 1986 onwards.

The Royal Air Force evaluated the YAV-8B technology-demonstrator in its current interim form during 1979 and it was clear that the aircraft met almost all the mission and operating demands, and probably showed itself to be a potentially more cost-effective aircraft in the long term than the 're-winged' Harrier.

One must obviously be aware of the very considerable labour employment benefits that would accrue in the United Kingdom from a decision to embark on a manufacturing programme of upwards of 500 aircraft for the RAF and US Marine Corps—not to mention the substantial long-term technological benefit to the nation of advanced manufacturing technique experience.

Chapter 11

The Harrier described

The design of the Harrier is remarkable insofar as it is not only required to be capable of radical operating modes but also has to include all the operating faculties of wholly conventional aircraft, and this has to be achieved with minimum aircraft weight. Efficient design has to be achieved with no loss in the ruggedness so essential to ground attack aircraft, especially when designed for use from advanced bases on semi-prepared and natural sites. The structure represents some 35 per cent of the aircraft's basic weight, and strenuous efforts have been made to keep this, together with the remaining 65 per cent, representing systems, powerplant and equipment, to a minimum. The most important basic structural parameters within which the Harrier is designed are:

a) Static strength for symmetric flight, maximum normal acceleration 7.8g specified, 11.7g ultimate.

b) Static strength for ground (undercarriage) proof vertical velocity of descent 12 ft/sec with capability of use from semi-prepared and natural grass sites.

c) Fatigue life for primary structure of 3,000 safe flying hours (15,000 equivalent flying hours with UK rules to be achieved on single specimen test).

d) Resistance to bird strikes essential to safe low-level operations. The specific bird strike resistance against a 1 lb bird at 600 knots to be achieved at the windscreen centre panel, the most vulnerable areas of the engine air intake and the wing leading edge.

The importance which has been attached to achieving low structure weight is reflected in the use of highly efficient structural materials. High strength steels, including maraging steel with strength exceeding 110 tons/sq in and titanium alloy bar, forgings and sheet in the 70-80 tons/sq in range, are used in the Harrier structure. (A carbon fibre ferry wing tip was flown to unfactored limits in 1977; at that time it was the largest item of composite primary structure to be flown in Europe.)

The Harrier is designed to operate in world-wide climatic conditions with a primary operational rôle extending from sea level to 10,000 ft, and a maximum useful operating height of about 45,000 ft. The design diving speed is Mach 1.2 or 635 knots corrected airspeed. These conditions do not result in novel structural problems. However, the unusual layout associated with vectored thrust gives rise to quite severe conditions on the external skins aft of the engine nozzles; in these areas noise levels of the order of 165 dB combine with skin temperatures of up to 200°C. The jet efflux also gives rise to turbulence in the tail region, and it has been found necessary to provide increase in tailplane strength to give adequate life against these effects.

Fuselage

The fuselage has been designed as a continuous structure with manufacturing joints at Frames 8 and 33, separating the nose and tail sections. Continuity of moment-resisting structure at the wing position is provided by port and starboard longerons which pass immediately below the wing lower surface, and diffuse into the forward and aft sections. The wing is attached at this position by six main fittings in pairs at three frames. These fittings are all designed to carry vertical reactions but other loads as follows: front, lateral only; centre, lateral, fore and aft; rear none. The wing is removed for engine change, and the vertical and horizontal tail surfaces are detachable.

The fuselage nose section comprises the pilot's cockpit, skinned with 19 swg aluminium alloy sheet, pressurised to 3½ lb/sq in maximum differential pressure, with a sliding hood, a fixed forward-facing flat windscreen and curved quarterlights. Forward of the front pressure bulkhead a short nose cone carries the pitot static head, the forward reaction control valve and several items of electronic and other equipment. The rocket-powered ejection seat is mounted on the rear sloping pressure bulkhead.

The windscreen main load-carrying panel of laminated stretched acrylic has been tested to show bird-strike resistance against a 1 lb bird at 600 knots, and is faced with a thin laminated glass front component, with air gap, to resist screen wiper abrasion. The windscreen is manufactured to high optical accuracy for weapon aiming, its width being dictated by the Head-up Display reflector glass. The hood is hot-moulded from 8-mm 'as cast' acrylic sheet and is bolted to metal side rails through glass-reinforced plastic edge members bonded to the acrylic edges.

The bifurcated engine air intake incorporates auxiliary inlet doors in the forward walls of the cowl to provide maximum air breathing at low forward speeds, and a boundary layer bleed slot in the cabin wall perimeter ducted to exits in the rear hood fairing. The intake is reinforced against bird strike over the leading edge and inner walls, and has been tested to show satisfactory resistance against the specific bird strike case, thus protecting the engine compressor from metallic debris release and the forward fuselage fuel tank from penetration or bursting from bird strike. The frames in this area are designed to carry front fuselage shear across the air intake to the centre fuselage side skins. Frames 9 and 11 carry the flight refuelling probe, when fitted.

The centre fuselage is an open-top U-structure which, with wing and fairings removed, allows the engine unit to be installed and removed; this section carries the maximum fuselage loadings. The aluminium alloy skin of up to 9 swg is chemically etched to reduce weight wherever possible. Frames 19A, 23 and 29 are designed to carry front, centre and rear wing attachment fittings; they are in turn designed to be replaceable without serious disruption of the main tension longeron at which they are mounted.

Frame 29 also supports the aft end of the fore and aft beams on which the main undercarriage is mounted, and is integrally machined in one piece from aluminium alloy plate. The engine is supported on fuselage Frame 19 by port and starboard trunnions near its centre of gravity, and also at the rear of the jet pipe by port and starboard links adjacent to the rear nozzle bearing flanges; these links are mechanically compensated so that fuselage torsional loads are not carried by the engine between main and aft mountings.

The engine jet efflux is discharged through two pairs of rotatable nozzles, which project through large reinforced holes in the fuselage side skins. The forward pair of nozzles are mounted directly to the fuselage structure on large diameter single-row ball bearings, and discharge relatively cool bypass air from the engine fan. The rear engine nozzles are mounted on the engine via a similar bearing and are clear of the fuselage structure, discharging the hot jet efflux. The fuselage skin immediately aft of the rear engine nozzles is protected by a low-expansion stainless steel heat shield; it is attached to strong points on the fuselage side by easily accessible bolts engaging anchor nuts, and the attachments are provided with thermal insulation. The hot part of the engine is surrounded by low-gauge titanium heat shields which protect the largely aluminium alloy fuselage structure from excessive engine heat.

Five integral fuel tanks are carried in the fuselage; port and starboard side tanks, each of 51½ gallons capacity, are located between the engine intake and front engine nozzles, and a further two side tanks, each of 39 gallons capacity, are located between front and rear nozzles; a central tank, containing 104 gallons, occupies the upper portion of the fuselage immediately aft of the wing.

The nose undercarriage is mounted on a pair of high strength titanium alloy fittings extending from fore and aft beams machined from aluminium alloy plate and supported by Frames 11 and 16; it retracts forward between the engine air intakes aft of the cockpit rear pressure bulkhead.

The main undercarriage is similarly supported between machined aluminium alloy plate beams extending from fuselage Frames 23 to 29. It retracts aft into a bay immediately aft of the engine and below the rear fuselage fuel tank. The main trunnion bearings of both nose and main undercarriage units are carried on plain PTFE lined bearings. The side hinged landing gear doors are sequenced to close on extension of the legs to reduce the entry of ground debris. The underfuselage area between the nose and main undercarriage is stressed to support a considerable weapon load; a detachable central pylon may be fitted, on either side of which provision is made for the attachment of self-contained 30 mm gun pods with 130 rounds of ammunition in each.

A capacious equipment bay occupies most of the fuselage cross section aft of the main undercarriage compartment and rear fuel tank. Much of the electronic equipment is contained herein on a large double-decked anti-vibration rack. The equipment may be quickly engaged in rear plug and socket quick-release mountings and is accessible through large load-carrying doors on both sides of the fuselage. It is in this region that the side skin plating is in etched titanium alloy to resist the effects of engine efflux heat and noise; the skins of 18 swg are chemically etched from 1.36 mm to 0.84 mm except along frame and stringer rivet lines.

The rear fuselage tapers rapidly in plan view and is provided with strongpoints for fin and tailplane attachment. The fin is mounted at two spar positions, the forward spar being attached to Frame 40 and the rear mounting, with tailplane hinge, to Frame 43. The rear fin and tailplane attachments are machined from high tensile steel and are bolted between twin back-to-back aluminium alloy frame pressings, the fin fittings extending upwards through a narrow spanwise aperture in the tailplane centresection box.

The tailplane is carried on port and starboard hinges at approximately the midpoint of the root chord. It is an all-moving surface and the power control unit is mounted vertically in the fuselage, being attached on the centreline of the tailplane forward of the hinges at the front of the centresection box. Both tailplane hinges and the power control unit attachment are provided with self-aligning spherical PTFE lined bearings, the port hinge bearing also featuring an inner PTFE lined cylindrical sleeve to permit small axial movement due to tailplane bending. The underfin incorporates a replaceable rubber bumper pad.

Wing

The wing is manufactured as a single unit comprising port and starboard halves permanently joined at a centreline rib. The main structural box extends from the centreline rib to the tip rib under which the outrigger is mounted. This box forms an integral fuel tank to half span, is bounded at front and rear by full-span spar webs, and an intermediate spar extends over the tank span.

The main box skins—two lower and three upper—are machined to provide integral spanwise and chordwise stiffeners. The lower (tension) skins extend full span and the upper skins to just outboard of the outer tank rib where, owing to the shallow depth, the

construction cannot follow the assembly procedures optimised for the fuel tank area; at this point a separate, stringer-reinforced, chemically-etched skin continues to the tip. The skin thicknesses are graded spanwise according to the load values and include integral local reinforcements to cater for tank access panels, pylon spigot holes, bolts and so on.

The design criteria vary for different spanwise stations on the wing, the inner three-quarters being determined by combat manoeuvring criteria with various combinations of external stores, the outer portion being designed with outrigger load considerations in mind, together with flight criteria when fitted with the extended ferry wing tip.

The outrigger units are mounted immediately outboard of the ailerons, at the tip of the main wing structural box. Provision is made at this point for the attachment of either the normal combat or extended ferry tips. The wing leading edge section contains a hydraulic services conduit, the reaction control ducting and an aileron primary circuit control extending to about two-thirds span. The leading edge has been designed to withstand the specified bird strike without damage to the internal services. (On later aircraft the bird strike resistance has been achieved by chemical etching, leaving 3.2 mm metal thickness at the nose radius).

Aluminium alloy fittings are provided at four stations in the wing main load-carrying box into which quickly detachable inner and outer wing store pylons may be assembled. These pylons are designed to mount a wide range of stores on twin-lug ejector-release units, including the use of twin-store carriers and the carriage of 100-gallon combat drop tanks or 330-gallon ferry tanks. The structural design of these pylons covers full flight envelope manoeuvres with a wide range of weapons and the combat tanks from all fuel states between tanks empty and two-thirds full.

The wing trailing edge between fuselage and outrigger carries plain flaps inboard and ailerons outboard, constructed of full-depth metal honeycomb core. The flaps are

Far left *Harrier port outrigger component, showing relation to position of wing RCV (without fairing panels attached)* (Hawker Siddeley Aviation, Neg No 701715).

Left *Close-up of Harrier nosewheel unit* (Hawker Siddeley Aviation, Neg No 701718).

Right *Harrier main undercarriage component, shown fully extended* (Hawker Siddeley Aviation, Neg No 701719).

mounted on three hinges and operated by tubular drive shafts from a single hydraulically operated jack mounted above the wing on the aircraft centreline. Each aileron is mounted on two hinges. A power control unit housed forward of the inboard hinge within the aerofoil profile actuates the aileron through an idling rod to a lever integral with the inboard hinge fitting in the aileron.

A fuel jettison pipe is located in the wing trailing edge between the flap and aileron, through which the contents of the external and wing tanks may be discharged in flight.

Tail surfaces

The tailplane is a single continuous unit, the exposed portions of which have 15 degrees anhedral. The main skins (thickness graded by chemical etching) and main spars are cranked at the root rib which forms the port and starboard boundary of a flat centresection in which are contained the hinge lugs and a lug to which the power control unit is attached. The main structural box is bounded by a front and rear spar. Aft of the rear spar the trailing edge is manufactured in full-depth aluminium alloy bonded honeycomb.

The fin is a conventional structure in aluminium alloy built on two spars which are reinforced at the lower ends with titanium alloy sections terminating in steel end fittings which provide a four-bolt attachment to the fuselage. The rudder is constructed employing full-depth aluminium alloy honeycomb.

Undercarriage

The Harrier employs a bicycle ('zero-track tricycle') undercarriage with main units retracting on the aircraft centreline into the fuselage and balancing outriggers mounted near the wing tips.

The main undercarriage is a twin-wheeled telescopic oleo-pneumatic strut; the twin wheels are rigidly connected by a live axle and are provided with an adaptive braking system which is designed to give maximum braking down to very slow taxy speeds.

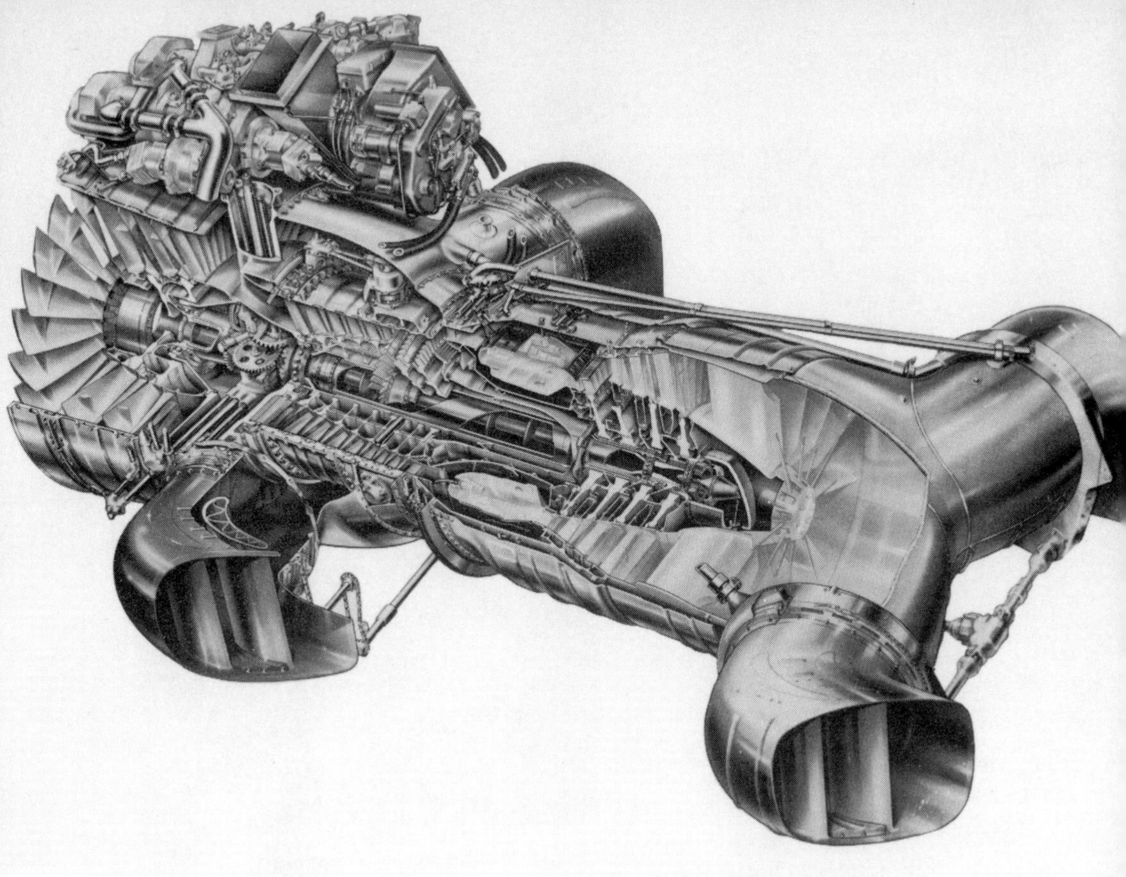

Cutaway of Rolls-Royce (Bristol) Pegasus 11 vectored-thrust turbofan (Rolls-Royce (Bristol) Ltd).

The nose undercarriage is a fully-castoring and steerable levered-suspension unit with a single trailing wheel; this unit contains an hydraulically-operated steering system arranged to give steering angles up to plus or minus 45 degrees. The suspension is by a liquid-spring shock absorber which is connected by a link to the fuselage such that a secondary contraction shortens the unit for retraction. The nose leg housing and the wheel fork are machined from aluminium alloy die forgings, and the turning tube is machined from a titanium alloy die forging.

The outrigger units are single-wheeled telescopic struts, retraction of which is accomplished by hydraulic jacks with mechanical internal locks. The outrigger leg is machined from an aluminium alloy die forging; the sliding member end fitting is machined from a high tensile steel die forging, and the sliding member itself is machined from maraging steel tube.

Powerplant

The Rolls-Royce Bristol Pegasus Mark 103 (as fitted in the Harrier GR Mark 3 and AV-8A aircraft) is an axial-flow, two-spool, turbofan engine with a bypass ratio of 1.29:1 at V/STOL rating. It is designed specifically to enable the gross thrust vector to be rotated to meet the requirements of V/STOL, conventional flight and to provide a measure of reverse thrust for braking and for thrust Vectoring in Forward Flight (VIFF).

The mechanically-independent low pressure and high pressure compressor systems are co-axial and counter-rotating to minimise gyro coupling. The three-stage titanium LP compressor (fan) is overhung from the front bearing and has no inlet guide vanes; it is driven by a two-stage LP turbine. The eight-stage steel-bladed HP compressor is provided with variable inlet guide vanes and is supercharged by the fan, and is driven by a two-stage HP turbine.

Combustion is effected in an annular combustion chamber into which fuel is fed by the engine fuel system which comprises a Dowty fuel control unit, flow distributors, gallery, dump valve, torch igniter and primer jet system.

The engine exhausts through two pairs of rotatable nozzles operated simultaneously and positioned symmetrically on each side. They are fabricated from sheet steel and incorporate two aerofoil section vanes equispaced across the nozzle throat. Bypass air from the LP compressor is ducted through the LP compressor delivery duct to the front pair of 'cold' nozzles. Discharge characteristics of the front nozzles at sea level VTO rating are 800 mph and 150°C.

Gases from the combustion chamber are expanded across the HP and LP turbines and are discharged through the rear pair of 'hot' nozzles. Discharge characteristics of the rear nozzles at sea level VTO rating are 1,200 mph and 670°C. Total thrust is divided almost equally between front and rear nozzles.

Reaction controls and flying controls

For hovering and very low speed flight, in which aerodynamic forces are absent from aileron, elevator and rudder, control is effected by downward-blowing reaction control valves at nose and tail for pitch, sideways-blowing valve at the tail for yaw, and upward/downward blowing valves at wing-tips for roll control. These reaction control valves are interconnected with the conventional aerodynamic surfaces (except front pitch and yaw valves), so as to provide continuous transition from reaction to aerodynamic control in accelerating transition, and *vice versa* in decelerating transition. Pressure air for the reaction control system is tapped from the engine at the 8th stage of the HP compressor.

Cockpit layout and escape system

The Specification for the Harrier required inclusion of the Ferranti FE 541 Inertial Nav-Attack System and Smiths Head-Up Display (HUD) as the primary flight information display.

The pilot's centre console incorporates the HUD mounted at the top to coincide with the pilot's eye datum in normal level flight. The unit displays, via a bright cathode ray tube and reflector glass, the information from the HUD system which is integrated into the electronic system; the display provides all flight information in all modes of flight, including navigation director, instrument flying, weapon aiming and V/STOL flying. A photocell directed forward through the windscreen compensates for varying outside light levels to maintain a preset level of CRT symbology relative intensity.

The other major item in the centre console is the navigation display and computer, providing projected moving map display driven by the inertial system at scale ground speed.

The port instrument panel is used as a standby flight information panel using conventional instruments with inputs separate from the integrated head-up navigation display system. The lower panel contains the undercarriage main and emergency controls, the undercarriage position indicator, flap selector and indicator.

The starboard instrument panel contains the instruments chiefly associated with engine and fuel system, and the lower section incorporates the Tacan indicator.

The combined engine throttle and nozzle control box is mounted on the port console and consists of a single box containing a throttle lever, nozzle lever, adjustable short take-

Above *Harrier GR Mark 1 cockpit. In the centre of the windscreen can be seen the head-up flight information display, and behind the control column the head-down moving-map indicator. On the port console are located the throttle box and undercarriage controls, and on the port instrument panel are the flight instruments, armament selector and jettison switches. On the starboard panel are the engine and fuel instruments, below which are the nav-attack system switches. On the starboard console are the communications controls and compass repeater. The central warning panel is located below the starboard quarter-light* (Hawker Siddeley Aviation, Neg No 50828).

Below *Harrier GR Mark 1 cockpit, close-up of starboard side instruments and controls. Top left, engine speed, jet pipe temperature, fuel flow and contents instruments; centre left, navigation control panel; top centre, communications selector switches and volume control; centre, central warning panel; the forward six lamps (red) indicate primary warning with attention-getters and audio warning; the rear 20 lamps (amber) are secondary warnings without audio* (Hawker Siddeley Aviation, Neg No 40628).

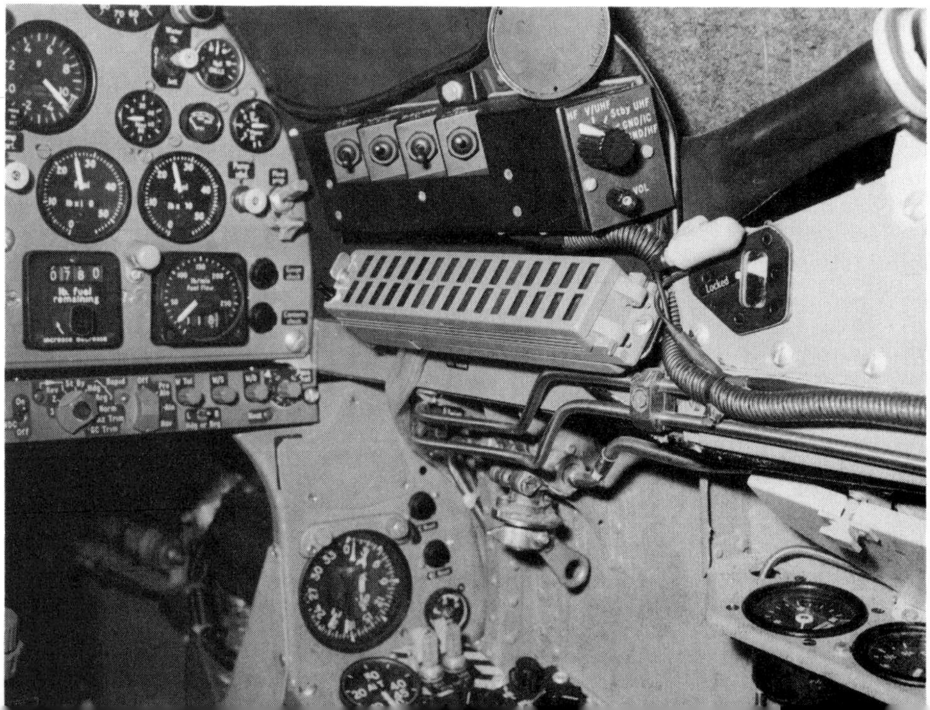

Above left *Harrier GR Mark 1 cockpit, close-up of port side instruments and controls. Top right, reading clockwise: angle of attack indicator, altimeter, attitude indicator, ASI and rate-of-climb indicator. Below the flight instruments is the weapon selector and jettison panel. Upper left is the pilot display unit control box* (Hawker Siddeley Aviation, Neg No 40328).

Above right *Sea Harrier FRS Mark 1 cockpit, starboard side. Reading from the rear of the console: cabin conditioning controls, TACAN and CCS panel, navigation display controls and computer, IFF panel, fuel and electrics panel. Mounted obliquely at the forward end of the console is the radar warning receiver display and controls. Not visible are the main radar display and fuel gauges, mounted on the starboard front instrument panel* (British Aerospace Corporation, Neg No 791152).

off stop, a fixed vertical take-off stop, a parking brake lock and a limiter-off switch. The throttle lever handle has a twist-grip control for stadiametric ranging for weapon aiming, and incorporates the engine re-light button, airbrake switch and press-to-transmit radio switch. The nozzle lever controls the angle of the Pegasus nozzles and is a telescopic spring-loaded lever; during decelerating transitions and in landing, this lever can be lifted up over the fixed VTO stop to provide the braking angle range of nozzle movement. The design of the throttle box has been undertaken in such a way as to enable the pilot to achieve optimum control without recourse to looking down at the unit during actual operation.

A Martin Baker Type 9A Mark 2 fully automatic rocket-assisted ejector seat is provided. The seat is fitted with canopy breakers incorporated in the upper structure, the purpose of which is to pierce the canopy before contact by the pilot's helmet; it provides a means of escape at all speeds and altitudes down to zero speed zero height, and from an aircraft with a high sink rate. The action of pulling upwards on the single firing handle, situated on the front of the seat pan, fires the ejection gun and restrains the pilot's body and legs in the seat. The ejection gun imparts a modest initial velocity before burn from the rocket—located beneath the seat pan—is initiated. Rocket burn lasts for about 0.4 seconds and burnout velocity of the seat and occupant from zero-zero initiation is around 130 mph with a peak trajectory of about 400 ft. Very soon after burnout, the seat is stabilised by a drogue parachute system which, after a further short time delay, then

Sea Harrier FRS Mark 1 cockpit, port side. From the rear of the console, reading clockwise: radar hand-controller, throttle and nozzle box, undercarriage and non-skid switches, UHF/VHF communications panel, armament panel and, on the centre panel, flight instruments. The missile control panel, below the flight instruments, has not been fitted. Engine instruments, not visible in this picture, are located above the armament panel (British Aerospace Corporation, Neg No 791151).

extracts the pilot's main parachute—the deployment of which separates the pilot from the seat.

For rapid escape on the ground, the pilot is provided with a canopy breaking system employing miniature detonating cord (MDC); this consists of a linear explosive charge which forms the core of a hollow lead tube of 1.5-mm diameter. This 'cord' is enclosed by a rubber backing strip around the periphery of the canopy, and the explosive is actuated by a detonator at the aft end of the canopy frame, and is initiated by mechanical operation of either a D-ring inside the canopy or two handles on the outside of the canopy (for external rescue). Being manually operated, the system is entirely independent of electrics.

In the Harrier two-seater the front cockpit is designed to follow as closely as possible that of the single-seater for obvious reasons of pilot familiarisation. The rear cockpit is equipped with full dual main flight controls (ie, engine throttle and nozzle levers, control column, rudder bar, etc); in addition, the other essential flight controls, switches and instruments common to the front cockpit are duplicated in the rear; some of these are arranged so that the rear pilot has over-riding authority in all situations involving safety of flight.

Flying the Harrier—the V/STOL flying technique

The four primary V/STOL manoeuvres employing vectored thrust may be defined as follows: vertical take-off and accelerating transition to wingborne flight; short take-off and accelerating transition to wingborne flight; decelerating transition from wingborne flight to hover; and vertical landing. The following are the piloting techniques of the Harrier in these manoeuvres.

VTO and accelerating transition: i Using the steerable nosewheel, line up the aircraft and apply the brakes. **ii** Move the nozzle lever to Hover Stop. **iii** Immediately open the throttle to full power. **iv** As the aircraft becomes airborne after two or three seconds, retract the undercarriage. **v** At about 50 ft—ie, clear of ground effects—select the flaps IN and move the nozzle lever progressively forward to hold height. **vi** At about 180 knots the aircraft is fully wingborne.

STO and accelerating transition: i Using the steerable nosewheel, line up the aircraft and apply the brakes. **ii** Set the ASI 'bug' to lift-off speed. **iii** Set the nozzle stop to 50 degrees. **iv** Open the throttle to 55 per cent RPM. **v** Release the brakes and slam open the throttle to full RPM. **vi** Hold the nozzle lever and at 'bug' speed move the nozzle lever to the stop. **vii** When airborne retract the undercarriage. **viii** At about 50 ft, select flaps IN; move the nozzle lever progressively forward to hold height. **ix** At about 180 knots the aircraft is fully airborne.

Decelerating transition to hover: i Carry out normal landing checks: wheels and flaps down. **ii** When downwind, select nozzles to 20 degrees to check the reaction controls. **iii** On the final approach, select nozzles to 40 degrees and maintain an angle of attack of about eight to nine degrees using the throttle. **iv** At about 50 ft and 1,200 yards from hover point, move the nozzle lever to Hover Stop. **v** Using the throttle, maintain the flight path as speed falls off. **vi** Adjust to the hover point using the control column. **vii** Hover at not less than 50 ft.

Vertical landing: i From the hover, by sensitive use of the throttle, reduce RPM by one to two per cent to establish a slow descent. **ii** During descent maintain position and height control with the control column. **iii** As soon as firm wheel-on-ground contact is felt, close the throttle to engine idle. **iv** Select nozzles fully aft and apply wheel brakes.

Leading particulars

Geometric data

Wings (Harrier Marks 1-4 and Sea Harrier Mark 1). Span (combat), 25 ft 3.226 in; (ferry), 29 ft 8.05 in. Root chord on aircraft centreline, 11 ft 8 in. Tip chord, geometric true, 4 ft 1.35 in. Aileron chord, 1 ft 6.0 in. Aileron area aft of hinge (each), 5.27 sq ft. Flap chord, 1 ft 5.6 in. Flap area (each), 6.95 sq ft. Wing leading edge notch from aircraft centreline, 5 ft 9.75 in. Leading edge fences from aircraft centreline, 9 ft 7.0 in and 6 ft 4.85 in. (All spanwise dimensions are measured along aerofoil true datum.) Aspect ratio, 3.175. Taper ratio, 0.336. Quarter-chord sweepback (true), 34°. Leading-edge sweepback (true), 40° 0′ 23″. Standard apex mean chord, 7 ft 11.508 in. Thickness/chord ratio, root 10 per cent, tip (combat), 3.3 per cent. Wing anhedral, 12° true on aerofoil datum.

Fuselage Overall length (Harrier Mark 1), 45 ft 6.62 in; (Harrier Mark 2), 55 ft 10.8 in; (Harrier Mark 3), 45 ft 8 in; (Harrier Mark 4), 56 ft 0.2 in; (Sea Harrier Mark 1), 47 ft 7.68 in. Fuselage datum, parallel to and 2 ft 6.50 in below top line of rear fuselage. Wing aerofoil datum 1.75° to fuselage datum. Maximum cross-sectional area (Marks 1 and 3), 30.31 sq ft; (Marks 2 and 4), 32.80 sq ft; (Sea Harrier Mark 1), 30.31 sq ft.

Tailplane (All Harriers and Sea Harrier). Span, 13 ft 11.08 in. Root chord, 5 ft 7.39 in. Tip chord, basic, 1 ft 9 in. Tip chord, actual, 1 ft 5.83 in. Tailplane pivot, 3 ft 1.5 in aft of tailplane apex on aircraft centreline. Area (total), 47.54 sq ft. Aspect ratio, 4.079. Moment of tailplane quarter-chord to wing quarter-chord on aircraft centreline, 16 ft 7.38 in. Mean chord, 3 ft 5 in. Tailplane movement +11° 15′, -10° 15′. Quarter-chord sweepback, 32° 53′ 25″. Leading-edge sweepback, 38° 43′ 7″. Thickness/chord ratio, root 7 per cent, tip 7 per cent. Anhedral, 15° 50′ 27″ on tailplane aerofoil datum.

Fin and rudder Net area excluding fuselage (Harrier Mark 1), 25.83 sq ft; (Harrier Marks 2 and 4), 32.9 sq ft; (Sea Harrier), 26.56 sq ft. Tip height above static ground line (Harrier Marks 1 and 3), approx 11 ft 6.5 in; (Harrier Marks 2 and 4), approx 12 ft 2 in;

(Sea Harrier), 11 ft 10.4 in. Moment of fin quarter-chord to wing quarter-chord on aircraft centreline (Harrier Marks 1 and 3), 15 ft 8.28 in; (Harrier Marks 2 and 4), 17 ft 11.4 in; (Sea Harrier), 15 ft 9.72 in. Quarter-chord sweepback (all versions), 47° 22′. Rudder area aft of hinge (all versions), 5.267 sq ft. Rudder movement normal to hingeline (all versions), ±15°. RWR antenna fairing centreline depressed 3° to fuselage datum, located 4 ft 0.55 in above rear fuselage top line at point of intersection with fin leading edge.

Airbrake (all versions). Area, 8.50 sq ft. Movement about hingeline, undercarriage down, 25°; undercarriage up, 66°.

Engine propulsion nozzles (all versions). Distance between nozzle centrelines (cold), 6 ft 3.36 in. Cold nozzle centreline 2 ft 0.5 in aft of wing apex measured in true plan. Nozzle rotation range (hot and cold), 98.5° from horizontally aft.

Reaction control valves Front (single-seaters), 12 ft 0.57 in; (two-seaters), 17 ft 6.85 in forward of wing apex; on single seaters the valve flow centreline is angled 7° 38′ forward of vertical to fuselage datum, on two-seaters, 5°. Rear RCV (single-seaters), 26 ft 11.94 in; (two-seaters), 32 ft 10 in aft of wing apex; valve flow centreline on all versions is angled 8° aft of vertical to fuselage datum. Wing RCVs (all versions), 11 ft 1.06 in from aircraft centreline (true); valve flow centreline (downwards) is angled 3° outwards from vertical.

Wing store pylons (all versions). Centreline of inboard pylon, 6 ft 3.12 in from aircraft centreline; centreline of outboard pylon, 10 ft 2.50 in from aircraft centreline.

Undercarriage Nosewheel, 26.00 × 8.75 - 11; single-seaters, 90 psi; two-seaters, 100 psi. Mainwheels, 26.00 × 7.75 - 13; single-seaters, 90 psi; two-seaters, 95 psi. Outrigger wheels (all versions), 13.50 × 6 - 4, 95 psi. Main undercarriage wheelbase (single-seaters), 11 ft 5 in; (two-seaters), 11 ft 4.6 in. Mainwheel effective rolling radius, 11.2 in. Outrigger track (all versions), 22 ft 2.12 in.

Air intake (all versions). Total throat area (both sides), 9.20 sq ft. Engine entry face area, 10.3 sq ft.

Flight refuelling probe (all versions). Front lip of probe 12 ft 2.77 in forward of wing apex. Probe nozzle centreline 4 ft 5.09 in to port of aircraft centreline and 2 ft 10.87 in above fuselage datum.

Weapon carriage

In addition to the twin 30-mm Aden gun pods with 300 total rounds of ammunition, the Harrier GR Marks 1 to 4 may carry the following:

1 Six underwing 68-mm or 2-in Matra Type 116M or 115 multiple rocket launchers; or **2** Up to five 1,000-lb free-fall or retarded bombs; or **3** Up to five cluster weapons; or **4** Up to ten Lepus flares; or **5** One centreline store and two underwing 100-gallon combat tanks; or **6** Two 330-gallon ferry tanks; or combinations of the above up to a total store weight of approximately 9,000 lb. Additional to the above the Sea Harrier may carry two Harpoon air-to-surface and two AIM-9 Sidewinder air-to-air missiles.

Weights

Empty (Harrier Mark 1), 12,200 lb; (Harrier Mark 2), 13,000 lb; (Harrier Mark 3), 12,640 lb; (Harrier Mark 4), 13,440 lb; (Sea Harrier), approx 12,950 lb. Loaded (maximum rolling take-off, all versions), 26,000 lb.

Performance

Sea level maximum speed, 642 knots (740 mph), all versions. Maximum diving speed, Mach 1.29. Ceiling, 51,200 ft. Typical low-level (lo-lo-lo) sorties (Harrier Mark 3): vertical take-off with 3,000 lb fuel, radius of action 50 miles; short take-off (300 yds to 50 ft) with 4,000 lb fuel, radius of action 160 miles; short take-off (700 yds to 50 ft) with 5,000 lb fuel, radius of action, 250 miles (Requirement criterion). Maximum endurance with one in-flight refuelling, 7 hours 18 min. Ferry range, unrefuelled, 2,340 miles.

Appendices

Glossary of abbreviations

A&AEE Aircraft and Armament Experimental Establishment
AFB (US) Air Force Base
ASM Air-to-surface missile
ASPJ Advanced, self-protection jamming system
ASR Air Staff Requirement
AST Air Staff Target
ASW Air-to-Surface Warfare
BIS (US) Navy Board of Inspection and Survey
BuAer (US) Bureau of Aeronautics
CA Controller (Air), MoS and MoA
Cat Category
CFE Central Fighter Establishment
CW centimetric wavelength
DB Development Batch
deld delivered
DSARC (US) Defence Systems Acquisition Review Council
ECM electronic countermeasures
EW Electronic Warfare
(F) Fighter
FAA Fleet Air Arm
FADEC Full Authority Digital Electronic Control
ff first flight
FGA Fighter, Ground Attack
FOD foreign object damage
FRADU Fleet Requirements Air Development Unit (also TU, Training Unit)
FRS Fighter/Reconnaissance/Strike
GOR General Operational Requirement
GR Ground Attack/Reconnaissance
HOTAS 'hands-on-throttle-and-stick'
HSA Hawker Siddeley Aviation
HUD head-up display
I/WAC Interface/Weapons Aiming Computer
JPT jet pipe temperature
LERX leading-edge root extension
LID lift improvement device
LRMTS laser ranging and marked target seeking

MBA Martin Baker Aircraft
McAir McDonnell Aircraft Company
MDC miniature detonating cord
MGB Medium Girder Bridge
Mintech Ministry of Technology
MoA Ministry of Aviation
MoD Ministry of Defence
MoS Ministry of Supply
MWDT Mutual Weapons Development Team
NASA National Aeronautics and Space Administration
NBMR NATO Basic Military Requirement
OCU Operational Conversion Unit
OR Operational Requirement
PCB plenum chamber burning
QFI Qualified Flying Instructor
RAE Royal Aircraft Establishment
RCV reaction control valve
RNAS Royal Naval Air Station
RSRE Royal Signals and Radar Establishment
RWR radar warning receiver
SAM Surface-to-air missile
SBAC Society of British Aircraft (Aerospace) Constructors
SEPECAT *Société Européenne de Production de l'Avion Ecole de Combat et Appui Tactique*
SNECMA *Société Nationale d'Etude et de Construction de Moteurs d'Aviation*
TI trial installation
TMR Thrust Measuring Rig
TSR Tactical Strike/Reconnaissance
USMC United States Marine Corps
VAK *Vertikal-Aufklärungs-und-Kampfflugzeug*
VIFF (Thrust) Vectoring in Forward Flight
VMA (US) Marine Corps Attack Squadron (also (T), Training)
VSS Vertical Support Ship
V/STOL Vertical/Short Take-off and Landing
VT Vosper Thornycroft
WOD wind over deck

1 Problems inherent in V/STOL operations

It is possible here to describe only very briefly the nature of problems associated with V/STOL operations, problems which have been studied in great detail by every experimental and operational establishment over the past 20 years. Through these exhaustive studies and by adherence to carefully evolved operational procedures, these problems are now fully understood and have been almost entirely overcome.

Broadly speaking the areas in which V/STOL manoeuvres differ significantly from normal airfield/runway operation lie in: a) engine thrust losses due to recirculation of hot gases; and b) foreign object damage (FOD) resulting from jet blast.

Exhaust gas recirculation

Fortunately, by the design nature of the Harrier, the hot gas exhaust nozzles of the Pegasus are located further aft from the engine air intakes than the 'cold' nozzles. However, when hovering at more than about 20 ft above the ground there is some 'mixing' of the two exhausts due to expansion and interaction of the ground sheets so that some recirculation of hot gases can occur with consequent loss of engine efficiency (and hence of thrust).

There are two obvious remedies to alleviate this effect, namely to point the aircraft into wind so that any such hot gas interaction may tend to be shifted aft away from the intake suction, and to commence transition as soon as possible after lift-off so that the rearward rotation of the nozzles will cause the interaction of the hot gases to take place behind the aircraft.

Of course, the choice of a rolling or short take-off, with the nozzles directing the exhaust aft, will entirely eliminate hot gas recirculation.

Foreign object damage (FOD)

This is unfortunately the most difficult problem to overcome in any V/STOL operation, depending as it must do on the nature of the operating site; that is to say that the most attractive dispersed site (such as a clearing in a wood) is probably the most difficult to divest of potential 'foreign objects'.

FOD may embrace anything from a light covering of the aircraft by dirt and dust (which might later be concentrated by suction to block a filter) to direct injestion of major debris, birds, maintenance equipment or clothing into the engine, possibly resulting in total destruction of the aircraft.

Service maintenance techniques are particularly stringent in ensuring that intake blanks are used wherever possible, and the forbidden practice of resting spanners and other tools on the intake lips is regarded as potentially lethal.

The Pegasus fan blades are constructed in high-strength titanium alloy, a particularly tough material capable of withstanding impact with small foreign objects, but stones and metal objects usually cause fairly serious damage. While some instances are known where foreign objects have been centrifuged by the fan out of the front nozzles without severe damage, other cases are known when bolts have passed through the fan into the high pressure compressor, causing blades to fail and pass down the engine starting a chain reaction of failure, surging and disintegration of the turbine.

When operating from 'unprepared' surfaces, such as grass clearings and compressed earthen patches, the effect of vertical jet blast is swift and destructive; a few seconds at full thrust is sufficient to parch the grass, dry out the topsoil and then break down the surface layer, leading initially to light erosion and eventually to 'digging a pit'. The debris which inevitably accompanies this excavation circulates in the deflected jet blast, fairly quickly entering the engine intakes.

Not unnaturally, VTOL pads and mats have been developed with considerable success. Yet early experience well demonstrated the vital necessity for such mats to be very securely anchored to the ground as the energy in the jet, if allowed to penetrate beneath the edge of the mat, is quite capable of lifting the entire mat off the ground with possible damage to the aircraft itself. (It is known that on one occasion a V/STOL aircraft—not a Harrier—while hovering about 60 ft above the edge of an insecurely anchored pad, lifted the entire 11-ton pad 4 ft into the air.)

Experience has shown that a custom-designed VTOL mat, provided that it is in good condition and is correctly secured, is more efficient than an apparently clean area of paved surface, such as a runway or road. Small imperfections, seams between concrete slabs or tarmac surfacing can erode rapidly and lead to major disintegration with all the ensuing FOD.

Once more the employment of rolling short take-off and landing considerably reduces the risk of FOD, and the relative freedom of ships' decks from foreign objects renders them ideal operating surfaces for V/STOL aircraft.

Living with FOD. A Harrier GR Mark 1A of No 20 (F) Squadron 'goes agricultural' during Exercise 'Grimm Charade' in North Rhine-Westphalia, Germany, during 1973 (Ministry of Defence, Neg No 2975/25).

2 P1127/Kestrel/Harrier ship operations, 1963-1982

Ship	Nationality	Tonnage	Date*	Aircraft
HMS *Ark Royal*	British	50,800	Feb 1963	P 1127
USS *Independence*	American	78,000	May 1966	Kestrel
USS *Raleigh* (LPD)	American	13,900	May 1966	Kestrel
HMS *Bulwark*	British	27,300	June 1966	Kestrel
HMS *Blake*	British	12,100	Aug 1967	Harrier
Andrea Doria	Italian	6,500	Oct 1967	Harrier
USS *LaSalle* (LPD)	American	13,900	May 1969	XV-6A
25 De Mayo	Argentinian	19,900	Sept 1969	Harrier
HMS *Eagle*	British	50,000	Mar 1970	Harrier
USS *Guadalcanal* (LPH)	American	18,300	Mar 1971	AV-8A
USS *Coronado* (LPD)	American	16,800	Mar 1971	AV-8A
Green Rover	British	11,520	Sept 1971	Harrier
USS *Guam* (LPH)	American	18,300	Jan 1972	AV-8A
Vikrant	Indian	19,500	July 1972	Harrier
Dédalo	Spanish	15,800	Oct 1972	Harrier
Minas Gerais	Brazilian	19,800	Oct 1973	Harrier
Jeanne d'Arc	French	12,365	Oct 1973	Harrier
Foch	French	27,300	Nov 1973	Harrier
USS *Tripoli* (LPH)	American	18,300	Aug 1974	AV-8A
USS *Inchon* (LPH)	American	18,300	Jan 1975	AV-8B
HMS *Intrepid*	British	12,120	Jan 1975	Harrier
HMS *Engadine*	British	9,000	Jan 1975	Harrier
USS *Ponce* (LPD)	American	16,800	Feb 1975	AV-8A
HMS *Fearless*	British	12,120	June 1975	Harrier
USS *Iwo Jima* (LPH)	American	18,300	Oct 1975	AV-8A
USS *New Orleans* (LPH)	American	18,300	Dec 1975	AV-8A
USS *Juneau* (LPD)	American	16,800	Feb 1976	AV-8A
HMS *Hermes*	British	28,700	Apr 1976	Harrier
USS *Franklin D. Roosevelt* (CV)	American	64,000	June 1976	AV-8A
USS *Ogden* (LPD)	American	16,800	Aug 1976	AV-8A
USS *Cleveland* (LPD)	American	16,800	Aug 1976	AV-8A
USS *Saratoga* (CVA)	American	80,000	July 1977	AV-8A
USS *Trenton* (LPD)	American	16,800	Oct 1976	AV-8A
HMAS *Melbourne*	Australian	19,966	Oct 1976	Harrier
USS *Shreveport* (LPD)	American	16,800	Oct 1977	AV-8A
USS *Okinawa* (LPH)	American	18,300	Mar 1978	AV-8A
USS *Saipan* (LHA)	American	39,300	July 1978	AV-8A
USS *Eisenhower* (CVN)	American	91,400	Aug 1978	AV-8A
USS *Tarawa* (LHA)	American	39,300	Dec 1978	AV-8A
RFA *Olwen*	British	10,890	Apr 1979	Sea Harrier
HMS *Invincible*	British	16,000	Nov 1979	Sea Harrier
MV *Atlantic Conveyor*	British	14,946	Apr 1982	Sea Harrier/ Harrier
HMS *Illustrious*	British	16,000	Aug 1982	Sea Harrier

* *Date of first embarkation or landing.*

3 Hawker/Hawker Siddeley V/STOL projects, 1957-1962

Project number	Engine configuration	Design Engineer	Date	Remarks
P 1126	Twelve lift engines	R.S. Williams	June 1957	Started after P 1127 but number booked earlier
P 1127	One vectored-thrust engine engine	R.S. Hooper	June 1957	First brochure issued August 1957
None	Four deflected-thrust engines plus two cruise engines	J.W. Fozard	Oct 1957	
P 1136	Four lift engines plus one cruise engine	J.W. Fozard	Apr 1959	
P 1137	Two rotatable tip pods plus two clang-box cruise engines	R.S. Williams	May 1959	
P 1139	Two lift engines plus one clang-box cruise engine	J.W. Fozard	Feb 1960	
P 1140	Three lift engines plus one clang-box cruise engine	J.W. Fozard	Mar 1960	
P 1143	Four rotatable tip pods plus three lift engines	R. Braybrook	July 1960	
P 1149	Six lift engines plus two cruise engines	J.W. Fozard	Feb 1961	
P 1150/1	One BS 100 vectored-thrust engine with PCB	R.S. Hooper	Feb 1961	
P 1152	Four lift engines plus one clang-box cruise engine	J.W. Fozard	Mid-1961	In competition with tenders from DH, Blackburn and Hawker Siddeley Advanced Projects Group
P 1154	One BS 100 vectored-thrust engine with PCB or two vectored-thrust RR Speys	R.S. Hooper	Oct 1961	Cf P 1150/3 and won NBMR-3 design competition

4 Allocation of prototype and development aircraft

Hawker P 1127 Two prototypes, *XP831* and *XP836,* designed and built as private ventures during 1958-60, but eventually purchased under HM Government Contract.

XP831 Commenced hovering trials at Dunsfold, 21-10-60, flown by A.W. Bedford, OBE; first untethered hovering flight, 19-11-63. Damaged in accident at Paris Air Show, 16-6-63. Repaired and returned to Dunsfold, 9-64. Preserved at RAF Museum (Sir Sydney Camm Memorial Hall), Hendon, 1973.

XP836 ff 7-7-61. Used to 'close the gap' between horizontal and vertical flight, 7-61 until 11-61. Crashed and destroyed at Yeovilton, 14-12-61, after cold nozzle became detached in flight; A.W. Bedford ejected safely at 200 ft.

Hawker P 1127 Four prototypes, *XP972, XP976, XP980* and *XP984,* purchased by HM Government Contract for aerodynamic and powerplant research.
XP972 ff 5-4-62. Aircraft suffered engine failure following bearing seizure and blade fouling in high-g turn, 30-10-62; force landed at Tangmere, suffered titanium fire and was extensively damaged following undercarriage failure. Hugh Merewether, escaped unhurt.
XP976 ff 12-7-62. Aircraft introduced inflatable intake lips and fin-mounted pitot head. Used for radio aerial trials at RAE. Scrapped at RAE, circa 1970.
XP980 ff 5-63. Aircraft introduced anhedral tailplane and streamwise wingtip fairings. Taxying trials and undercarriage load measurements, RAF Gaydon, 1972-73.
XP984 ff 10-63. Aircraft introduced swept wing, wing leading edge extensions and cold steel nozzles. Force landed, Thorney Island, 19-3-65; aircraft damaged but repaired. Crashed and destroyed in landing at RAE, Bedford, 31-10-75.

Hawker Siddeley Kestrel FGA Mark 1 Nine evaluation aircraft, *XS688-XS696,* ordered for Tripartite evaluation trials at the Central Fighter Establishment, West Raynham, Norfolk, during 1964-65. Aircraft introduced fully-swept wing, nose camera, taller fin, bulged and slightly longer fuselage for 15,000-lb thrust Bristol Siddeley Pegasus, and (later) extended tailplane. Six aircraft shipped to USA as XV-6A for Tri-Service Trials at Patuxent River, and aboard USS *Raleigh* and USS *Independence.* USAF trials at Edwards AFB, and flown by USAF, Army, Navy and Marine Corps pilots.
XS688 ff 7-3-64; short tailplane; evaluation No *8.* SBAC Display, 9-64. Shipped to USA; carried BuAer No *64-18262.* (Fitted with extended tailplane, 7-64.) Displayed at USAF Museum, Wright Patterson AFB.
XS689 ff 28-5-64; extended tailplane; evaluation No *9.* Shipped to USA; carried BuAer No *64-18263.* To Edwards AFB carrying NASA No *521.*
XS690 ff 5-8-64. Evaluation No *0.* Shipped to USA; carried BuAer No *64-18264* for Tri-Service Trials; trials from USS *Guam,* 1968. Dumped in Virginia River at completion of trials.
XS691 ff 5-9-64. Evaluation No *1.* Shipped to USA; carried BuAer No *64-18265* for Tri-Service Trials; to Edwards AFB, 5-67, carrying New Trials No *5*; scrapped after completion of trials.
XS692 ff 7-11-64. Evaluation No *2.* Shipped to USA; carried BuAer No *64-18266* for Tri-Service Trials; later cannibalised for spares.
XS693 ff 15-11-64. Evaluation No *3.* Performed first night VTO, 1-2-65, and was the first to be delivered to CFE, 8-2-65; retained in UK after Tripartite evaluation. Fitted with Pegasus 6 engine at Brough; ff 10-6-67. Crashed at Filton 21-9-67; pilot, Squadron Leader H. Rigg, escaped safely.
XS694 ff 10-12-64. Evaluation No *4.* Shipped to USA; carried BuAer No *64-18267* for Tri-Service Trials; ground-looped, extensively damaged and scrapped.
XS695 ff 17-2-65. Evaluation No *5.* Crashed at A&AEE, Boscombe Down, but later delivered to RAE, Farnborough.
XS696 ff 5-3-65. Evaluation No *6.* Crashed at West Raynham following ground-loop during take-off. Pilot rescued.

Hawker Siddeley Harrier GR Mark 1 (Development batch) Six pre-production aircraft, *XV276-XV281.* Aircraft used for systems trials, armament and stores clearance; engine flight development and handling (Pilot's Notes, etc), HSA, RAE, A&AEE and Rolls-Royce Ltd.
XV276 ff 31-8-66. Continuing flight trials, HSA Dunsfold, 1966-73. Engine flamed out and aircraft crashed, Dunsfold, 10-4-73, with throttle stop out of adjustment; pilot ejected safely.
XV277 ff 9-11-66, H. Merewether. Retained by manufacturers for performance and handling trials. Later employed on store clearance trials.
XV278 ff 31-12-66, A.W. Bedford. Retained by manufacturers for various store TIs, including preliminary installation of LRMTS nose profile, 1972.
XV279 ff 4-3-67, A.W. Bedford. Employed on engine handling and performance trials, Dunsfold and Filton, 1967-70.
XV280 ff 29-4-67, A.W. Bedford. Employed on miscellaneous trials by manufacturers, Rolls-Royce (Bristol), A&AEE, RAE, etc.
XV281 ff 14-7-67, D.M.S. Simpson. Manufacturer's trials at Dunsfold and Filton, 1967-68. To RAE for all-weather trials, and later for ski-ramp launch trials, circa 1977. Boscombe Down, 1981.

5 Allocation of production aircraft

Hawker Siddeley Harrier GR Mark 1 First production batch of 60 aircraft, *XV738-XV762, XV776-XV810,* ordered in 1966 to meet Air Staff Requirement 384. Bristol Siddeley Pegasus 6 (Mark 101) vectored-thrust turbofan rated at 19,000-lb thrust with water injection.

XV738 ff 28-12-67; employed on engine trials by Rolls-Royce Bristol from 16-4-68; deld to No 3 (F) Sqn, 10-75.

XV739 ff 21-4-68; trials at Boscombe Down from 16-4-68; deld to No 1 (F) Sqn, Wittering, 15-3-73; crashed in Cyprus following pitch-down in vertical climb from hover; pilot ejected but broke his leg, 24-9-73.

XV740 ff 3-7-68; trials at Boscombe Down from 22-7-68; deld to No 4 (F) Sqn, Wildenrath, 1-75.

XV741 ff 5-8-68; trials at Boscombe Down from 16-8-68; deld to No 4 (F) Sqn, Wildenrath, 7-72; No 3 (F) Sqn, 9-72.

XV742 ff 13-9-68; retained by HSA for trials and TIs; temporarily painted in US Marine Corps markings for demonstrations.

XV743 ff 19-12-68; crashed at Dunsfold, 27-1-69. Aircraft entered uncontrollable roll during turn in transition following VTO; US Marine Corps pilot killed.

XV744 ff 5-3-69, John Farley; deld to No 1 (F) Sqn, at Boscombe Down preparatory for Trans-Atlantic Air Race; Harrier Conversion Unit, Wittering, 9-70; No 1 (F) Sqn and No 233 OCU, 11-70 to date.

XV745 ff 25-3-69; deld No 1 (F) Sqn, Wittering, 3-70; Harrier Conversion Unit, Wittering, 9-70; No 233 OCU, Wittering, 11-70. *Converted to Harrier GR Mark 3.* Written off after collision with *XV754* at Wittering, 19-1-76; pilot did not eject and was killed.

XV746 ff 3-4-69; deld to No 1 (F) Sqn, Wittering, 18-4-69; No 233 OCU, Wittering, 12-75. Aircraft crashed into mountainside near Tromso, Norway, 12-3-76; pilot believed to have ejected but was killed.

XV747 ff 18-4-69, Tony Hawkes; deld Harrier Conversion Unit, Wittering, 3-70; No 233 OCU, 11-70; No 4 (F) Sqn, 4-75.

XV748 ff 30-4-69, Tony Hawkes; deld Harrier Conversion Unit, Wittering, 3-70; No 1 (F) Sqn, 9-72; taken on temporary loan by HSA for Lugano Air Show, 19-6-73 to 26-6-73; thereafter held by No 233 OCU. *Converted to Harrier GR Mark 3.*

XV749 ff 17-4-69; deld No 1 (F) Sqn, 3-70; aircraft crashed while flying over the Wash following bird-strike, 26-4-72; pilot ejected safely.

XV750 ff 13-5-69; deld to RAF, 28-5-69; to No 1 (F) Sqn, Wittering, 3-70; aircraft damaged by bird-strike during STO at Wittering, 6-4-70; repaired and deld to No 20 (F) Sqn, Wildenrath, 4-72. Aircraft crashed in Holland, 6-9-73, following engine failure; pilot ejected safely but with minor injuries.

XV751 ff 28-5-69, John Farley; deld to RAF, 2-7-69. Aircraft suffered Cat 4 damage at West Raynham, 5-8-69; aircraft entered rapid descent in decelerating transition and crashed inverted in cabbage field. Was returned to HSA for repair; ff 22-10-70, Andy Jones; deld to RAF 24-2-71; No 233 OCU, 4-71. *Converted to Harrier GR Mark 3,* 3-73. Deld No 20 (F) Sqn, 4-73; No 3 (F) Sqn, 2-77; No 1 (F) Sqn, 2-79.

XV752 ff 30-5-69 Duncan Simpson; deld to RAF, 27-8-69; to Harrier Conversion Unit, Wittering, 3-70; to No 1 (F) Sqn, 11-72. *Converted to Harrier GR Mark 3.* No 1 (F) Sqn, 11-73; No 233 OCU, 8-77.

XV753 ff 1-7-69, Tony Hawkes; deld to RAF, 15-8-69; No 1 (F) Sqn, Wittering, 3-70; No 233 OCU, 9-72. *Converted to Harrier GR Mark 3.* No 233 OCU, 11-73; No 1 (F) Sqn, 4-76; No 233 OCU, 8-77.

XV754 ff 4-7-69; deld to RAF, 13-8-69; No 1 (F) Sqn, 3-70 *Converted to Harrier GR Mark 3.* Written off after mid-air collision with *XV745* at Wittering, 19-1-76; pilot did not eject and was killed.

XV755 ff 15-8-69, Don Riches; deld to RAF, 18-9-69; to No 233 OCU, 1970; to No 1 (F) Sqn, 8-72. *Converted to Harrier GR Mark 3.*

XV756 ff 20-8-69, Don Riches; deld to RAF, 19-9-69; to No 233 OCU, 1970; to No 1 (F) Sqn, 10-73. *Converted to Harrier GR Mark 3.*

XV757 ff 29-8-69, Barry Tonkinson; deld to RAF, 19-9-69; service with No 233 OCU and No 1 (F) Sqn, Wittering, 3-70 to date. *Converted to Harrier GR Mark 3.*

XV758 ff 6-9-69, Don Riches; deld to RAF, 30-1-70. Demonstrated aboard HMS *Bulwark,* 17/18-9-69; No 233 OCU, 1970. *Converted to Harrier GR Mark 1A.* Deld to No 3 (F) Sqn, Wildenrath, 6-74. Aircraft damaged Cat 4 after striking runway at Wildenrath following loss of power at 30 ft, 3-10-74; to Bitteswell for repair ff 20-10-77, Don Riches. *Converted to Harrier GR Mark 3.* Deld to No 3 (F) Sqn, 1-12-77.

XV759 ff 20-9-69, Barry Tonkinson; deld to RAF, 12-3-70. *Converted to Harrier GR Mark 1A.* Served with No 233 OCU and No 1 (F) Sqn, Wittering, 1970 to date.

XV760 ff 25-9-69, Barry Tonkinson; deld to RAF, 30-1-70. *Converted to Harrier GR Mark 1A.* Served with No 233 OCU, 1970 to date.

XV761 ff 14-2-70, Tony Hawkes, deld to RAF, 25-3-70. To No 233 OCU, 1970. *Converted to Harrier GR Mark 1A.* To No 3 (F) Sqn, Wildenrath, 1-73; to No 4 (F) Sqn, 2-74. *Converted to Harrier GR Mark 3.*

XV762 ff 8-10-69, Tony Hawkes; deld to RAF, 27-2-70. To No 233 OCU, 1970. *Converted to Harrier GR Mark 1A and later Mark 3.* Deld to No 1 (F) Sqn, 4-76; to No 233 OCU, 6-76. Aircraft taken on loan by manufacturers for demonstration to Chinese Delegation, Dunsfold, 12-78.

XV776 ff 26-2-70; deld to RAF, 3-4-70; to No 1 (F) Sqn, 4-70. *Converted to Harrier GR Mark 1A and later Mark 3.* Aircraft crashed when flying from Wittering at 33,000 ft following main engine bearing failure, 9-4-75; pilot ejected safely.

XV777 ff 13-3-70; deld to RAF, 1-5-70; to No 1 (F) Sqn, 5-70. Aircraft crashed at Wittering during decelerating transition to vertical landing, 1-5-72; pilot ejected safely.

XV778 ff 16-3-70, Tony Hawkes; deld to RAF, 15-4-70; aircraft demonstrated at Hanover Air Show, 24-4-70; No 1 (F) Sqn, 1970. *Converted to Harrier GR Mark 1A and later Mark 3.*

XV779 ff 26-3-70, Don Riches; deld to RAF, 29-5-70; No 1 (F) Sqn, 5-70; No 4 (F) Sqn, 7-70; No 20 (F) Sqn, 8-72. *Converted to Harrier GR Mark 1A and later 3.* to No 3 (F) Sqn, Wildenrath, 2-77.

XV780 ff 26-3-70; deld to RAF, 28-5-70; to No 1 (F) Sqn, 5-70; No 4 (F) Sqn, Wildenrath, 7-70. Aircraft crashed in Germany following bird strike, 27-6-72; pilot ejected safely.

XV781 ff 18-4-70, John Farley; deld to RAF, 29-5-70; No 1 (F) Sqn, 5-70; No 4 (F) Sqn, Wildenrath, 7-70; No 20 (F) Sqn, 8-72. *Converted to Harrier GR Mark 1A.* To No 3 (F) Sqn, 5-73. *Converted to Harrier GR Mark 3.*

XV782 ff 19-5-70, Tony Hawkes; deld to RAF, 15-7-70; No 1 (F) Sqn, 7-70; No 4 (F) Sqn, 8-70. *Converted to Harrier GR Mark 1A and later Mark 3.*

XV783 ff 9-6-70, Tony Hawkes; deld to RAF, 25-6-70; No 4 (F) Sqn, 8-70; *Converted to Harrier GR Mark 1A.* No 20 (F) Sqn, 4-74. *Converted to Harrier GR Mark 3.* No 4 (F) Sqn, 2-77.

XV784 ff 2-7-70, Barry Tonkinson; deld to RAF, 14-8-70; No 4 (F) Sqn, 8-70. *Converted to Harrier GR Mark 1A and later Mark 3.*

XV785 ff 29-7-70; deld to RAF, 25-9-70; No 233 OCU, 9-70; No 20 (F) Sqn, 11-70; No 3 Sqn, 7-72; No 4 (F) Sqn, 9-72. *Converted to Harrier GR Mark 1A and later Mark 3.*

XV786 ff 20-8-70, Tony Hawkes, deld to RAF, 29-9-70; No 233 OCU, 9-70; No 20 (F) Sqn, Wildenrath, 12-70. *Converted to Harrier GR Mark 1A.* No 4 (F) Sqn, 4-74. *Converted to Harrier GR Mark 3.* No 1 (F) Sqn, 10-77; to Belize, 4-78; No 4 (F) Sqn, Belize, 10-78.

XV787 ff 9-9-70, Tony Hawkes; deld to RAF, 11-11-70; No 1 (F) Sqn, 11-70. *Converted to Harrier GR Mark 1A and later Mark 3.*

XV788 ff 7-4-70; deld to RAF, 7-5-70; No 1 (F) Sqn, 11-70. *Converted to Harrier GR Mark 3.* Aircraft crashed at Belize, 1-12-75, after pilot experienced engine surge at 450 knots at 1,000 ft; pilot ejected safely.

XV789 ff 21-4-70, Barry Tonkinson; deld to RAF, 23-6-70; No 1 (F) Sqn, 6-70; No 4 (F) Sqn, Wildenrath, 8-70. *Converted to Harrier GR Mark 3.* Aircraft taken on loan by manufacturers for 1978 SBAC Farnborough Display.

XV790 ff 4-6-70, Don Riches; deld to RAF, 30-6-70; No 4 (F) Sqn, 8-70; No 20 (F) Sqn, 8-72. *Converted to Harrier GR Mark 3.* No 4 (F) Sqn, 2-77.

XV791 ff 13-5-70; deld to RAF, 9-6-70; No 1 (F) Sqn, 6-70; No 4 (F) Sqn, 7-70; No 20 (F) Sqn, 8-72. Aircraft crashed at Wildenrath, 9-7-73, following bird-strike; pilot ejected safely.

XV792 ff 22-5-70, Tony Hawkes; deld to RAF, 17-6-70; No 1 (F) Sqn, 6-70. Aircraft crashed at Gardemoen, Oslo, 21-11-71, and suffered Cat 4 damage; pilot suffered loss of directional control during landing on snow and the aircraft turned on to its back. Returned to HSA for repair on 31-12-71. ff 16-8-73, Duncan Simpson; to No 3 (F) Sqn, 2-11-73 as Harrier *GR Mark 1A.* No 4 (F) Sqn, 9-77; No 3 (F) Sqn, 10-77.

XV793 ff 2-7-70, Barry Tonkinson; deld to RAF, 27-8-70; No 233 OCU, 1970. *Converted to Harrier GR Mark 1A and later Mark 3.* No 20 (F) Sqn, 3-73; No 3 (F) Sqn, 2-77; No 1 (F)

Sqn, 8-78; No 4 (F) Sqn, 10-78 (Belize).
XV794 ff 12-6-70; deld to RAF, 28-7-70; No 4 (F) Sqn, 8-70. Aircraft crashed at Wildenrath, 4-5-72, following bird-strikes and ingestion; pilot ejected safely.
XV795 ff 24-7-70, Duncan Simpson; deld to RAF, 15-9-70; No 1 (F) Sqn, 9-70. *Converted to Harrier GR Mark 1A and later Mark 3.* No 233 OCU, 8-77; No 1 (F) Sqn, 8-78; No 4 (F) Sqn, Belize, 10-78; No 3 (F) Sqn, Wildenrath, 2-79.
XV796 ff 6-8-70; deld to RAF, 28-8-70; No 1 (F) Sqn, 9-70. Aircraft crashed after flame-out at Ouston, Northumberland, 6-10-70; pilot ejected safely.
XV797 ff 3-9-70; deld to RAF, 30-9-70; No 233 OCU, 11-70; No 20 (F) Sqn, 12-70; No 4 (F) Sqn, 8-72. *Converted to Harrier GR Mark 1A.* Aircraft crashed in Holland in uncontrollable dive, 23-1-74; pilot ejected but killed following parachute harness failure.
XV798 ff 15-9-70; deld to RAF, 28-10-70; No 20 (F) Sqn, 1970. Aircraft crashed on approach to vertical landing at Wildenrath, 23-4-71; pilot ejected safely through trees.
XV799 ff 17-9-70; deld to RAF, 29-10-70; No 233 OCU, 11-70. Pilot flew into high ground in Scotland, 13-9-72, and was killed; aircraft destroyed.
XV800 ff 28-9-70; deld to RAF, 20-11-70; No 20 (F) Sqn, 1-71. *Converted to Harrier GR Mark 1A and later Mark 3.* No 4 (F) Sqn, 4-74. Aircraft crashed after flame-out at 50 ft after take-off at Wildenrath, 16-5-75; pilot ejected safely.
XV801 ff 20-11-70, Andy Jones; deld to RAF (first Harrier delivered direct to Germany), No 20 (F) Sqn, 11-1-71. *Converted to Harrier GR Mark 1A and later Mark 3.* No 4 (F) Sqn, 3-73; No 20 (F) Sqn, 4-74; No 3 (F) Sqn, 2-77.
XV802 ff 25-11-70; deld to No 20 (F) Sqn, 1-71; aircraft flew into wooded area and crashed, Stadtoldendorf, 21-3-72; pilot killed.
XV803 ff 12-5-71; deld to No 1 (F) Sqn, 7-71; aircraft crashed at Wittering following nozzle runaway, 3-8-71; USAF pilot killed as seat rocket pins were not removed.
XV804 ff 13-11-70; deld to No 233 OCU, 2-71. *Converted to Harrier GR Mark 1A and later Mark 3.*
XV805 ff 11-5-71; deld to No 20 (F) Sqn, 22-6-71. *Converted to Harrier GR Mark 1A.* Aircraft crashed at Wildenrath after bird-strike, 30-7-73; pilot, Major Gibson, USMC, ejected safely at 500 ft.
XV806 ff 21-4-71; deld to No 20 (F) Sqn, 15-6-71. *Converted to Harrier GR Mark 1A and later Mark 3.* No 4 (F) Sqn, 4-74.
XV807 ff 16-9-71; deld to No 233 OCU, 20-10-71. *Converted to Harrier GR Mark 1A and later 3.* No 3 (F) Sqn, 7-75; No 233 OCU, 7-77.
XV808 ff 23-1-71; deld to No 4 (F) Sqn, 26-3-71; No 20 (F) Sqn, 7-72. *Converted to Harrier GR Mark 1A and later Mark 3.* No 3 (F) Sqn, 2-77.
XV809 ff 9-3-71; deld to No 20 (F) Sqn, 2-4-71; No 4 (F) Sqn, 8-72. *Converted to Harrier GR Mark 1A and later Mark 3.*
XV810 ff 25-3-71; deld to No 20 (F) Sqn, 26-4-71. *Converted to Harrier GR Mark 1A and later Mark 3.* No 4 (F) Sqn, 2-77.

Hawker Siddeley Harrier GR Mark 1 One replacement aircraft, *XW630.* Standard of preparation as for first production batch.
XW630 ff 10-6-71; deld to No 20 (F) Sqn, 6-71; No 4 (F) Sqn, 8-72. *Converted to Harrier GR Mark 1A and later Mark 3.* No 20 (F) Sqn, 6-74; No 3 (F) Sqn, 2-77.

Hawker Siddeley Harrier GR Mark 1 Second production batch of 17 aircraft, *XW916-XW924, XW763-XW770* (batch flown in this order). Rolls-Royce (Bristol) Pegasus 6 (Mark 101) engines.
XW916 ff 11-6-71; deld to No 20 (F) Sqn, 11-71; No 3 (F) Sqn, 1-72. *Converted to Harrier GR Mark 1A and later Mark 3.* No 20 (F) Sqn, 8-73; No 4 (F) Sqn, 2-77.
XW917 ff 30-6-71; deld to No 4 (F) Sqn, 8-71; No 3 (F) Sqn, 2-72. *Converted to Harrier GR Mark 1A and later Mark 3.*
XW918 ff 10-7-71; deld to No 4 (F) Sqn, 7-71; No 3 (F) Sqn, 1-72. Aircraft struck farm building and crashed during demonstration at Wildenrath, 12-1-72; pilot killed.
XW919 ff 23-7-71; deld to No 233 OCU, 9-71; No 1 (F) Sqn, 11-72. Aircraft badly damaged in accident at Lyneham, 28-6-73, but repaired and *converted to Harrier GR Mark 3.* No 1 (F) Sqn, 4-76; No 4 (F) Sqn, Belize, 10-78.
XW920 ff 2-9-71; deld to No 20 (F) Sqn, 10-71; No 3 (F) Sqn, 1-72. Aircraft crashed in Sardinia, 21-6-72, following fuel system failure due to shearing of low pressure governor shaft; pilot ejected safely.
XW921 ff 17-9-71; deld to No 20 (F) Sqn, 10-71; No 3 (F) Sqn, 1-72; No 4 (F) Sqn, 7-72. *Converted to Harrier GR Mark 1A and later*

Mark 3. No 4 (F) Sqn, Belize, 1-79.
XW922 ff 26-8-71; deld to No 1 (F) Sqn, 10-71; No 233 OCU, 11-72. *Converted to Harrier GR Mark 1A and later Mark 3.* No 1 (F) Sqn, 5-76; No 233 OCU, 6-76.
XW923 ff 8-9-71; deld to No 1 (F) Sqn, 10-71. *Converted to Harrier GR Mark 1A and later Mark 3.* Served with No 233 OCU and No 1 (F) Sqn, 12-76 to date.
XW924 ff 15-9-71; deld to No 20 (F) Sqn, 10-71; No 4 (F) Sqn, 8-72. *Converted to Harrier GR Mark 1A and later Mark 3.* No 4 (F) Sqn, Belize, 4-79.

XW763 ff 30-9-71; deld to No 4 (F) Sqn, 11-71; No 3 (F) Sqn, 9-73 to date. *Converted to Harrier GR Mark 1A and later Mark 3.*
XW764 ff 14-10-71; deld to No 4 (F) Sqn, 11-71; No 3 (F) Sqn, 1-72. Aircraft damaged (Cat 3) but repaired, 7-75, and *deld as Harrier GR Mark 3.*
XW765 ff 1-11-71; deld to No 20 (F) Sqn, 12-71; No 3 (F) Sqn, 2-72 to date. *Converted to Harrier GR Mark 1A and later Mark 3.*
XW766 ff 1-11-71; deld to No 20 (F) Sqn, 12-71; No 3 (F) Sqn, 2-72 to date (Aircraft damaged (Cat 3, 10-72) but repaired.) *Converted to Harrier GR Mark 1A and later Mark 3.*
XW767 ff 24-11-71; deld to No 20 (F) Sqn, 12-71; No 3 (F) Sqn, 2-72. *Converted to Harrier GR Mark 1A and later Mark 3.* Served with No 1 (F) Sqn and No 233 OCU, 2-76 to date.
XW768 ff 9-12-71; deld to No 3 (F) Sqn, 4-72; No 20 (F) Sqn, 9-72. *Converted to Harrier GR Mark 1A and later Mark 3.* No 4 (F) Sqn, 2-77.
XW769 ff 10-1-72; deld to No 3 (F) Sqn, 3-72. *Converted to Harrier GR Mark 1A and later Mark 3.* Served with No 1 (F) Sqn and No 233 OCU, 10-76 to date.
XW770 ff 4-1-72. Stored until 9-6-72; deld to No 3 (F) Sqn, 1-73. *Converted to Harrier GR Mark 3.* Aircraft crashed after flame-out at 600 ft, Wildenrath, 6-7-76; pilot ejected safely.

Hawker Siddeley Harrier T Mark 2 Two development two-seat aircraft, *XW174* and *XW175,* ordered in 1967 to conform to Air Staff Requirement 386. Rolls-Royce (Bristol) Pegasus 6 (Mark 101) engines rated at 19,000 lb thrust.
XW174 ff 24-4-69, Duncan Simpson. Retained for development flight trials, HSA, Dunsfold. Aircraft crashed, 4-6-69, at Larkhill following fuel system fault. Pilot, Duncan Simpson, ejected but injured.
XW175 ff 14-7-69. Aircraft retained for development flight trials (eg, weathercock stability investigation, etc), HSA, Dunsfold.

Hawker Siddeley Harrier T Mark 2 and 2A. First production batch of 12 two-seat aircraft, *XW264-XW272, XW925-XW927,* ordered in 1967 to conform to Air Staff Requirement 386. Rolls-Royce (Bristol) Pegasus 6 (Mark 101) engines rated at 19,000 lb thrust. First ten delivered as T Mark 2s, remaining two as T Mark 2As.
XW264 ff 3-10-69. Not delivered to RAF but retained by HSA for store and weapon clearance. Aircraft written off after force landing at Boscombe Down, 11-7-70, following fuel system fault; aircraft burned but pilot, Barry Tonkinson, safe.
XW265 ff 28-2-70. Retained for CA Release clearance trials. Accepted by MoD, 21-5-70.
XW266 ff 1-2-70; deld to Harrier Conversion Unit, Wittering, 28-7-70; No 233 OCU, 11-70. *Converted to Harrier T Mark 2A and later Mark 4.* No 1 (F) Sqn, 6-77.
XW267 ff 3-7-70; deld to Harrier Conversion Unit, Wittering, 28-8-70; No 233 OCU, 11-70. *Converted to Harrier T Mark 2A and later Mark 4.*
XW268 ff 5-11-70; deld to No 233 OCU, 7-1-71. *Converted to Harrier T Mark 2A and later Mark 4.* No 1 (F) Sqn, 5-77, No 233 OCU, 7-77.
XW269 ff 12-2-71; deld to No 4 (F) Sqn, 1-4-71 to date (1-81). *Converted to Harrier T Mark 2A and later Mark 4.*
XW270 ff 24-11-70; deld to No 233 OCU, 10-3-71. *Converted to Harrier T Mark 2A and later Mark 4.* No 1 (F) Sqn, 8-76; No 233 OCU, 9-76.
XW271 ff 26-5-71; deld to No 1 (F) Sqn, 20-7-71. *Converted to Harrier T Mark 2A and later Mark 4.* Served with No 1 (F) Sqn and No 233 OCU, from 8-76 to date.
XW272 ff 4-5-71; deld to No 20 (F) Sqn, 10-6-71. *Converted to Harrier T Mark 2A and later Mark 4.* No 4 (F) Sqn, 2-77.

XW925 ff 26-8-71; deld to No 233 OCU, 1-10-71. *Converted to Harrier T Mark 2A and later Mark 4.* No 1 (F) Sqn, 5-76.
XW926 ff 6-4-72; deld as first Harrier T Mark 2A, No 3 (F) Sqn, 11-5-72. *Converted to Harrier T Mark 4.* No 233 OCU, 10-75.

XW927 ff 8-6-72; deld as second Harrier T Mark 2A, No 233 OCU, 28-7-72. *Converted to Harrier T Mark 4.*

Hawker Siddeley AV-8A Harrier Mark 50
First production batch of 12 aircraft (BuAer Nos *158384* to *158395*) purchased by US Navy Department for US Marine Corps. Funding voted during 1970 for FY 1971. Aircraft delivered with Rolls-Royce (Bristol) Pegasus Mark 102 engines but ten aircraft retroactively fitted withPegasus Mark 103 engines.
159384 ff 20-11-70; deld 19-1-71. Served with VMA-513.
158385 ff 24-12-70; deld 5-2-71. Served with VMA-513 and later VMA-231.
158386 ff 3-2-71; deld 15-3-71. Served with VMA-513. Aircraft failed to recover from dive attack, Chesapeake Bay, 18-6-71; pilot killed.
158387 ff 16-2-71; deld 12-3-71. Served with VMA-513.
158388 ff 16-4-71; deld 11-5-71. Served with VMA-513. Aircraft crashed at Beaufort after bird-strike, 27-3-73; pilot ejected safely.
158389 ff 7-4-71; deld 30-4-71. Served with VMA-513.
158390 ff 20-5-71; deld 10-7-71. Served with VMA-513 and later VMA-231.
158391 ff 7-5-71; deld 28-5-71. Served with VMA-513.
158392 ff 19-6-71; deld 13-7-71. Served with VMA-513.
158393 ff 28-10-71; deld 29-11-71. Served with VMA-513.
158394 ff 23-12-71; deld 31-1-72. *Aircraft modified to become first McDonnell Douglas YAV-8B, 1974-75.*
158395 ff 18-2-72; deld 21-3-72 (airlifted). *Aircraft modified to become second McDonnell Douglas YAV-8B, 1974-75.*

Hawker Siddeley AV-8A Harrier Mark 50
Second production batch of 18 aircraft (BuAer Nos *158694* to *158711*), purchased by US Navy Department for US Marine Corps. Funding voted during 1971 for FY 1972. All aircraft delivered with Rolls-Royce (Bristol) Pegasus Mark 103 engines. Aircraft retained Ferranti 541 inertial nav-attack system.
158694 aa 12-4-72; deld 4-5-72. Served with VMA-513.
158695 ff 11-5-72; deld 31-5-72. Served with VMA-513.
158696 ff 6-6-72; deld 13-7-72. Served with VMA-513.
158697 ff 23-6-72; deld 10-7-72. Served with VMA-513.
158698 ff 18-7-72; deld 19-9-72. Served with VMA-513 abroad USS *Guam* (LPH-9).
158699 ff 22-8-72; deld 22-9-72. Served with VMA-513 aboard USS *Guam* (LPH-9).
158700 ff 8-8-72; deld 6-9-72. Served with VMA-513.
158701 ff 30-8-72; deld 7-9-72 (airlifted). Served with VMA-513.
158702 ff 18-9-72; deld 11-10-72. Served with VMA-513.
158703 ff 21-9-72; deld 6-10-72.
158704 ff 20-10-72; deld 11-12-72. Served with VMA-542.
158705 ff 6-10-72; deld 26-10-72 (airlifted). Served with VMA-542.
158706 ff 16-10-72; deld 7-12-72. Served with VMA-513 aboard USS *Guam* (LPH-9).
158707 ff 27-10-72; deld 29-11-72 (airlifted). Served with VMA-542.
158708 ff 17-11-72; deld 28-12-72. Served with VMA-542 and later VMA-231. Aircraft crashed after engine failure at night off Kadena, Okinawa, 29-11-77, pilot ejected safely.
158709 ff 18-11-72. Served with VMA-513 and later VMA-542. Aircraft crashed during landing at Jacksonville, 10-1-76; pilot ejected safely.
158710 ff 22-11-72; deld 2-1-73. Served with VMA-513 aboard USS *Guam* (LPH-9).
158711 ff 27-11-72; deld 19-12-72. Served with VMA-542.

Hawker Siddeley AV-8A Harrier Mark 50
Third production batch of 30 aircraft (BuAer Nos *158948* to *158977*), purchased by US Navy Department for US Marine Crops. Funding voted during 1972 for FY 1973. All aircraft delivered with Rolls-Royce (Bristol) Pegasus Mark 103 engines. First 29 aircraft retained Ferranti 541 inertial nav-attack system; 30th aircraft equipped with Baseline system.
158948 ff 29-12-72; deld 2-2-73. Served with VMA-542. Aircraft crashed on landing, 5-6-74; pilot ejected but was killed.
158949 ff 28-12-72; deld 22-1-73. Served with VMA-542.
158950 ff 17-1-73; deld 20-2-73. Served with VMA-542.
158951 ff 13-2-73; deld 13-3-73. Served with VMA-542.
158952 ff 6-2-73; deld 8-3-73. Served with VMA-542. Aircraft crashed, 2-78, following engine failure; pilot ejected but slightly hurt.

158953 ff 6-3-73; deld 27-3-73. Served with VMA-542. Aircraft crashed off Cherry Point, 27-7-77; pilot killed.
158954 ff 13-3-73; deld 6-4-73. Served with VMA-542.
158955 ff 28-3-73; deld 17-4-73. Served with VMA-542.
158956 ff 18-4-73; deld 18-4-73. Served with VMA-542.
158957 ff 18-5-73; deld 9-7-73. Served with VMA-542. Aircraft crashed at Cherry Point, 27-8-76, following engine failure; pilot ejected safely.
158958 ff 11-5-73; deld 28-6-73. Served with VMA-542.
158959 ff 25-5-73; deld 5-7-73. Served with VMA-542.
158960 ff 13-6-73; deld 17-7-73. Served with VMA-542.
158961 ff 2-7-73; deld 27-7-73. Served with VMA-542.
158962 ff 3-7-73; deld 31-7-73. Served with VMA-542.
158963 ff 24-7-73; deld 30-8-73. Served with VMA-542.
158964 ff 27-7-73; deld 7-9-73. Served with VMA-542.
158965 ff 7-8-73; deld 30-8-73.
158966 ff 23-8-73; deld 21-9-73.
158967 ff 18-9-73; deld 4-10-73. Served with VMA-542. Engine failed at high altitude and failed to re-light, 11-2-77; aircraft crashed but pilot ejected safely.
158968 ff 21-9-73; deld 2-11-73. Served with VMA-513.
158969 ff 26-9-73; deld 26-10-73. Served with VMA-513.
158970 ff 1-11-73; deld 30-11-73. Served with VMA-513. Aircraft flew into mountainside at Las Vegas during dive bombing, 6-9-77; pilot killed.
158971 ff 22-10-73; deld 9-11-73. Served with VMA-513. Aircraft crashed from hover during demonstration, Beaufort, 27-7-74; pilot injured.
158972 ff 7-11-73; deld 28-11-73. Served with VMA-513.
158973 ff 16-11-73; deld 7-12-73. Served with VMA-513.
158974 ff 21-11-73; deld 20-12-73. Served with VMA-513. Aircraft ran out of fuel and crashed, Iwakuni, 30-8-76; pilot ejected safely.
158975 ff 11-12-73; deld, 22-1-74. Served with VMA-513.
158976 ff 7-12-73; deld, 4-1-74. Served with VMA-513.
158977 ff 7-12-73; deld, 7-2-74, after Baseline system trials. Trials at Patuxent River, 1974.

Hawker Siddeley AV-8A Harrier Mark 50
Fourth production batch of 30 aircraft (BuAer Nos *159230* to *159259*), purchased by US Navy Department for US Marine Corps. Funding voted during 1973 for FY 1974. All aircraft delivered with Rolls-Royce (Bristol) Pegasus 103 engines; aircraft equipped with Baseline system.
159230 ff 2-1-74; deld 25-1-74. Served with VMA-513. Aircraft crashed into sea off Iwakuni, 6-12-76; pilot killed.
159231 ff 19-12-73; deld 25-1-74. Served with VMA-513.
159232 ff 11-1-74; deld 13-2-74. Served with VMA-513.
159233 ff 20-3-74; deld 5-4-74.
159234 ff 20-3-74; deld 5-6-74.
159235 ff 21-3-74; deld 21-6-74. Served with VMA-231. Aircraft crashed during vertical landing, Cherry Point, 13-2-75; pilot killed.
159236 ff 22-3-74; deld 19-6-74. Served with VMA-231. Aircraft flew into the ground near Beaufort, 4-7-75; pilot did not eject and was killed.
159237 ff 3-4-74; deld 10-7-74. Served with VMA-231. Aircraft crashed into sea after engine failure at 600 feet, Mayport, 16-6-76; pilot ejected safely.
159238 ff 3-4-74; deld 26-6-74. Served with VMA-231.
159239 ff 11-4-74; deld 30-7-74. Served with VMA-231.
159240 ff 26-4-74; deld 23-7-74. Served with VMA-231.
159241 ff 3-5-74; deld 29-8-74. Served with VMA-231.
159242 ff 24-5-74; deld 15-8-74. Served with VMA-231.
159243 ff 19-6-74; deld 13-9-74. Served with VMA-231.
159244 ff 26-6-74; deld 20-9-74. Served with VMA-231. Aircraft crashed after engine failure at low level, Beaufort, 4-7-75; pilot ejected safely.
159245 ff 16-7-74; deld 7-8-74. Served with VMA-231. Aircraft crashed during landing at Cherry Point, 9-10-74; pilot killed.
159246 ff 23-7-74; deld 22-8-74. Served with VMA-231.
159247 ff 25-7-74; deld 5-9-74. Served with VMA-231.

159248 ff 21-8-74; deld 27-9-74. Served with VMA-231.
159249 ff 10-9-74; deld 4-10-74. Served with VMA-231.
159250 ff 23-9-74; deld 22-10-74. Served with VMA-231. Aircraft crashed into the sea during rocket attack while flying from USS *Saratoga* off Cape Hatteras, North Carolina, 12-7-77; pilot killed.
159251 ff 8-10-74; deld 6-11-74. Served with VMA-231.
159252 ff 25-10-74; deld 18-11-74. Served with VMA-231.
159253 ff 8-11-74; deld 18-12-74.
159254 ff 27-11-74; deld 23-12-74.
159255 ff 13-12-74; deld 13-1-75.
159256 ff 4-12-74; deld 6-1-75. Served with VMA(T)-203.
159257 ff 19-12-74; deld 20-1-75. Served with VMA(T)-203.
159258 ff 7-1-75; deld 30-6-76.
159259 ff 24-1-75; deld 3-3-75.

Hawker Siddeley AV-8A Harrier Mark 50 Fifth production batch of 12 aircraft (BuAer Nos *159366* to *159377*), purchased by US Navy Department for US Marine Corps under Contract No K/A10a/15. Funding voted during 1974 for FY 1975. All aircraft delivered with Rolls-Royce (Bristol) Pegasus 103 engines; aircraft equipped with Baseline system.
159366 ff 25-3-75; deld 20-6-75. Served with VMA(T)-203.
159367 ff 25-4-75; deld 27-6-75. Served with VMA(T)-203.
159368 ff 13-5-75; deld 30-6-75.
159369 ff 24-6-75; deld 25-7-75.
159370 ff 5-8-75. Served with VMA(T)-203.
159371 ff 20-8-75; deld 17-10-75.
159372 ff 12-9-75; deld 28-10-75. Served with VMA(T)-203. Aircraft crashed during landing transition, 6-4-77; pilot killed.
159373 ff 2-7-76; deld 4-8-76.
159374 ff 24-8-76; deld 8-10-76.
159375 ff 6-11-75; deld 5-1-76. Served with VMA(T)-203.
159376 First flight and delivery details not known.
159377 ff 12-12-75; deld 29-1-76. Served with VMA(T)-203. Aircraft crashed during pilot's first transition, 19-3-77; pilot ejected safely.

Hawker Siddeley TAV-8A Harrier T Mark 54 Production batch of eight two-seaters (BuAer Nos *159378* to *159385*), purchased by US Navy Department for US Marine Corps under Contract No K/A10a/15. Funding voted during 1975 for FY 1975-76.
159378 ff 16-7-75; deld 1-10-75. Served with VMA(T)-203.
159379 ff 17-10-75; deld 16-1-76. Served with VMA(T)-203.
159380 ff 12-12-75; deld 6-2-76. Served with VMA(T)-203.
159381 ff 19-3-76; deld 12-4-76. Served with VMA(T)-203. Aircraft crashed during landing transition and overturned, 19-4-77; both pilots unhurt.
159382 ff 10-8-76; deld 16-9-76. Served with VMA(T)-203.
159383 ff 4-5-76; deld 28-6-76. Served with VMA(T)-203.
159384 First flight and delivery details not known.
159385 ff 7-10-76; delivery details not known. Served with VMA(T)-203.

Hawker Siddeley Harrier Mark 52 Single two-seat demonstration aircraft, *G-VTOL*, built as private venture and owned by manufacturers. ff 16-9-71. Demonstration flights at home and overseas. Powered in turn by Rolls-Royce (Bristol) Pegasus 102 and 103 engines. Also registered *ZA250.*

Hawker Siddeley Harrier T Mark 4 Production batch of two aircraft, *XW933* and *XW934* ordered in 1972, and delivered with Rolls-Royce (Bristol) Pegasus 103 engines.
XW933 ff 4-5-73; deld to No 20 (F) Sqn, 22-8-73; Nos 3 (F) Sqn, 1-75. (First Harrier delivered new to RAF as T Mark 4.)
XW934 ff 16-10-73; deld to No 1 (F) Sqn, 21-12-73; A&AEE, Boscombe Down, 4-74. Served with No 1 (F) Sqn and No 233 OCU from 7-74 to date.

Hawker Siddeley Harrier GR Mark 3 Production batch of 12 aircraft, *XZ128-XZ139*, ordered during 1974 under Contract No KA/9a/31 for delivery during 1975-76. Powered by Rolls-Royce (Bristol) Pegasus 11 (Mark 103) engines rated at 21,500 lb thrust.
XZ128 ff 9-1-76; deld to No 233 OCU, 15-3-76; No 1 (F) Sqn, 5-76 (to Belize, 4-78). (First Harrier to be built and delivered as GR Mark 3.)
XZ129 ff 24-2-76; deld to No 233 OCU, 6-4-76; No 1 (F) Sqn, 6-76.

XZ130 ff 24-2-76; deld to No 3 (F) Sqn, 7-4-76; No 20 (F) Sqn, 6-76; No 3 (F) Sqn, 1-77; No 4 (F) Sqn, 2-77; No 1 (F) Sqn, 7-78.
XZ131 ff 5-4-76; deld to No 4 (F) Sqn, 30-4-76 to date.
XZ132 ff 15-4-76; deld to No 3 (F) Sqn, 14-5-76; No 1 (F) Sqn, 8-78; No 233 OCU, 10-78.
XZ133 ff 21-5-76; deld to No 233 OCU, 9-7-76; No 1 (F) Sqn, 2-77.
XZ134 ff 2-7-76; deld to No 3 (F) Sqn, 29-7-76.
XZ135 ff 25-8-76; deld to No 20 (F) Sqn, 2-11-76; No 3 (F) Sqn, 1-77; No 4 (F) Sqn, 3-77.
XZ136 ff 9-9-76; deld to No 1 (F) Sqn, 5-11-76.
XZ137 First flight date not known. Deld to No 4 (F) Sqn, 6-1-77.
XZ138 First flight date not known. Deld to No 3 (F) Sqn, 25-3-77.
XZ139 First flight date not known. Deld to No 3 (F) Sqn, 22-3-77.

Hawker Siddeley Harrier T Mark 4 Production batch of four two-seat aircraft, *XZ145-XZ147* and *XZ445*, ordered during 1975 for delivery in 1976. Powered by Rolls-Royce (Bristol) Pegasus 103 engines.
XZ145 ff 20-1-76; deld to No 3 (F) Sqn, 8-3-76.
XZ146 ff 4-8-76; deld to No 1 (F) Sqn, date unknown. Believed fitted with 'laser nose'.
XZ147 First flight date and delivery details not known. Served with No 1 (F) Sqn and No 233 OCU, 1-77 to date.

XZ445 First flight date and delivery details not known.

Hawker Siddeley AV-8A Matador (Harrier Mark 50) Six single-seat aircraft ordered by the Spanish Government via the United States of America during 1973. Aircraft were added to the end of the US Navy AV-8A Contract and therefore carried standard BuAer Nos *159557* to *159562*. Aircraft shipped to the USA, and thence shipped aboard Spanish carrier *Dédalo.*
159557 ff 26-2-76; deld 1-4-76. Served with *Escuadrilla 008* aboard carrier PH-01 *Dédalo,* Spanish Naval Air Arm, 1977 to date. *'008-1'*
159558 ff 14-4-76; deld 10-5-76. Served with *Escuadrilla 008* aboard carrier PH-01 *Dédalo,* Spanish Naval Air Arm, 1977 to date. *'008-2'*
159559 ff 11-6-76; deld 7-7-76. Served with *Escuadrilla 008* aboard carrier PH-01 *Dédalo,* Spanish Naval Air Arm, 1977 to date. *'008-3'*
159560 ff 18-9-75; deld 7-11-75. Served with *Escuadrilla 008* aboard carrier PH-01 *Dédalo,* Spanish Naval Air Arm, 1977 to date. *'008-4'*
159561 ff 24-10-75; deld 12-12-75. Aircraft crashed during training period at Whiteman, USA, 11-6-76; aircraft pitched-up during short take-off. Pilot ejected safely (Stencel ejection seat).
159562 ff 3-12-75; deld 22-1-76. Served with *Escuadrilla 008* aboard carrier PH-01 *Dédalo,* Spanish Naval Air Arm, 1977 to date. *'008-6'*

Hawker Siddeley TAV-8A Matador (Harrier Mark 54) Two two-seat aircraft ordered by the Spanish Government via the United States of America during 1973. Aircraft carried standard BuAer Nos *159563* and *159564.* Aircraft shipped to USA, and thence shipped aboard Spanish carrier *Dédalo.*
159563 ff 21-1-76; deld 25-2-76. Served with *Escuadrilla 008* aboard carrier PH-01 *Dédalo,* Spanish Naval Air Arm, 1977 to date. *'008-7'*
159564 ff 28-5-76; deld 5-7-76. Served with *Escuadrilla 008* aboard carrier PH-01 *Dédalo,* Spanish Naval Air Arm, 1977 to date. *'008-8'*

Hawker Siddeley AV-8S Matador (Harrier Mark 55) Four single-seat aircraft ordered by the Spanish Government via the United States of America during 1977. Aircraft carried standard BuAer Nos 161174 to 161177. Aircraft shipped direct to Spain. First flight and delivery dates not yet known. Carried markings *'008-9'* to *'008-12'*

Hawker Siddeley TAV-8S Matador (Harrier Mark 58) One two-seat aircraft ordered by the Spanish Government via the United States of America during 1977. Aircraft carried BuAer No *161178* and Spanish Naval Air Arm markings *'008-14'*, and shipped direct to Spain. First flight and delivery date not yet known.

British Aerospace Sea Harrier Three development (pre-production) aircraft, *XZ438-XZ440,* ordered from Hawker Siddeley Aviation Limited, Kingston-upon-Thames, in 1975, powered by 21,500-lb thrust Rolls-Royce (Bristol) Pegasus 104 vectored-thrust turbofans.
XZ438 ff 30-12-78, M.H.B. Snelling. Retained

by manufacturers at Dunsfold, 1978-81, for performance and handling trials.

XZ439 ff 30-3-79, M.H.B. Snelling. Store trials at Dunsfold and A&AEE, Boscombe Down. Present at sea trials, HMS *Hermes,* 1979.

XZ440 ff 6-6-79, M.H.B. Snelling. Handling and performance trials, Dunsfold, Boscombe Down, RAE and Rolls-Royce (Bristol). Present at sea trials, HMS *Hermes, 1979.*

British Aerospace Sea Harrier FRS Mark 1 Production batch of 31 aircraft, *XZ450-XZ460, XZ491-XZ500, ZA174-ZA177, ZA190-ZA195,* ordered from Hawker Siddeley Aviation Limited, Kingston-upon-Thames, in 1975, powered by 21,500-lb thrust Rolls-Royce (Bristol) Pegasus 104 vectored-thrust turbofans.

XZ450 ff 20-8-78, J.F. Farley. Was first Sea Harrier to fly on account of low instrumentation; SBAC Display, Farnborough, September 1978. Retained for trials at Dunsfold, 1978-81. No 800 Sqn. Shot down by ground fire over Goose Green, Falkland Is., 4-5-82; pilot killed.

XZ451 ff 25-5-79, H. Frick. Deld No 700A Sqn, FAA, Yeovilton, 18-6-79. Squadron number *100.* Transferred to No 899 Sqn. To Falkland Is., HMS *Invincible*, 5-82.

XZ452 ff 17-8-79, M.H.B. Snelling. Deld No 700A Sqn, FAA, Yeovilton, 12-10-79. Squadron Number *101.* Transferred to No 899 Sqn. Suffered Cat 3 damage, 5-3-80. Collided with *XZ453* in bad weather off Falkland Is., 6-5-82; pilot killed.

XZ453 ff 5-12-79, J.F. Farley. Deld No 700A Sqn, FAA, Yeovilton, 31-1-80. Squadron number *105.* Transferred to No 899 Sqn. Collided with *XZ452* in bad weather off Falkland Is., 6-5-82; pilot killed.

XZ454 ff 12-12-79, H. Frick. Deld No 800 Sqn, FAA, Yeovilton, 15-2-80. Squadron number *250.* Crashed into English Channel and lost, 1-12-80; pilot ejected safely.

XZ455 ff 9-10-79, H. Frick. Deld No 700A Sqn, FAA, Yeovilton, 9-11-79. Squadron number *102.* Transferred to No 899 Sqn. To Falkland Is., HMS *Hermes*, 5-82.

XZ456 ff 9-11-79, H. Frick. Deld No 700A Sqn, FAA, Yeovilton, 4-1-80. Squadron number *103.* Transferred to No 899 Sqn. Hit and damaged by ground fire near Port Stanley, Falkland Is., pilot ejected and rescued, 28-5-82.

XZ457 ff 15-12-79, J.F. Farley. Deld No 700A Sqn, FAA, Yeovilton, 31-1-80. Squadron number *104.* Transferred to No 899 Sqn. To Falkland Is., HMS *Hermes*, 5-82; destroyed two Mirage IIIs and one Skyhawk.

XZ458 ff 10-1-80, H. Frick. Deld No 800 Sqn, FAA, Yeovilton, 22-2-80. Squadron number *251.* Transferred to No 809 Sqn; to South Atlantic by air, 30-4-82.

XZ459 ff 21-3-80. H. Frick. Deld No 800 Sqn. FAA, Yeovilton, 15-5-80. Squadron number *252.* To Falkland Is., HMS *Hermes*, 5-82.

XZ460 ff 10-4-80, T. Scott. Deld No 800 Sqn, FAA, Yeovilton, 29-5-80. Squadron number *253.* To Falkland Is., HMS *Hermes*, 5-82.

XZ491 ff 20-6-80, H. Frick. Deld A&AEE, Boscombe Down, 18-8-80, for Service trials; returned to Dunsfold, 6-11-80, for manufacturer's trials. To South Atlantic by air with No 809 Sqn, 30-4-82.

XZ492 ff 25-10-80, J.F. Farley. Deld No 800 Sqn, FAA, Yeovilton, 29-12-80. Squadron number *254.* To Falkland Is., HMS *Hermes*, 5-82; destroyed one Skyhawk.

XZ493 ff 26-11-80, J.F. Farley. Deld No 801 Sqn, FAA, Yeovilton, 6-1-81. Squadron number *001.* To Falkland Is., HMS *Invincible*, 5-82.

XZ494 ff 24-10-80, J.F. Farley. Deld No 899 Sqn, FAA, Yeovilton, 5-12-80. Squadron number *106.* To Falkland Is., HMS *Hermes*, 5-82.

XZ495 ff 1-81. To Falkland Is., HMS *Invincible,* with No 801 Sqn, 5-82.

XZ496 ff 9-12-80, T. Scott. Deld No 801 Sqn, FAA, Yeovilton, 1-81. Squadron number *002.* To Falkland Is., HMS *Hermes*, with No 800 Sqn, 5-82; destroyed one Skyhawk.

XZ497 ff 2-5-82 T. Scott

XZ498 ff 20-2-81 H. Frick. To Falkland Is., HMS *Invincible,* with No 801 Sqn, 5-82.

XZ499 ff 12-6-81 T. Scott. To South Atlantic by air with No 809 Sqn, 30-4-82; destroyed one Mirage III.

XZ500 ff 28-5-81 T. Scott. To Falkland Is., HMS *Hermes,* with No 800 Sqn, 5-82; destroyed one Skyhawk.

ZA174 ff 15-9-81 H. Frick; 899 Sqn; hit by ground fire, Falkland Is., 28-5-82; pilot ejected and rescued.

ZA175 ff 28-10-81 J.F. Farley. To Falkland Is., HMS *Invincible*, with No 801 Sqn, 5-82.

ZA176 ff 25-11-81 H. Frick. To South Atlantic

by air with No 809 Sqn. 30-4-82; destroyed one Mirage III.
ZA177 ff 5-12-81 M.H.B. Snelling. To South Atlantic by air with No 809 Sqn, 30-4-82; destroyed two Mirage IIIs.

ZA190 ff 5-11-81 J.F. Farley. To South Atlantic by air with No 809 Sqn, 30-4-82.
ZA191 ff 4-12-81 H. Frick. To Falkland Is., 5-82, with No 899 Sqn.
ZA192 ff 29-1-82 J.F.Farley. To Falkland Is., as reserve aircraft, 5-82. Crashed on take-off from HMS *Hermes*, South Atlantic, 24-5-82; Lt. Cdr. G.W. Batt, DSC, killed.
ZA193 ff 13-1-82 J.F. Farley. To Falkland Is., as reserve aircraft, 5-82; destroyed one Mirage III.
ZA194 ff 23-4-82 M.H.B. Snelling. To South Atlantic by air with No 809 Sqn, 30-4-82; destroyed one Mirage III.
ZA195 Not flown at time of writing.

British Aerospace Harrier GR Mark 3 Attrition batch of 24 production aircraft, *XZ963-XZ973, XZ987-XZ999* ordered from British Aerospace Corporation, Kingston-upon-Thames, in 1978. Full production and modification standard with Rolls-Royce (Bristol) Pegasus 103 turbofans, LRMTS/FE 541 and RWR equipment.

XZ963 ff 26-3-80, T. Scott. Deld No 1 (F) Sqn, Wittering, 8-5-80. Shot down by SAM, Goose Green, Falkland Is., 21-5-82; pilot wounded.
XZ964 ff 14-3-80, T. Scott. Deld No 1 (F) Sqn, Wittering, 22-4-80.
XZ965 ff 27-6-80, T. Scott. Deld to RAF Germany, 28-8-80.
XZ966 ff 18-7-80, T. Scott. Deld No 1 (F) Sqn, Wittering, 4-9-80.
XZ967 ff 17-7-80, H. Frick. Deld No 233 OCU, Wittering, 3-9-80.
XZ968 ff 31-10-80, H. Frick. Deld to RAF Germany, 19-12-80.
XZ969 ff 13-11-80, M.H.B. Snelling. Deld to RAF Germany, 15-12-80.
XZ970 ff 5-12-80, T. Scott. Deld to RAF Germany, 13-1-81.
XZ971 ff 20-2 81 H. Frick.
XZ972 ff 5-6-81 T. Scott; No 1 (F) Sqn; hit by ground fire, Falkand Is., 30-5-82; pilot, Sqn.Ldr. J.J. Pook, DFC, ejected and rescued.
XZ973 ff 14-8-81 J.F. Farley; written off in fatal accident, North Wales, 12-2-82.

XZ987 ff 9-9-81 T. Scott.
XZ988 ff 27-8-81 H. Frick.
XZ989 ff 3-10-81 T. Scott; No 1 (F) Sqn; hit by ground fire, Falkland Is., and damaged in crash landing, 9-6-82; Wg. Cdr. Squire unhurt.
XZ990 ff 4-11-81 J.F.Farley.
XZ991 ff 28-11-81 J.F. Farley.
XZ992 ff 27-11-81 J.F. Farley.
XZ993 ff 14-12-81 M.H.B. Snelling.
XZ994 ff 18-12-81 H. Frick.
XZ995 ff 22-2-82 M.H.B. Snelling.
XZ996 ff 13-1-82 T. Scott.
XZ997 ff 21-1-82 M.H.B. Snelling.
XZ998 ff 14-4-82 T. Scott; No 1 (F) Sqn; hit by ground fire, Falkand Is., 27-5-82; Sqn. Ldr. R.D. Iveson ejected and evaded capture.
XZ999 ff 25-5-82 H. Frick.

British Aerospace Harrier T Mark 4 Seven two-seat aircraft *ZB600-ZB603* for Royal Air Force, and *ZB604-ZB606* for Royal Navy (not yet flown at time of writing).

British Aerospace Indian Sea Harrier FRS Mark 51 Six single-seat naval fighters. *601-606* (Nos *602-606* not flown at time of writing).
601 ff 6-8-82 H. Frick; carried temporary registration *G-9-478* and *IN601* at SBAC Display, 9-82.

British Aerospace Indian Harrier T Mark 60 Two two-seat aircraft, *621* and *622* (not yet flown at time of writing).

6 Senior technical, administrative and flight executive personnel, Hawker P 1127 and Harrier programmes, 1957-82

Barkey, Herman D. Vice-President (Aircraft Engineering), McDonnell Aircraft Company, McDonnell Douglas Corporation, St Louis, Missouri, USA.
Bedford, Alfred William, OBE, AFC, FRAeS. Chief Test Pilot, Hawker Aircraft Ltd, 1956-65; Sales Manager (Harrier), Hawker Siddeley Aviation (and British Aerospace), from 1967.

Boddington, Lewis, CBE, MIMechE, FRAeS. Director, Aircraft Research and Development (RAF), MoA, 1959-60.

Camm, Sir Sydney, CBE, FRAeS. Chief Designer, Hawker Aircraft Ltd, 1925-66. Director, Hawker Aircraft Ltd, 1935-63; Director of Design, Hawker Siddeley Aviation, 1963-66.

Cawood, Dr Walter, CB, CBE, BSc, PhD, FRAeS. Director General of Scientific Research (Air), 1955-58; Deputy Controller of Aircraft Research and Development, MoA, 1958-60; Chief Scientist, War Office, from 1960.

Chaplin, Ronald Henry, OBE, BSc, FRAeS. Chief Designer and Executive Director, Hawker Aircraft Ltd, from 1959 until 1962.

Chapman, Colonel (later General) Bill, USAF. Director, Mutual Weapons Development Team, Paris, 1956-60.

Cook, F.G.R., BSc, AMIMechE, AFRAeS. RAF Strike Aircraft Research and Development, Ministry of Aviation and Department of Trade and Industry (Aviation Group).

Davies, Handel, CB, MSc, FRAeS, FAIAA. Director General, Scientific Research (Air), MoS, 1957-59; Deputy Director (A), RAE, 1959-63; Deputy Controller (Aircraft), Research and Development, MoA and Mintech, 1963-66.

Farley, John. Deputy Chief (later Chief) Test Pilot, Hawker Siddeley Aviation, and British Aerospace Corporation, Dunsfold, 1967 to date.

Fletcher, Air Marshal Sir Peter Carteret, KCB, OBE, DFC, AFC. Controller of Aircraft, Ministry of Aviation and Department of Trade and Industry (Aviation Group), 1970. (Previously Director of Operational Requirements, Air Ministry, 1961-63.)

Fozard, John William, DCAe, BSc Hons(Eng), CEng, FRAeS. Senior Project Designer, Hawker Aircraft Ltd, 1955-60; Deputy Head of Project Office, 1960-62; Chief Designer (P 1154), 1962-64; Chief Designer (Harrier), 1965-68; Deputy Chief Engineer, since 1968.

Frick, Heinz. Production Test Pilot, Rolls-Royce Ltd (Bristol Engine Division); joined British Aerospace Corporation, Dunsfold, November 1978.

Gabbay, Ellis Joseph, PhD, BSc(Eng), BA, FIMechE, FRAeS, AFAIAA. Chief Systems Engineer, Hawker Aircraft Ltd, 1956-62.

Hawkes, Tony. Production Test Pilot (Harrier), Hawker Siddeley Aviation, Dunsfold.

Hawkins, Jim. Production Test Pilot (Harrier), Hawker Siddeley Aviation and British Aerospace Corporation, Dunsfold, from July 1973 (at time of writing flying BAe Hawk aircraft).

Hooker, Dr Stanley, CBE, FRS, DSc, DIC, DPhil, MIMechE, ARCSc, FRAeS. Technical Director, Bristol Siddeley Engines Ltd and Rolls-Royce Ltd, Bristol Engine Division, 1956 to date.

Hooper, Ralph S., DCAe, DAe, CEng, MIMechE, FRAeS. P 1127 Project Engineer, 1957-63, Hawker Aircraft Ltd; Assistant Chief Designer (Projects), Hawker Siddeley Aviation, 1963-68; Executive Director and Chief Engineer, HSA and British Aerospace Corporation, Kingston and Brough, since 1968.

Jackson, Jackie Carl. Experimental Test Pilot, McDonnell Aircraft Company, McDonnell Douglas Corporation, St Louis, Missouri, USA.

Jones, Andy. Production Test Pilot (Harrier), Hawker Siddeley Aviation and British Aerospace Corporation, Dunsfold, from October 1970 (at time of writing flying BAe Hawk aircraft).

Jones, Ernest Turner, CB, OBE, MEng, FRAeS. Director General of Technical Development (Air), 1955-58, Ministry of Aviation; Deputy Controller (Overseas Affairs), Department of Trade and Industry, 1959-61.

Lewis, Gordon Manns, MA, FIMechE, FRAeS. Project Engineer, Bristol Siddeley

Engines Ltd, 1957. Director of Advanced Engineering, Rolls-Royce Ltd, Bristol Engine Division, since 1968.

Lickley, Robert Lang, BSc, DIC, CEng, MIMechE, FRAeS. Director, Hawker Aircraft Ltd, 1960-61; Deputy Managing Director, Hawker Siddeley Aviation, 1961-63; Assistant Managing Director, since 1965.

Lidbury, John T., FRAeS. Managing Director, Hawker Aircraft Ltd, 1956-59; Joint Managing Director, Hawker Siddeley Aviation, from 1959.

Marsh, Robert Bulkeley, FRAeS. Chief Project Engineer, Hawker Aircraft Ltd and Hawker Siddeley Aviation, 1956-64; Assistant Chief Engineer (Kingston), from 1969.

Merewether, Hugh, BSc. Assistant Chief Test Pilot, Hawker Aircraft Ltd and Hawker Siddeley Aviation, 1956-64.

Morgan, Sir Morien Bedford, KCB, MA, CEng, FRAeS. Scientific Adviser to the Air Ministry, 1959-60; Deputy Controller (Aircraft), Research and Development, Ministry of Aviation, 1960-63; Controller of Aircraft, MoA, 1963-66; Director, RAE, 1969.

Nicholson, Lewis Frederick, CB, MA, FRAeS. Head of Aerodynamics Department, RAE, 1953-59; Director General, Scientific Research (Air), Ministry of Aviation, 1959-63; Deputy Director (Air), RAE, 1963-66; Deputy Controller of Aircraft (Research and Development), Department of Trade and Industry (Aviation Group), from 1969.

Pelly, Air Chief Marshal Sir Claude Bernard Raymond, GBE, KCB, MC. Controller of Aircraft, Ministry of Supply (and MoA), 1956-59.

Plantin, Charles Peter, BSc(Eng), CEng, FRAeS. Chief Structures Research and Development Engineer, Hawker Aircraft Ltd.

Plummer, Charles Alphonso, Jr. Experimental Test Pilot, McDonnell Aircraft Company, McDonnell Douglas Corporation, St Louis, Missouri, USA.

Ramey, Madison L. Vice-President (Engineering Technology), McDonnell Aircraft Company, McDonnell Douglas Corporation, St Louis, Missouri, USA.

Riches, Don. Production Test Pilot (Harrier, Armament Installations), Hawker Siddeley Aviation and British Aerospace Corporation, Dunsfold, from March 1973.

Rochefort, Henry Ernest James, Wh Sch, ACGI, DIC, CEng, MIMechE, FRAeS. Head of Research, Hawker Aircraft Ltd, and Hawker Siddeley Aviation, since 1969; Assistant Chief Designer (Structures), 1961-69.

Scott, Taylor. Production Test Pilot (Harrier), British Aerospace Corporation, Dunsfold, September 1979 to date.

Seddon, Dr John, BSc, PhD, FRAeS, AFAIAA. Superintendent (Tunnels), RAE, 1959-66; Director, Scientific Research (Air), Mintech, 1966-68; Director General since 1969.

Shaw, Ronald Andrew, OBE, MA, FRAeS. Assistant Director (Aircraft Research), Ministry of Aviation, 1953-66.

Simpson, Duncan, FRAeS. Chief Production Test Pilot, Hawker Aircraft Ltd, 1964-66; Chief Test Pilot, Hawker Siddeley Aviation (Dunsfold), 1967-70.

Snelling, Mike. Production Test Pilot (Harrier), Hawker Siddeley Aviation, and British Aerospace Corporation, Dunsfold, from September 1973 to date.

Sutton, Frederick Vere Kent, BSc(Eng), CEng, AMIMechE, FRAeS. Chief Flight Development Engineer, Hawker Aircraft Ltd, Hawker Siddeley Aviation and British Aerospace Corporation, Dunsfold (1960-78). Flight Test Manager, 1978 to date.

Tonkinson, Barry. Production Test Pilot (Harrier), Hawker Siddeley Aviation, Dunsfold.

Vessey, Hugh Frederick, BSc, FRAeS, MIInfSc. Head of Transonic Tunnels, RAE, 1954-60.

Williams, David, DSc, MIMechE, FRAeS. Deputy Chief Scientific Officer, Structural Research, RAE, until 1961.

Bibliography

Works are listed chronologically.

The Hawker P1127 V/STOL Strike Fighter. A.W. Bedford. *Journal of the Royal Aeronautical Society,* London, December 1962.

Plenum Chamber Burning Feature Studies. Various authors. *Aviation Week & Space Technology,* New York, September 20 1965.

Combined Lift and Propulsion. J.H. Dale and R.M. Lucas. RM Paper No 68-37, 6th Congress of the International Council of the Aeronautical Sciences, Munich, 1968.

The Harrier—An Engineering Commentary. J.W. Fozard. First J.D. North Memorial Lecture, 1969. *Aeronautical Journal of the Royal Aeronautical Society,* London, September 1969.

Marines Plan for Harrier Introduction. William S. Hieronymous. *Aviation Week & Space Technology,* New York, September 14 1970.

Engineering Solutions to some Conflicts between Transonic Flight and Jet V/STOL. J.W. Fozard. RM Paper No 70-57*bis.* 7th Congress of the International Council of the Aeronautical Sciences, Rome, 1970.

Technical Development in Aviation. N.E. Rowe. *The Aeronautical Journal,* the Royal Aeronautical Society, London, September 1970.

Hawker Aircraft Since 1920, Francis K. Mason. Putnam & Co, London (Second Edition), 1971.

US Marine Corps/Department of Defense V/STOL Exercise Validates AV-8A Harrier Goals. Brooke Nihart. *Armed Forces Journal,* USA, May 1972.

AV-8A Harrier Experience in the US Marine Corps. Major-General T.H. Miller, USMC, and Lieutenant-Colonel C.M. Baker, USMC, *Interavia* 2/1973.

Royal Air Force Experience of the Harrier. Air Marshal Sir Ruthven Wade. Second Sir Sydney Camm Memorial Lecture, 1973. Royal Aeronautical Society, London, 1973.

The Harrier—A Story of Two Decades. R.S. Hooper. 19th Chadwick Memorial Lecture, 1974. Royal Aeronautical Society, London, 1974.

Payload Without Penalty—A Suggestion for Improving the Take-off Performance of Fixed-Wing V/STOL Aircraft. Lieutenant Commander D.R. Taylor, RN. RAeS Paper No 267. *The Aeronautical Journal,* Royal Aeronautical Society, London, August 1975.

Sea Harrier—The first of the New Wave. J.W. Fozard. 23rd R.J. Mitchell Memorial Lecture, 1976. Royal Aeronautical Society, Southampton Branch, 1976.

Advanced AV-8B Development Approved. Aviation Week & Space Technology, New York, August 2 1976.

The AV-8B Wing: Aerodynamic Concept and Design. T.R. Lacey and K. Miller. AIAA V/STOL Conference, Palo Alto, California. McDonnell Aircraft Company, Saint Louis, Missouri, June 1977.

The Jet V/STOL Harrier: An Evolutionary Revolution in Tactical Air Power. John W. Fozard. British Aerospace Aircraft Group, Kingston-Brough Division, July 1977.

The Royal Air Force View on Vectored Thrust. Air Commodore H.A. Merriman. (Presented by) British Aerospace, Tokyo, Japan, June 1978.

Contribution and Legacy—Have We Used it Well? R.S. Hooper. 5th Sir Sydney Camm Memorial Lecture, 1979, Royal Aeronautical Society, London, 1979.

AV-8B Advanced Harrier. G. Warwick. *Flight International,* London, December 29 1979.

Ski-Jump—A Great Leap for Tactical Airpower. J.W. Fozard. 1st Atlantic Aeronautical Conference, Williamsburg, Virginia, March 1979.

Vectored Thrust Jet V/STOL: An Evaluation of the Harrier AV-8A and the Pegasus Engine. Rolls-Royce Ltd (Aero Division), Bristol, issue 2 of December 1978, updated May 1980.

Other references

Diary of Events, P1127, Kestrel and NBMR-3 Projects. Sir Sydney Camm, J.W. Fozard, R.S. Hooper and R.B. Marsh. Unpublished. Hawker Aircraft Ltd, 1957-65.

Blue Fox—Sea Harrier Radar. Ferranti Ltd. *Pacific Defence Reporter.*

Harrier Foreign Object Damage Avoidance. J.W. Fozard. Hawker Siddeley Aviation Ltd, 1971.

La croisée des chemins pour l'aviation navale de combat ('The Crossroads for Naval Combat Aviation'). British Aerospace Aircraft Group, May 1979.

Various other issues of the following periodicals: *The Aeroplane and Astronautics, Flight International, Flying Review International, Aviation Week & Space Technology, Interavia* and *Air Force/Space Digest.*

Index